Himalaya's

OBJECTIVE QUESTIONS AND ANSWERS FOR MANAGEMENT STUDIES

(For B.B.M., B.B.A., B.C.S., B.Com., M.B.A., M.Com., C.A., ICWA, Central and State Civil Services, Professional, Competitive and Entrance Examination of various Boards/Universities)

Dr. P. PERIASAMY,

M.B.A., Ph.D.

Reader,

Dept. of Business Management,

Erode Arts College,

Erode - 638 009.

Himalaya Publishing House

MUMBAI ● DELHI ● NAGPUR ● BANGALORE ● HYDERABAD

FIRST EDITION : 2004

Edition - 2011

Published by : Mrs. Meena Pandey
for **HIMALAYA PUBLISHING HOUSE,**
"Ramdoot", Dr. Bhalerao Marg, Girgaon,
Mumbai - 400 004.
Phones: 2386 01 70/2386 38 63,
Fax: 022-2387 71 78
Email: himpub@vsnl.com
Website: www.himpub.com

Branch Offices :

Delhi : "Pooja Apartments", 4-B, Murari Lal Street,
Ansari Road, Darya Ganj,
New Delhi - 110 002.
Phone: 2327 03 92, Fax: 011-2325 62 86

Nagpur : Kundanlal Chandak Industrial Estate,
Ghat Road, Nagpur - 440 018.
Phone: 272 12 16, Telefax: 0712-272 12 15

Bangalore : No. 16/1 (old 12/1), 1st Floor,
Next to Hotel Highlands, Madhava Nagar,
Race Course Rd., Bangalore: 560 001.
Phones: 228 15 41, 238 54 61, Telefax: 228 66 11

Hyderabad : No. 2-2-1 167/2H, 1st Floor,
Near Railway Bridge, Tilak Nagar,
Main Road, Hyderabad - 500 044.
Phone: 555 01 745, Fax: 040-2756 00 41

Printed by : **7 Hills Printers,** Hyderabad.

Dedicated

to

my beloved mother

MOTHER MARY

Dr. P. Muthusamy, M.Com., M.B.A., Ph.D.,
(Formerly Director, School of Management,
Bharathiar University,Coimbatore)
21. Kaveri Nagar, Kuniyamuthur,
Coimbatore - 641 008.

FOREWORD

Dr. P. Periasamy had compiled the Question Bank on Management covering exhaustively all the subjects. He has taken enormous effort to go through the questions of many universities and set questions which are very important for Under Graduate and Post Graduate students in management studies. The publication of this book gains value as the UGC, Universities and other organisations are emphasising on the objective type of question papers for assessing the performance of candidates.

I congratulate Dr. P. Periasamy of the sincere effort and wish him all success.

(Dr. P. MUTHUSAMY)

PREFACE TO THE FIRST EDITION

At present, the UGC, Universities, Colleges, Human Resource Development Institutions and various professional Organizations in India are thinking of changing the educational systems and examination patterns. Upgradation, Vocationalization, Reasearch and Development, Innovations and Indepth subject knowledge are the new visions of educations, needed not only to improve the quality of education but also to fulfil our goals in the present and future. In this regard students and academicians from Science, Management, Commerce and Arts need exensive and thorough knowledge of Business Management, Finance, Production, Personnel Management, Business Law and Export Trade. It is for this purpose that this book has been prepared.

The book is intended primarily as a guide and reference book for pass and honours students, as well as professionals and non-professionals preparing for the Semester and Non-semester Examinations conducted by various colleges, Universities, Distance Education Institutions and also for the Competitive Examinations conducted by Central and State governments. The book has more than 2300 Multiple choice objective type questions with answers. It covers that contents of more than eighteen management papers of different universities and colleges. Each paper, on an average, consists of more than 175 questions with answers.

I thank Shri D.N. Pandey and Shri Neeraj Pandey and Shri K. Sivadasam, Area Manager, Tamil Nadu of Himalaya Publishing House for the interest they have shown in my subject and agreeing to publish this book in time.

I am deeply indebted to my professors Dr.P. Muthusamy and Dr. S. Sumant for their invaluable help in the preparation of this book.

ERODE ARTS COLLEGE (AUTONOMOUS)
ERODE

DR. P. PERIASAMY

C O N T E N T S

Cost – Line of Balance – Maintenance Management – Equipment – Replacement Management – Capital Budgeting.

Purchasing Management: Purchasing Principles, Procedure and systems – Negotiating Skills – Evaluation of purchasing Performance – Stores Management – Types of Stores – Stock – Yards – Organisation of Stores – Storage Stock verification – Safety and Security Preservation of Materials – Waste and Scrap Disposal – Stock Maintenance and Stores According system.

III. MARKETING MANAGEMENT AND SALES PROMOTION

MARKETING : Definition of Market and Marketing – Concepts – Classification of Markets – Marketing and Selling – objectives – Importance and Social functions of Marketing – Marketing Management – Marketing Environment : Various factors Affecting the marketing functions.

Marketing Mix – System and Process : Meaning, definitions of Marketing Mix – Elements of the Marketing Mix – Forces affecting Market Mix- Marketing system and Process.

Marketing Functions : Functions of Exchanges, Buying and Selling, Functions of Physical Supply – facilitating functions- Marketing Finance – Marketing Information – Transpirations – Storage and Ware housing.

Marketing Management : Meaning and Definition of Marketing Management – Scope of Marketing Management – Nature and importance of Marketing Management – Functional Areas of Management – Guiding Philosophies of Marketing Management –Principles of Marketing Management – Marketing Organisational Structures.

Market Segmentation : Definition – Importance of Market Segmentation – Requirements for Successful Segmentation – Bases for Market Segmentation – Strategies and Elements of Market Segmentation – Market Targeting – Market Positioning – Strategies – Strategies option for Competitors in a Competitive Market.

Consumer Behaviour : Meaning and Major factors influencing Consumer Behaviour – Buying motives – Theories contributed by Social Sciences – Maslow's Classification of Basic Needs. Types Satisfaction – Reason for purchases – Emotional and Rational Buying Motives – Measurement of Consumer satisfaction Consumer Retention.

Channels of Distribution : Meaning – Basis of Channel – Distribution – Factors influencing the Selection of a channel – Level of channel – Meaning – Definition and classifications of Middlemen – Agent – Middlemen – Merchant – Middlemen – of wholesalers – Retailers – Importance of Retailers – Meaning – Functions and Services of the Retailers – Essential Requisites for success in Retailing – Methods of Retailing.

Sales Forecasting : Definition of Sales of Forecasting – Objectives Importance – Uses – Needs – Methods of Sales Forecasting – Factors and Procedure for Forecasting.

Product Planning and Development : Meaning – Definition and Market Characteristics of a products – Classification of Goods for products – Products policies Importance – Scope Definition and Areas conferred by the product policy. Product planning and Development Scope of Product Planning and development – Product Life cycle – Stages in Product Life cycle – Product Mix – Factors determining the product Mix – Product Mix Strategies. Product – Diversification – New Product Development – Process – Failure of a Product.

Branding – Brand, Brand Name, and Brand Mark Characteristics of a Good Brand – Advantages and Disadvantages of Branding. Brand Equity – Trade Marks – Packaging – Labeling.

Pricing: Meaning – Objectives – Factors influencing Pricing Decisions – Kinds of Pricing – Pricing strategies – Pricing of New Products – Price changes.

Sales Promotion : Meaning, Definition, Scope and Benefits of Sales Promotion – Objectives, Importance and Types of Sales Promotion – Promotional Mix – Personal Selling – Qualities and objectives of Personal Selling – Essentials of Salesmanship – Uses of Salesmanship.

Advertising : Meaning, definition, Elements, Functions and Advantages of Advertising – Kinds of Advertising – Advertising Copy – Definition – Aims – elements of an advertisement Copy – Media–Classification of the advertising Media – Advertising Agencies – Meaning and Definition – Need for an Advertising Agency – Effectiveness Advertising.

Marketing Services : Definitions of Services – Characteristics of Services - Pricing of Services – Classification of Services – The Marketing Concept and Service Marketing – Methods of Price Determination – Consumer Protection Act 1986- Scope of the Act – Consumer Protection Councils – Consumerism – Meaning and Definition of Consumerism – Rights of the Producers and consumers – Scope of Consumerism Consumer Organisations.

IV. RESEARCH METHODOLOGY AND MARKETING RESEARCH

Marketing Research : Conceptual frame work – Nature – Scope Importance – Market Research Vs Marketing Research – Relationship with other disciplines – Organisation of Marketing research department ; Problem – Discovery and Formulation ; Marketing Research Process – Steps in Marketing research – Problem definition – Research design – field work – date analysis – Report Preparation Characteristics of good marketing research – marketing Research Plan ; scientific Method – Steps in Scientific research Process – Hypothesis – conceptual frame work – Testing of hypothesis.

Research Design : Exploratory research – Importance and Methods of Exploratory research – Descriptive research – Importance – Case research design – Panel analysis – Experimental Design - concept Uses and Types of Experimental Design.

Data Collection : Secondary Data – concept – Merit and Limitation of Secondary data – Types and sources of Secondary data; Primary Data – Types of Primary data – Methods of communication – Survey method and its Administration – Survey Technique – Personal interview – Telephone Survey – Mail Survey – Survey Technique – Problems relates to Interviewers and Respondents ; Questionnaire Design – Distinguishing Questionnaire and Interview Schedule – Constructing the Questionnaire and Determining types of questions.

Attitude Measurement and Scaling Techniques : Concept – Numerical Scales – Nominal Scales – Ordinal Scales Ratio Scales – Consumer attitudes – Rating Scales – Paired compressions – Rank Order Rating Scale – Semantic Differential – Thurston Differential – Multidimensional Scaling.

Observation Method : Concept – Uses – Methods of Observation

Sampling Concept : Method of Sampling Meaning - Types of Sampling. Sampling errors - Problems of Sampling – Data Collection Errors.

Data Analysis : Processing Collected data, Data Analysis and Interpretation – Percentage – Averages – Dispersion – Developing Hypothesis – Test – Z test – Chi – Square Analysis – F - Test - One – Way classification – Two – Way Classification – Measurement of Association – Correlation Analysis – Regression Analysis – Factor Analysis – Cluster Analysis.

Presentation of Research Project: Written reports – Factors and suggestions for written reports – Types of reports.

Product Research : New Product research – Generating ideals – Idea Screening – Concept Development and Testing – Business analysis – Product development – Test Marketing – Commercialisation – Product life cycle research – Product Mix research.

Advertising Research : Definition – Product appeal research – Copy Testing – Pre testing – Post tests – Media Selection research –Print – Media – Broadcast Media.

Motivation Research : Nature of Motivation research – Kinds of information Sought – Motivation research technique.

Sales Control Research : Sales forecasting – Sales analysis – Sales Potential – Methods for developing Market potentials – Direct ata Method – Corollary Data Method – Use of Surveys to determine Potentials.

V. EXPORT MANAGEMENT, INTERNATIONAL MARKETING AND EXPORT PROMOTION

EXPORT MANAGEMENT: Meaning, Definition, features, Scope, and functions of export management. Similarities and Difference between Export Management and home management Importance of Export Management. Factors affecting Export Management.

International Marketing and International Trade Agreements: Need and Main features of International Marketing, Advantages and benefits of International Marketing Trade Barriers : Objectives, Classification –Advantages Barriers. Tariff Barriers and Non-Tariff Barriers – Advantages and difference between Tariff and non – Tariff Barriers. Tariff and Import – Quotas And Valorem Duty and Specific Duty. Bilateral Trade Agreement, GATT – Objectives, Importance and short – comings. UNCTAD – objectives, functions, limitations of UNCTAD. Trade Blocks. Different Trading Blocs.

Export Marketing Organisations and their Role: Methods of Export Marketing Definition, Types of Export Marketing Organisations. Merchant Exporter. Distinction between Manufacturer export and Merchant Exporter, Export House and Trading House.

Export Costing and Export Pricing: Definition, objectives and Importance of Export Pricing. Factors Determining Export Price. Methods of Costing used in exports. Full cost Approach, Marginal Cost Approach – Direct and Indirect cost involved in Export Price. Skimming the cream pricing policy and penetrations price, FOB and CIF, Cost Assistance and Duty Draw backs, Total Cost Price and Marginal cost price.

EXPORT FINANCE: Meaning and Need of Export Finance, Pre-shipment Finance – Features, Types and Procedure foe obtaining pre-shipment Credit. Past – shipment – Finance – Features Types and Procedure for obtaining Post – Shipment Finance. Difference between Pre-Shipment and Post – Shipment – Finance.

Role of Commercial Bank in Export Finance – EXIM Bank. Objectives and Functions of EXIM Bank. Various Policies issued by ECGC.

EXPORT PROCEDURE: Registration Procedure for an Export House, Procedure to be followed to export goods from India. Measures during Pre- Shipment Stage – Quality control of Pre – Shipment procedure for Realisation of export incentives offered by Government of India.

EXPORT DOCUMENTATION: Documents required in export transaction. Types of Export Documents, Letter of Credit – Procedure, Types of Letter of Credit. Performa Invoice, Commercial Invoice Certificate of origin – Importance – Types, Mate's Receipt and Bill of Leading. Shipping Bills, Airway Bills. Bill of Lading and its Types. GR Form and AR-4 Forms.

ORGANISATIONS FOR EXPORT PROMOTION : Various Export Promotion Organisation – Role or functions of Export Promotion Councils ; Commodity Boards. Functions of Commodity Boards. Indian Institute of Packaging, Indian Institute of Foreign Trade – features and objectives of Indian Council of Arbitration. Export Inspection Council. Export Process Zone – Trade Fair Authority of India – World Trade Centre – Marine Products and Export Development Authority.

Export Promotion Measures and Incentives of Indian Exporters: Meaning of Export Incentives and Assistance – Various Export Promotion Measures given by Government of India Various Export Promotion Measures. Cash Incentives – Tax Incentives and Relief's. Excise Duty Relate – Overseas Marketing facilities. Facilities to exporters for export Production – Export Incentives and Assistance to Indian Export.

VI. HUMAN RESOURCE AND PERSONNEL MANAGEMENT

Personnel Management: Meaning – Definition – Concept – Objectives of Personnel Management – Characteristics – Qualities – Role of Personal Manager – Impact of Environment on organization objectives – Techniques and Methods and different approaches of Personnel Management: Functions of Personnel Management – Meaning – Classifications – Functions Areas and Scope of Personnel Policies, Procedures and Programmes – Personnel - Policies – Essential Characteristics – Sources –

Types – Methods and Principles – Factors Responsible for the Development of Personnel Management in India – Growth – Labour Welfare officer – Functions – Qualifications – Role of Personnel Manager in India.

Organisational Structure: Meaning – Process – Functions – concepts – Merits – Drawback of Organisation Structure. Scope of organisation – Organisation Authority and Responsibility: Personnel Records – Reports – Audit – Research – Essentials – Objectives – Need for Personnel Audit - Scope and Uses of Reports and Audits. Types of Audit – Methods of Analysis – Personnel Research – Meaning – Coverage – Types – Objectives – Methods – Procedure – Sources – Tools of Personnel Research.

Human Resource Planning : Meaning – Definition – Need – Benefits – Process – Responsibility – Component of Human Resource Planning – Job Analysis – Job Description – Job Specification – Meaning – Objectives – uses – factors – Methods – Merits and Demerits.

Recruitment and Selection Process : Meaning – Factors – Steps – Forecast – Sources of Recruitment – Method and Assessment of Recruitment Programme – Selection – Procedure – Essentials steps in Selection Procedure.

Psychological Testing Interviews, Placement and Induction: Purpose – Nature and Characteristics – Classification – Advantages – Developing a Test Programme – Guidelines – Interviews – Types – Guidelines for interviews – Qualities – Interviews Technique – Defects – Errors in Interviewing. Placement – Orientation – Induction – objectives – Procedure – Techniques of Induction Programmes.

Promotion, Transfers, Separation, Absenteeism and Turnover: Meaning – Purpose – Types – Procedure – System – Policy of Promotion – Demotion – Causes – Transfer – Purpose – Policy – Procedure of Demotion – labour Turnover – Impact – Magnitude – Causes of Labour Turnover – Measures to Control Labour Turnover.

Employee Training: Meaning – Need – Importance – Responsibility – Principles – Policy – Steps – Programmes – Methods of Training – Executive Development Managerial functions – objectives – Importance – Concepts – Components – Factors – Methods and Different Programmes – Techniques of Management Development.

Performance Appraisal: Meaning – Importance – Process – Methods – Techniques of Performance Appraisal – Modern Methods – Components of Appraisal Evaluation. Factors – Objective – Ethics of Performance Appraisal.

Job Evaluation Techniques : Definition – Objectives – Principles – Basic Procedure – Advantages – Limitations – Methods – Systems – Essentials of Job evaluation Technique.

Wage and Salary Administration: Nature – Purpose – Factions Principles of Wage and Salary Administration - Theory of Wages – Kinds of Wages – Importance and Components of remuneration. Reward and Incentives – features – Determinates – Types – objectives – Incentive Schemes Employee benefits and employee Services.

Human Relations : Group Dynamics – Human Relations – Human Needs – Personality – Motivation – Motivation Theories and Models Employee Morale – Communication – Leadership – Management of Grievances – Management of Grievances.

Employee Safety and Industrial Health and Labour Management Relations: Employee Staff – Industrial Accident – Nature – Causes – Accident – Measurement – Safety Programme and Policy – Accident prevention – Importance – Occupational Diseases – Programmes – Industrial Dispute – Forms – Types – Relations – Definition – Content – Objectives – Scope of Industrial Relation. Trade Unions – Definition – Characteristics – Principles – Objectives – Growth and Factors affecting Trade Unions – Functions and Features of Trade Unionism.

Human Resource Management : Human Resource Management and Economic Liberalisation – Human Resource Accounting – Human Resource Audit – Human Resource Research – Exit Policy – its effects – The job and the Challenges.

VII. FINANCIAL MANAGEMENT AND PROJECT MANAGEMENT

Business Finance : Nature and Scope – Importance of finance – Meaning and objectives of Financial Management – Liquidity Vs. Profitability – Methods of Financial Management – Importance of Financial Management – Financial Planning – Estimating Capital Requirements – Fixed Capital – Working Capital, Capitalisation – Pattern of financing, Capital Structure – Optimum Capital Structure – Factors Determinty Capital Structure – Time Floatation.

Working Capital Management: Concept – Nature – Types and Adequacy of Working Capital – Management of Working Capital – Management of Cash, Inventories – Accounts Receivable and Accounts Payable – Over and Under – Trading – Working Capital Control and.Banking Policy.

Capital Budgeting: Concept of Capital Budgeting – Capital Expenditure Budget Importance of Capital Budgeting – Rationale of Capital Expenditure – Kinds of Capital Investment Proposals Factors Affecting Capital Investment – Decisions – Capital Budgeting Appraisal Methods – Capital Rationing – Risk Analysis of Capital Budgeting – Risk Defined Incorporation of Key Factors.

Cost of Capital : Concept – Importance – Classification of Cost if Capital – Controversy Regarding Cost of Capital – Determination of Cost of Capital.

Leverages: Meaning of Leverage – Types of Leverages – Significance of Leverages.

Source of Finance: Classification of Source of Finance – Security Financing – Internal Financing – Loan Financing Specialised Financial Institutions.

Dividends, Bonus And Rights: Dividends–Bonus Shares–Rights of Shares.

Working Capital : Concepts–Types of Working Capital Methods of Working Capital – Policies and Principles of Work Capital – Cash Management : Meaning Concepts and factors of Cash Management; Cash forecast–objectives and Types of cash forecast.

Inventory Management: Meaning–Types and Objectives of Inventory Management–Factors and Valuation of inventory analysis.

Project Management: Preparation of Project Report–Appraisal of Project PERT and CPM.

VIII. FINANCIAL ACCOUNTING

Nature of Accounting : Definition – Objectives – Necessity – Limitation of Accounting – Nature and Meaning of Accounting Principles – Essential Features – Kinds of Accounting Principles – Concepts – Objectivity of Concepts – Conventions – Definition – Explanations Sale of Goods – Rendering Services – Holding of Assets – Double Entry Book keeping – Transaction Analysis – Income measurement – Nature – Income – Need – Different ways of inventory valuation – Impact of Price – Level Changes – Different methods Adjusting Profit for Inflation.

Balance Sheet : Valuation of Principle – Meaning of Balance Sheet – Asset – Definition – Classification of Assets – Business Combination – Fixed Assets – Valuation of fixed Assets – Current Assets – Valuation of Current Assets – Long Term Investments – Liabilities – Classification of Liabilities – Functions – Advantages – Limitations of Balance Sheet.

Review of Accounting Cycle: Recording, Posting and Preparation – of Trail Balance – General Journal – Nature of Account – Rules for Debiting and Crediting – Journal – Classification Cash Book – Classification – Posting – Process of Posting – Preparation of Trail Balance – Balancing Accounts.

Final Account : Trading and Profit and Loss Account. Balance Sheet – Preparation – Methods of Accounting for Income – Adjustment Entries – Provisions – Adjustment Entries for preparation of Trading, Profit and Loss Account and Balance Sheet.

Rectification of Errors: Meaning – Rectification by Journal Entry – Suspense Account – Effect and Rectification of Errors – Explanation of difficult – rectification.

Bank Reconciliation Statements: Meaning – Definition – Causes of difference – Errors in the Pass Book and Cash Book – Procedure and Preparation of Bank Reconciliation Statement.

Inventory Valuation: Meaning – Objectives – Methods of Inventory Valuation – Presentation of Inventory in Financial Statement – Valuation of Stock on the date of financial accounts.

Bill of Exchange : Definition – Meaning – Accounting aspects – Drawn – Accepted – Discharged – Indorsement – Discounting – Collection – Dishonour of Bills – Noting Charges – Renewal.

Capital and Revenue – Expenditure and Receipts.

Accounting for Non-Trading Concern: Meaning – Definition – Income and Expenditure of Non Trading Concern – Accounting treatment of General and Special funds – Calculations of Subscription.

Manufacturing Accounts : Cost of Materials – Labour Cost – Expenses – Prime – Cost – Factory Cost – Cost of Production – Types of Manufacturing Account – Cost Sheet.

Consignment Account : Meaning – Definition – Methods of Consignment Account – Valuation of Stock.

Joint Venture : Meaning – Difference between Partnership and Joint Venture – Accounting treatment – Set of Books – Methods of Accounting for Joint Venture.

Average Due Date and Account Current: Account Current – Calculation of Interest – Different Methods of Average Due Date and Account Current.

Depreciation Accounting: Meaning – Definition – Basis of Depreciation – Objectives providing depreciation – Causes – Factors influencing depreciation – Method of allocating depreciation – Depreciation revaluation – Depreciation policy – Depreciation accounting – Reserve and provisions – Nature – Characteristics and Types of reserves – Advantages –Accounting treatment for reserves and provisions.

IX. MANAGEMENT ACCOUNTING

Management Accounting : Meaning – Definition – Development of Accounting – Concepts – Functions – Objectives and Principles of Management – Accounting – Utility and Limitations of Management Accounting – Difference between Management Accounting, Financial Accounting and Cost Accounting.

Financial Analysis : Meaning and Types of Financial Statements – Formats – Nature and Limitations of Financial Statements – Analysis – Types – Steps – Tools of Financial Analysis and Interpretations.

Accounting Ratios: Meaning – Classification of Ratios – Profitability – Turnover Ratios – Financial Ratios – Categories of Ratios – Advantages and Limitations of Accounting Ratios – Capital Gearing – Inter firm – Intra – firm Comparison.

Fund Flow Statements : Need for Fund Flow Statement – Meaning – Uses of Fund Flow Statement – Fund Flow Statement and Income Statement – Preparation of Fund Flow Statement. Statement of Changes in Working Capital – Factors Determining Working Capital.

Cash Flow Statements : Meaning – Preparation of Cash Flow Statements – Difference between Cash Flow Analysis and Funds Flow Analysis – Utility and Analysis of Cash Flow Analysis.

Budgetary Control : Meaning – Definition of Budget and Budgetary Control – Tools of Budgetary Control – Limitations of Budgetary Control – Classification Budgets – Performance of Budgeting – Control Ratios.

Capital Budgeting: Nature of Capital Expenditure – Concept of Capital Budgeting – Procedure – Methods of Capital Budgeting – Investment Proposals.

X. COST ACCOUNTING:

Definition of Cost, Costing, Cost Accounting – Scope and Objectives of Cost Accounting – Difference between Cost Accounting and Financial Accounting – Cost Accounting Vs Management Accounting – Advantages and Limitation of Cost Accounting. Elements of cost – Classification of Overheads Cost Sheet – Treatment of Stocks.

Materials Control : Meaning – Objectives – Essentials Advantages of Material Control. Materials Management – Purchase Control – Purchasing departments – Methods – Procedure of Purchasing -

Store keeping – Inventory Control - Stores layout – Classification and Codification of Materials – Receipt and issue of materials –Material records – Inventory Control techniques – Economic ordering Quantity – Pricing of Material Issues – Material losses.

Labour Control: Personnel Department – Labour Turnover Work Study – Time keeping department – payroll department – Remuneration and Incentives – Time Rate System – Piece Rate System – Premium and Bonus Plan.

Overheads : Meaning – definition – Importance of Overheads – Classification and Codification of Overheads – Procedure and Methods of overhead techniques – Absorption of Overheads – Methods of Absorption of Overheads – Administrative Overheads Selling and Distribution Overheads.

Reconciliation of Costing: Job Costing – Features – Objectives – Essential of job costing – Advantages and Limitations of job costing – Job costing Procedure – Forms used in job costing – Batch Costing – Contract Costing – Meaning and characteristics of job costing and contract costing – Unit or Output – Costing – Operating and operation costing – Meaning – Methods and Technique of Service Costing – Importance – Special features of operating costing – Process costing – Meaning – Charactertics – Types – Advantages and Disadvantages of Process costing – Process costing and job costing – costing procedure – Importance aspects of process costing.

Marginal Costing and Profit Planning: Meaning – Definitions of Marginal costing – Salient Features of Marginal Costing – Advantages and Limitations of Marginal Costing – Absorption Costing Vs Marginal costing–Differential Costing – Key factor – Break – Even Analysis – Margin of safety – Cost Volume Profit Relationship – Relevant – Costs – Special Decisions.

Standard Costing and Variance Analysis : Meaning of Standard Cost – Relevance of Standard cost for variance Analysis – Significance of Variance Analysis – Computation of Material – Labour – Overhead and Sales Variances – Accumulation and Disposal of Variances.

BUSINESS LAW, COMPANY LAW, AND INDUSTRIAL LAW

XI. BUSINESS LAW:

Law of Contract: Nature of contract – Offer and Acceptance – Consideration – Capacity to contract – Free Consent – Legality of Object – Agreements not Declared Void – Contingent Contracts – Performance of Contract – Discharge of Contract – Free Consent – Legality of Object – Agreements not Declared Void – Contract – Remedies of Breach of Contract – Quasi – Contracts

Indemnity and Gurantee : Contract of Indemnity – Contract of Gurantee – Kinds of Gurantee – Nature of Surety's liability – Rights and Discharge of Surety.

Bailment and Pledge: Contract of Bailment and Pledge – Requisites of Bailment – Classification of Bailments Duties of bailee and bailor – Termination of bailment – Rights of Pawnee – Pledge by Non – owners.

Contract of Agency : Agent – Rules of Agency – Creation of Agency – Right of Agents – Delegation of Authority – Relation of Principal with Third parties – Personal liability of Agent – Termination of Agency.

Sale of Goods : Formation of Contract – Conditions and Warranties – Transfer of property – Performance of contract – Rights of an unpaid Seller.

Law of Partnership: Nature of Partnership – Relation of Partners – Dissolution of Firm.

Negotiable Instruments : Negotiable Instruments, Notes–Bills and Cheques – Parties to a Negotiable Instrument – Negotiation – Hindis – Dishonour and Discharge of a Negotiable Instrument.

Law of Insurance : Law of Insurance – Life Insurance –Fire Insurance – Marine Insurance.

Carriage of Goods : Carriage by Land–Carriage By Sea and Carriage by Air.

XII. COMPANY LAW

Nature of Company: Meaning – Definitions – Charactertics Advantages and Limitations – Kinds of Companies – Basis of incorporation–Liability and Members – Private Company and Public Company – Classification on the basis of control and ownership – Conversion of Private into a public Company Duties of the Secretary – Privileges of a Statutory Public Company.

Formation of Company: Promotion – Promotion Incorporation and Registration – Functions of a promoter – Certificate of In Corporation – Commencement of Business – Memorandum of Association – Meaning, Contents and Purpose – Articles of Association – Nature, Contents and Scope – The Prospects – Meaning – Contents and Conditions.

Capital of a Company : Share Capital of a Company – Kinds – Classification and Methods of Raising Capital – Company Shares – Their Nature and kinds – Procedure for Issue and Transfer – Borrowed Capital – Short term and long term borrowings.

Ownership and Management: Members of a company – Meaning Rights and Duties – Directors of a Company – Powers –Manager – Appointment, Rights and Duties.

Meetings of a Company : Company Meetings – Conduct – Kinds – Law and Practice – Minutes of the Meetings – Secretary of a Company – Position- Powers and Duties – Specimen Forms and Documents.

Return on Investment: Dividend – Nature and Payment Procedure – Dividend Warrant – Dividend Mandate – Interim Dividend – Final Dividend – Duties of Secretary regarding payment of Dividend.

Accounts and Audit: Accounts of a company – Accounts Returns and Books of a company.

Protection to Share Holders : Majority and Minority – Majority Rule and Minority Rights – Prevention of oppression and Mismanagement.

Liquidation of a Company: Meaning – Definition – Methods and Procedure – Its Consequences – Liquidator – Powers and Duties Reconstruction – Arrangements, and Amalgamation.

Government and Company: Company Law in India – Administration of Company Law – Registrar of Companies – Investigation By the Government.

XIII. INDUSTRIAL LAW

1. The Factories Act – 1948 — 2. The Work Men's Compensation Act – 1923.

XIV. OFFICE MANAGEMENT

Office Management : Principles and Scope – Objectives – Activities and Functions of office Management.

Administrative Arrangements and Facilities.

Records Management.

Forms and Management and Control.

Office Supplies and Stationery.

Mail Service and Communication.

Collection and Recording of data.

Office Report and Précis Writing.

Office Cost Reduction and Cost Saving.

Office Supervision.

Work Measurement and Standards.

Work simplification.

Office Personnel Relation.

XII. COMPANY LAW

Nature of Company: Meaning – Definitions – Characteristics Advantages and Limitations – Kinds of Companies – Basis of incorporation Liability and Members – Private Company and Public Company – Classification on the basis of control and ownership – Conversion of Private into a public Company. Duties of the Secretary – Privileges of a Statutory Public Company.

Formation of Company: Promotion – Promotion Incorporation and Registration – Functions of a promoter – Certificate of In Corporation – Commencement of Business – Memorandum of Association – Meaning, Clauses and Purpose – Articles of Association – Nature, Contents and Scope – The Prospectus – Meaning – Contents and Conditions.

Capital of a Company: Share Capital of a Company – Kinds – Classification and Methods of Raising Capital – Company Shares – Their Nature and Kinds – Procedure for Issue and Transfer – Borrowed Capital – Short term and long term borrowings.

Ownership and Management: Members of a company – Meaning Rights and Duties – Directors of a Company – Powers – Manager – Appointment, Rights and Duties.

Meetings of a Company: Company Meetings – Conduct – Kinds – Law and Practice – Minutes of the Meeting – Secretary of a Company – Position, Powers and Duties – Specimen Forms and Documents.

Returns on Investment: Dividend – Nature and Payment Procedure – Dividend Warrant – Dividend Mandate – Interim Dividend – Final Dividend – Duties of Secretary regarding payment of Dividend.

Accounts and Audit: Accounts of a company – Accounts Returns and Books of a company.

Protection to Share Holders: Majority and Minority – Majority Rule and Minority Rights – Prevention of oppression and Mismanagement.

Liquidation of a Company: Meaning – Definition – Methods and Procedure – Its Consequences – Liquidator – Powers and Duties – Reconstruction – Arrangements and Amalgamation.

Government and Company: Company Law in India – Administration of Company Law – Registrar of Companies – Investigation By the Government.

XIII. INDUSTRIAL LAW

1. The Factories Act – 1948. – 2. The Work Men's Compensation Act – 1923.

XIV. OFFICE MANAGEMENT

Office Management : Principles and Scope – Objectives – Activities and Functions of office Management.

Administrative Arrangements and Facilities.

Records Management

Forms and Management and Control

Office Supplies and Stationery.

Mail Services and Communication

Collection and Recording of data

Office Report and Precis Writing.

Office Cost Reduction and Cost Saving.

Office Supervision

Work Measurement and Standards.

Work simplification

Office Personnel Relation

I

PRINCIPLES OF MANAGEMENT

1. **Management is referred to**
   (a) Noun (b) Verb (c) Adjective (d) Pro-Noun
2. **Decentralisation means __________**
   (a) Determinations of results expected (b) Creating an accounts
   (c) Transfer of Authority from one individual to another
   (d) Doing things in a central place
3. **Unity of Command means**
   (a) An employee receives order from more than one superior
   (b) An employee receives order from one Superior
   (c) An employee receives order from Subordinates
   (d) None of the above
4. **A Programme is a __________**
   (a) Fixed Plan (b) Multi – Use Plan
   (c) Single – Use Plan (d) List of Schedule
5. **Middle Management refers to**
   (a) Departmental Managers (b) Transmit orders downwards
   (c) Motivate lower Management (d) All of the above
6. **Authority refers to**
   (a) Getting work done (b) Right to get work done
   (c) Being in a Managerial Position (d) Sports Authority of India

7. Scalar Chain refers to

(a) All the Managers in a company

(b) Chain of Command

(c) Chain of Communication

(d) Chain of Managers from top to bottom linked step-wise

8. ______ and ______ Management functions are closely related

(a) Planning and Organization (b) Planning and Control

(c) Staffing and Organization (d) Control and Co-ordinations

9. Who said "Management is What Manager does"

(a) Louis Allen (b) H.Fayol (c) Elton Mayo (d) Freud

10. According to Whom Administration and Management to be same

(a) Terry (b) P.F. Drucker (c) H.Fayol (d) None of these

11. Management is ____________

(a) An Art (b) A Science (c) A Profession (d) All the above

12. Who is the father of Scientific management?

(a) H.Fayol (b) F.W. Taylor (c) Koontz (d) Elton Mayo

13. Functional approach to Management was developed by

(a) Koontz (b) Taylor (c) Henry Fayol (d) None of these

14. Elton Mayo who is the founder of ___________

(a) Behavioralal Sciences Approach to Management

(b) Functional Approach to Management

(c) Scientific Approach to Management

(d) None of these

15. According to Henry Fayol the Management Functions are Planning, Organizing, Control, Command and ___________

(a) Direction (b) Evaluating (c) Motivating (d) Co-ordination

16. ______ are specific guides to action rather than thinking

(a) Objectives (b) Plan (c) Policies (d) Procedures

17. A________ means a definite plan of work made in sequence and in conformity with the organization's objectives

(a) Rules (b) Policies (c) Programme (d) Plan

18. A Statement of expected results expressed in numerical forms is called as ______

(a) Budget (b) Strategies (c) Goals (d) Programme

19. Conscious choice among alternative courses of action, is termed as ________

(a) Budget (b) Decision Marketing

(c) Strategies (d) Rule

20. A Vertical Hierarchy is associated with ______ Organization

(a) Line (b) Line and Staff (c) Committee (d) Functional

21. Communication can be in the form of ______

(a) Written (b) Oral (c) Formal (d) All the above

22. Body language in implies:

(a) Authority (b) Responsibility (c) Communication (d) Organization

23. Who Wrote a book "The making of Scientific Management"

(a) Thomas Gerad Rose (b) W.Taylor

(c) Fayol.H (d) Urwick and Breach

24. According to Taylor a single foreman can supervise ________ workers

(a) Seven (b) Eight (c) Nine (d) Eighteen

25. Who wrote the book "The Philosophy of Management"?

(a) C. McClelland (b) Oliver Sheldon (c) Maslow (d) Varoom

26. Taking remedial action is the important aspect of

(a) Co-ordination functions (b) Staffing functions

(c) Control functions (d) Organizing functions

27. Which of the following is the oldest type of organization?

(a) Bureaucratic organization (b) Committee organization

(c) Functional organization (d) Line organization

28. Functional staff are associated with ______

(a) Line Bosses (b) Committee Members

(c) Functional Managers (d) Top Executives

29. Henry Fayol wrote a book on ______

(a) The making of Scientific Management

(b) The Philosophy of Management

(c) General and Industrial Management

(d) None of the above

30. Each employee receiving orders from one superior refers to

(a) Unit of Command (b) Unity of Direction

(c) Order (d) Scalar Chain

31. ________ principle is refers to the elimination of the personal element from the work of the organization

(a) Unity of Direction

(b) Division of work

(c) Subordination of individual interest to the general interest

(d) None of the above

32. Any line of authority from the highest executive to the lower one, the purpose of communication refers to ______

(a) Unity of Command (b) Unity of Direction

(c) Scalar Chain (d) Esprit de Corps

33. Arrangement of things and persons is the principles relates to

(a) Order (b) Equity (c) Centralisation (d) Discipline

34. 'Union is Strength' is the principle denotes

(a) Imitative (b) Esprit de corps (c) Equity (d) Division of work

35. Overall determination of policies and major objectives refers to

(a) Administration (b) Management (c) Both a and b (d) Profession

36. Which of the following is relates to administration?

(a) Legislative function (b) Executive function

(c) Active direction of the human effort (d) Management function

37. Deciding in advance what to do is refers to ________

(a) Planning (b) Forecasting (c) Policies (d) Rules

38. Who is the father of "The making of scientific management"?

(a) Herbert G. Hicks (b) Charles Babbage

(c) Urwick and Breach (d) Thomas Gerald Rose

39. Who was developed the concept of law of situation?

(a) Mary Parker Follett (b) F.W. Taylor

(c) Charles Babbage (d) Adam smith

40. The principles and methods of management accountancy was developed by ______

(a) Alfred Marshal (b) Thomas Gerald Rose

(c) Oliver Sheldon (d) Urwick

41. ________ refers to strict adherence to the rules formulated and procedure evolved.

(a) Discipline (b) Control (c) Co-ordinations (d) Morale

42. _______ refers to the obligation to perform the work in the manner desired and directed by the superior authorities

(a) Authority (b) Responsibility (c) Accountability (d) None of these

43. According to H.Fayol _______ is the right to give orders and the power to extract obedience

(a) Delegation (b) Responsibility (c) Power (d) Authority

44. Which of the following principles are closely associated?

(a) Authority and Responsibility (b) Authority and Accountability

(c) Responsibility and Accountability (d) Authority and Power

45. Which of the following is not pre-requisites of maintaining discipline?

(a) Good supervisors at all levels (b) Clean and fair agreements

(c) Judicious application of penalties (d) None of these

46. Which of the following is not a fundamental principles of delegation?

(a) Unity of command (b) Desire of dominance

(c) Assignment of duty in terms of results (d) Parity of authority and responsibility

47. Delegations of Authority to be effective must ensure that ______

(a) Establishment of clear and definite objectives

(b) Clear cut assignment of duties

(c) Establishing of adequate control

(d) All the above

48. Team work and unity among personnel refers to

(a) Unity of Command (b) Equity

(c) Espirit de Corps (d) Scalar Chain

49. Which of the following is not a technique of control function?

(a) Auditing (b) Budgeting (c) Inventory control (d) Span of control

50. _______ has the effect of reduces the burden of the top management

(a) Centralisation (b) Decentralisation

(c) Delegation of Accountability (d) Departmentalisation

51. Decentralisation is suitable for _________

(a) Big concern (b) Small concern (c) Medium concern (d) All the above

52. Superior – subordinate relations on the basis of interactions results in _________

(a) Formal organization (b) Informal organization

(c) Functional organization (d) Committee organization

53. The concept of management "getting things done by other people" is described by

(a) Mescon – 1985 (b) Marry Parker Follett – 1941

(c) Robinsion – 1989 (d) John Harvey Johes – 1993

54. Fayol's Approach on the Management operation functions refers to _________

(a) Planning, Organising, Controlling and Direction

(b) Development of Incentive System

(c) Adaptation of Modern Technology

(d) Scientific Selection, Training and placement

55. Max Weber's ideals is based on ______

(a) Taylorism (b) Structure of the Organization

(c) Time and Motion study (d) Scientific Management

56. Elton Mayo emphasised the concept of _______

(a) Complex Man (b) Social Man

(c) Administrative Man (d) Organizational Man

57. In Taylor's scheme of functional foremanship, who lays down the important work to be performed?

(a) Speed Boss (b) Gang Boss (c) Route Clerk (d) Repair Boss

58. Which of the following is not related to middle level management?

(a) Director (b) Supervisors

(c) Foremens (d) Production managers

59. Production manager is a part of the ______ management.

(a) Top level (b) Middle level (c) Lowel level (d) None of the above

60. Overall directions and Co-ordination are the major activities of ______

(a) Senior level executives (b) Middle level managers

(c) Junior level supervisors (d) None of the above

61. ______ is refers to conscious choice among alternative courses of action.

(a) Decision making (b) Control (c) Co-ordination (d) Direction

62. The ______ function involves a consideration of the alternative courses of action available.

(a) Control (b) Organization (c) Planning (d) Direction

63. To guide the future direction of managerial activities and decisions for handling major problems refers to

(a) Programmes (b) Procedure (c) Strategies (d) Budgets

64. 'Look Ahead' in business relates to ______

(a) Business forecasting (b) Budgeting

(c) Strategies (d) Planning

65. According to ______ Decision making may be defined as a conscious choice among alternative courses of action.

(a) G.L.S. hackle (b) Philip Kotler (c) D.E.Mc Farland (d) T. Copeland

66. Which of the following is the charectertics of decision making?

(a) Is a goal oriented process (b) Is a selection process

(c) Is a continuous process (d) All the above

67. Decision making is an important aspect of ______

(a) Planning (b) Organising (c) Control (d) All the above

68. Which of the following is the process of Decision making?

(a) Identifying the problem

(b) Analysing the problem

(c) Developing alternative solution for the problem

(d) All the above

69. Deciding the best course of action on the basis of ______

(a) Past experience (b) Experiment

(c) Research and Analysis (d) All the above

70. Decision taken by the board of directors and the chief executive in the interest of the organization as a whole is known as ______

(a) Individual decisions (b) Basic or routine decisions

(c) Group decisions (d) Operating decisions

71. Decisions with regard to the quality and price of the product refers to ______

(a) Major and supplementary decisions (b) Organization and personal decisions

(c) Basic and routine decisions (d) Policy and operating decisions

72. State the important element of co-ordination?

(a) Resistance (b) Integration (c) Semantic (d) Emotional attitude

73. If co-ordination takes place between the two parties within the organization it is called ______

(a) Internal co-ordination (b) External co-ordination

(c) Vertical co-ordination (d) Horizontal co-ordination

74. Functional Organization is suitable for ______

(a) Small undertakings (b) Manufacturing undertakings

(c) Non-Manufacturing undertaking (d) Large undertaking

75. Which of the following relates to Line Authority?

(a) Executive authority (b) Right to command

(c) Wider power (d) All the above

76. Which of the following is not related to staff authority?

(a) Advisory authority (b) Right to command

(c) Limited power (d) Mere appendage to the authority

77. The legal adviser in the line and Staff Organization is:

(a) Promoters (b) Auditors (c) Workforce (d) Staff

78. F.W. Taylor has evolved ______foremanship as one of the principles of management

(a) Functional (b) Scientific (c) Modern (d) Professional

79. Which of the following obstacle relate to delegation on the part of the superior

(a) Lack of self-confidence (b) Lack of information

(c) Fear of criticism (d) Inability to direct

80. ______ refers to everything that goes to enhance the importance of a subordinate's role

(a) Decentralisation (b) Centralisation

(c) Delegation (d) Departmentalisation

81. Dividing the work, people and grouping them on some logical basis is called ______

(a) Departmentalisation (b) Delegation

(c) Centralisation (d) Decentralization

82. ______ refers to concentration of power of decision making at one point or in few hands

(a) Decentralization (b) Centralisation (c) Departmentation (d) Delegation

83. Effective delegation of authority depends on the subordinate's ______

(a) Education (b) Experience

(c) Awareness (d) Ability and potential

84. Delegation refers to ______

(a) An Art (b) A Science (c) A Profession (d) Group Activity

85. Which of the following relates to Delegation of Authority?

(a) Decreases superior's responsibility (b) Increase superior's responsibility

(c) No effect on superior's responsibility (d) Increase superior's accountability

86. Delegation of Authority signifies the delegation of ______________

(a) Authority (b) Responsibility (c) Accountability (d) Work

87. _______ is the obligation to carryout the responsibility and exercise of authority in term of performance of standards established.

(a) Responsibility (b) Authority (c) Accountability (d) Delegation

88. Delegation of Authority serves the functions of ____________

(a) Contralisation of responsibility (b) Concentration of power

(c) Distribution of workload (d) Decentralisation authority

89. __________ is the power to make decision which guide the actions of others

(a) Authority (b) Accountability

(c) Responsibility (d) None of these

90. The person who makes the decisions is the _______

(a) Executives (b) Subordinates (c) Superiors (d) Both a and c

91. _________ cannot be delegated as in the case of authority

(a) Responsibility (b) Accountability

(c) Authority (d) None of the above

92. The general manager asking the personnel manger to select staff on his behalf is an example of _________

(a) Delegation of Responsibility (b) Delegation of Authority

(c) Delegation of Accountability (d) Delegation of Work

93. Matrix Structure stands for ________

(a) Project Management (b) Product Management

(c) Both a and b (d) Marketing Management

94. Clover Leaf Organization was advocated by _______

(a) Ackoff (b) B. C.J. Livegood (c) Koontz (d) A.C. Filley

95. Matrix Organization aims at _________

(a) Better control of project (b) Better customer relation

(c) Lower programme cost (d) All the above

96. Who is the author of the book "The System Age (1974)?

(a) Jelinek Mariann (b) Ackoff

(c) Koontz and O'Donnel (d) Livegood .J

97. Circular Organizational Structure is developed on the basis of ________

(a) Hierarchical system (b) Worker's satisfaction

(c) Traditional system (d) Specific objectives

98. _______can be delegated as in the case of authority

(a) Responsibility (b) Accountability (c) Powers (d) Both a and c

99. Vertical Organizational chart is also termed as _________

(a) Pyramidical chart (b) Top to Down chart

(c) Left to Right chart (d) Both a and b

100. Which of the following Organization Chart moves from left to right?

(a) Vertical Chart (b) Horizontal Chart

(c) Circular Chart (d) Concentric Chart

101. Which of the following manuals give general duties and responsibilities of the top executives?

(a) Policy Manuals (b) Company Organization Manuals

(c) Department Manuals (d) All the above

102. Vertical Chart moves from ______

(a) Top to Down (b) Down to Top (c) Left to Right (d) Right to Left

103. Delegation generally moves ______

(a) Downward (b) Upward (c) Vertical (d) Horizontal

104. Which of the following is an important objective of budgeting?

(a) Planning (b) Co-ordination (c) Control (d) All the above

105. ________ is established by virtue of the power of sanctions?

(a) Formal Organization (b) Informal Organization

(c) Matrix Organization (d) Committee Organization

106. ______ refers to written description of the authority and responsibility relationship of all positions

(a) Organization Chart (b) Organization Manuals

(c) Organization Structure (d) Modification of Organization

107. ________ is an useful aid in gaining an insight in to the organizational relationship that exist in a particular enterprise.

(a) Organization Chart (b) Organization Manuals

(c) Organization Structure (d) Matrix Structure

108. ______ is established on the result of the spontaneous efforts of individuals and groups to influence the conditions of their experience.

(a) Formal Organization (b) Informal Organization

(c) Functional Organization (d) Committee Organization

109. Which of the following type of organization has a subordinate to work under more than one boss?

(a) Functional (b) Line and Staff (c) Line (d) Committee

110. _______ means a special kind of plan formulated to meet the challenges posed by competitors

(a) Schedule (b) Programme (c) Strategy (d) Objectives

111. Unit of Command is violated in the _______ organization

(a) Line (b) Line and Staff (c) Functional (d) All the above

112. Which of the following is most democratic form of organization?

(a) Line (b) Line and Staff (c) Functional (d) Committee

113. ________ defined as that function with in the organization with responsibility for overall operations of the enterprise.

(a) Administrative Management (b) Principles of Management

(c) Functional Management (d) Personnel Management

114. Which of the following relates to staffing function?

(a) Expert advise (b) Oversee work

(c) Selecting suitable persons (d) Take remedial action

115. The co-ordination functions of management aims at

(a) Providing manpower resources

(b) Bringing harmony in various activities

(c) Prompt decision making

(d) Achive targets

116. Directing function of management relates to

(a) Issuing of orders (b) Supervising

(c) Guiding and Teaching (d) All the above

117. Each subordinate must have only one superior to whom he is directly accountable refers to ________

(a) Unity of Command (b) Scalar Chain

(c) Delegation of Authority (d) Direction

118. The line of authority must be clearly defined is the important concept of ________

(a) Division of Labour (b) Scalar Chain

(c) Unity of Command (d) Delegation of Authority

119. Bringing harmony in various activities is the main aim of ________

(a) Control Functions (b) Staffing Functions

(c) Planning Function (d) Co-ordinations Functions

120. Administration refers to

(a) Determinative (b) Executive (c) Theoretical (d) Practical

121. Line and Staff system is combination of

(a) Line and Functional system of Organization

(b) Line and Committee system of Organization

(c) Line and Matrix structure of Organization

(d) Staff and Committee system of Organization

122. High degree of discipline and span of control are prime concepts of ________

(a) Line Organizations (b) Functional Organizations

(c) Line Organizations (d) Line and Staff Organizations

123. Military Organization is also termed as ______

(a) Line Organization (b) Functional Organization

(c) Formal Organization (d) Informal Organization

124. ______ is group of people who meet by plan to discuss or make a decision for a particular subject.

(a) Functional Organization (b) Committee Organization

(c) Line and Staff Organization (d) Line Organization

125. Line Committee is also called as ______

(a) Executive Committee (b) Plural Executive

(c) Both a and b (d) Advisory Committee

126. Matrix Structure is also termed as ______

(a) Grid Structure (b) Organization Structure

(c) Circular Structure (d) Clover leaf Structure

127. The term operating management stands for

(a) Top Management (b) Middle level Management

(c) Lower level Management (d) None of the above

128. The classical period is also called as______

(a) Scientific Management period (b) Neo-classical period

(c) Modern period (d) None of the above

129. Hawthorne Experiments was developed by ____

(a) Kast and Rosenzwieg (b) Elton Mayo

(c) Koontz (d) Louis Allen

130. Which of the following is the components of methods of planning?

(a) Objectives (b) Policies and Rules

(c) Procedure and programs (d) All the above

131. Continuing decision which applies to repetitive situations refers to ______

(a) Strategies (b) Programs (c) Objectives (d) Policies

132. ______ represent the end towards which all the managerial functions are directed

(a) Budgets (b) Procedures (c) Rules (d) Objectives

133. Which one of the following merit offered by policies?

(a) It helps in co-ordinations

(b) It provides stability in the organization

(c) It provides stability in the organization

(d) All the above

134. Original policies are formulated by ______

(a) Top level Management (b) Middle level management

(c) Lower level Management (d) None of the above

135. Which of the following does not relate to externally imposed polices?

(a) Government (b) Public Agencies

(c) Trade union and Trade Associations (d) Business Organizations

136. Policies formulated on the basis of objectives of the organization and their achievement refers to

(a) Implied polices (b) Appealed polices

(c) Originated policies (d) Externally imposed policies

137. Which of the following does not relate to planning?

(a) Determination of objectives (b) Setting rules and procedures

(c) Determining projects (d) Delegation of authority

138. Which of the following process does not relate to organization?

(a) Determination and enumeration of activities

(b) Grouping and assignment of activities

(c) Setting policies and strategies

(d) Delegation of authority

139. Controlling function is closely associated with ______

(a) Motivation (b) Leadership

(c) Communication (d) All the above

140. Which of the following is special feature of staffing functions?

(a) It is concerned with people (b) It initiates organised action

(c) Intangible in nature (d) Both a and c

141. Formulating policies is the principal function of ________

(a) Middle level Management (b) Lower level Management

(c) Top Management (d) None of these

142. Middle Level Management is concerned with the _______

(a) Determination of objectives

(b) Formulation of policies

(c) Execution of the policies and plans

(d) Preservation the morale the workers

143. Maintaining of the standard, quality and workmanship of the product is the important functions of

(a) Lower level Management (b) Middle level Management

(c) Top level Management (d) None of these

144. The power to command others would imply ______

(a) Royalty (b) Directorship (c) Brute force (d) Authority

145. The number of persons a manager can effectively manage refers to the ______

(a) Expertise (b) Co-ordination

(c) Unity of Command (d) Span of Control

146. Koontz and O'Donnel defined ________ as "the ability of a manager to introduce subordinates to work with confidence and zeal.

(a) Leadership (b) Motivation (c) Unity of Command (d) Authority

147. A leader seeking to exercise very little control or influence over group members should make a/an _______ leader

(a) Autocratic (b) Demogratic (c) Laissez-Faire (d) Professional

148. The desire to become what one is capable of becoming would be a/an _____ human needs

(a) Esteem (b) Physiological (c) Safety (d) Self realisation

149. Hygiene Theory of Motivation was developed by _____

(a) Maslow (b) Koontz and O'Donnel

(c) Varoom (d) Herzberg

150. Policy Making is an important process of _______

(a) Planning (b) Organising (c) Controlling (d) Co-ordination

151. The planning process begins with clearly laying down by

(a) Policies (b) Procedure

(c) Goals and Objectives (d) Programs

152. According to David C. McClelland, an individual major motives to work include the need for _______

(a) Achievement (b) Affiliations (c) Power (d) All the above

153. Military Organization is the best example of _______ Organization.

(a) Line (b) Line and staff (c) Committee (d) Functional

154. Which of the following is an important process of organizations?

(a) Definitions of the objectives (b) Enumeration of the activities

(c) Classifications of activities (d) All the above

155. Line Organization is also called as _______

(a) Scalar Organization (b) Traditional Organization

(c) Hierarchical Organization (d) All the above

156. Which of the following is the oldest and simplest form of organization?

(a) Line Organization (b) Line and Staff Organization

(c) Functional Organization (d) Committee Organization

157. The jobs of speed boss and Route clerk are likely is to be encountered in the _____ organization.

(a) Committee (b) Line (c) Functional (d) Military

158. Authority flows vertically from top management to the lowest subordinate refers to ______

(a) Line Organization (b) Line and Staff Organization

(c) Functional Organization (d) Committee Organization

159. _______ is refers to co-ordination takes place between the various links of the different levels of the organization unit.

(a) Internal Co-ordination (b) External Co-ordination
(c) Vertical Co-ordination (d) Horizontal Co-ordination

160. Clearly fixed responsibility is the main advantages of ______

(a) Functional Organization (b) Committee Organization
(c) Line Organization (d) Line and Staff Organization

161. The most important element in an organization is ______

(a) Production (b) Money (c) Material (d) People

162. Achievement Tests is also known as ______

(a) Proficiency Test (b) Interest Test
(c) Aptitude Test (d) Personality Test

163. Induction training is also known as ______

(a) Orientation (b) Refresher (c) Indoctrination (d) Both a and c

164. Communication in an organization should ideally flow ______

(a) From top to bottom (b) From bottom to top
(c) From right to left (d) Both a and b

165. Considerable employee motivation results in ______

(a) Specialisation (b) Boosting morale
(c) Meet targets (d) None of the above

66. _______ means very little control is exercised over group members

(a) Autocratic Leadership (b) Democratic Leadership
(c) Lessez-Fair Leadership (d) Professional Leadership

167. According to theory X, workers _______

(a) Desire to work (b) Exercise self direction
(c) Prefer to be directed (d) Desire to pretend to be bosses

168. Expectancy Theory of motivation is associated with ______

(a) Drucker (b) Maslow (c) Herzberg (d) Vroom

169. Collective Bargaining Theory is developed by ______

(a) Dunlop (b) Drucker (c) Mc. Farland (d) H.Fayol

170. Management by Exception implies that _______problems are looked after by the top management

(a) All sorts of (b) Only important (c) Only routine (d) Day to day

171. Grapevine is a term relating to ______

(a) Informal communication (b) Formal communication
(c) Written communication (d) Oral communication

172. Span of Management is also called as _______

(a) Span of Supervision (b) Span of Authority
(c) Span of Managerial Responsibility (d) All the above

173. ________ refers to activities which can be grouped according to the process involved or the equipments used

(a) Departmentation by Process (b) Departmentation by Product

(c) Departmentation by Function (d) Departmentation by Number

174. Management by Objectives (MBO) was first proposed by ________

(a) Peter Drucker (b) Greiner (c) Pofer, Michael (d) Gilbreth

175. Which of the following principle relates to of Management by Objectives ?

(a) Establishment of objectives

(b) Performance

(c) Appraisal of performance based on the objectives

(d) All the above

176. ________ is the process of searching for prospective employees and stimulating them to apply for jobs in the organizations.

(a) Selection (b) Recruitment (c) Promotions (d) Tests

177. Which of the following method of recruiting is not from external sources

(a) Advertisement (b) Employment Exchange

(c) Personnel Consultants (d) None of these

178. Performance test is useful for

(a) Selecting experienced workers

(b) Identify the brilliant candidates

(c) Measuring overall learning ability

(d) Evaluate the interest of the candidate

179. Which of the following test is used to measure the mental ability or mental alertness of the applicant

(a) Performance Tests (b) Intelligence Tests

(c) Personality Tests (d) Aptitude Tests

180. Which of the following equation relates to Vroom's Theory of Motivation?

(a) Motivation = Valance x Expectancy

(b) Motivation = Valance x Expectancy

(c) Motivation = Valance x Efforts

(d) None of the above

181. According Vroom's Theory of Motivation, performance may be stated as ________

(a) Performance = Attractiveness x Effort

(b) Performance = Attractiveness x Expectancy

(c) Performance = Valance x Expectancy

(d) Performance = Attractiveness x Valance

182. Which of the following refers to SMART?

(a) Specific, Measurable, Attitude, Result and Time
(b) Specific, Measurable, Attainable, Result and Target
(c) Skill, Measurable, Action, Result and Time limit
(d) Specific, Measurable, Attainable, Result and Time limit

183. Leadership Theory of X and Y was developed by ______

(a) John Adair (b) Douglas Mc Gregor
(c) Relph stogdill (d) Donnell and Hall

184. The Path-Goal Theory of Leadership was developed by ______

(a) Hersey and Blanchard (b) Robert House
(c) Vroom and Yetton (d) Stoner and E-Freeman

185. Hersey and Blanchard's Situational Theory of Leadership mainly focuses on ______

(a) Hardwork (b) Confidence (c) Maturity (d) Experience

186. Under Expectancy Theory of Motivation, Motivation increases with ______ in valance

(a) Decrease (b) Increase (c) Not effect (d) None of the above

187. In Herzberg's Theory of Motivation, the hygine factor cause ______ among employees.

(a) Satisfaction (b) Dissatisfaction
(c) Most satisfaction (d) None of the above

188. Dunlop has given the theory on ______

(a) Collective Bargaining (b) Motivation
(c) Expectancy theory (d) Theory X and Y

189. Which of the following is not a functions of management?

(a) Co-operations (b) Co-ordinations
(c) Planning (d) Direction

190. Which of the following technique is used to achieve effective co-ordinations

(a) Group meetings (b) Direct contract
(c) Effective communications (d) All the above

ANSWERS

1. (a) Noun
2. (c) Transfer of authority from one individual to another
3. (b) An employee receives order from one superior
4. (a) Fixed Plan
5. (d) All of the above
6. (b) Right to get work done
7. (d) Chain of Manager from top to bottom linked step-wise
8. (b) Planning and control
9. (a) Louis Allan
10. (d) None of these
11. (d) All the above
12. (b) F.W. Taylor
13. (c) Henry Fayol

14. (a) Behavioralal Sciences Approach to Management
15. (d) Co-ordinations
16. (d) Procedures
17. (c) Programme
18. (a) Budget
19. (b) Decision Making
20. (a) Line
21. (d) All the above
22. (c) Communication
23. (d) Urwick and Breach
24. (b) Eight
25. (b) Oliver Sheldon
26. (c) Control function
27. (d) Line Organization
28. (a) Line Bosses
29. (c) General and Industrial Management
30. (a) Unity of Command
31. (c) Subordination of individual interest to the general interest
32. (c) Scalar Chain
33. (a) Order
34. (b) Esprit de Corps
35. (b) Management
36. (a) Legislative function
37. (a) Planning
38. (c) Urwick and Breach
39. (a) Marry Parker Follett
40. (b) Thomas Gerald Rose
41. (a) Discipline
42. (b) Resposibility
43. (d) Authority
44. (a) Authority and Responsibility
45. (d) None of the above
46. (b) Desire of dominance
47. (d) All the above
48. (c) Espirit de Corps
49. (d) Span of Control
50. (b) Decentralisation
51. (a) Big Concern
52. (b) Informal Organization
53. (b) Marry Parker Follett – 1941
54. (a) Planning, Organising, Controlling and Direction
55. (b) Structure of the Organization
56. (b) Social Man
57. (c) Route Clerk
58. (d) Production Managers
59. (b) Middle level
60. (a) Senior level executives
61. (a) Decision making
62. (c) Planning
63. (c) Strategies
64. (a) Business Forecasting
65. (b) Philip Kotler
66. (d) All the above
67. (d) All the above
68. (d) All the above
69. (d) All the above
70. (c) Group Decisions
71. (a) Major and supplementary Decisions
72. (b) Integration
73. (a) Internal co-ordination
74. (c) Non-Manufacturing undertakings
75. (d) All the above
76. (b) Right to command
77. (d) Staff
78. (a) Functional
79. (d) Inability to direct
80. (a) Decentralisation
81. (a) Departmentation
82. (b) Centralisation
83. (d) Ability and potential
84. (a) An Art
85. (a) Decreases Superior's Responsibility
86. (a) Authority
87. (c) Accountability
88. (c) Distribution of workload
89. (a) Authority
90. (d) Both a and c
91. (b) Accountability
92. (b) Delegation of Authority
93. (c) Both a and b
94. (b) B.C.J. Livegood

95. (d) All the above
96. (b) Ackoff
97. (a) Hierarchical System
98. (d) Both a and c
99. (d) Both a and b
100. (b) Horizontal Chart
101. (b) Company Organization Manuals
102. (a) Top to Down
103. (a) Downward
104. (d) All the above
105. (a) Formal Organization
106. (b) Organization Manuals
107. (a) Organization Chart
108. (b) Informal Organization
109. (c) Line
110. (c) Strategy
111. (d) All the above
112. (d) Committee
113. (a) Administrative Management
114. (c) Selecting suitable persons
115. (b) Bringing harmony in various activities
116. (d) All the above
117. (a) Unity of Command
118. (b) Scalar Chain
119. (d) Co-ordination Function
120. (a) Determinative
121. (a) Line and Functional system
122. (d) Line and Staff Organization
123. (a) Line Organization
124. (b) Committee organization
125. (c) Both a and b
126. (a) Grid structure
127. (c) Lower level Management
128. (a) Scientific Management period
129. (b) Elton Mayo
130. (d) All the above
131. (d) Policies
132. (b) Procedures
133. (d) All the above
134. (a) Top level Management
135. (d) Business Organization
136. (c) Originated Policies
137. (d) Delegation of Authority
138. (c) Setting policies and strategies
139. (d) All the above
140. (d) Both a and c
141. (c) Top Management
142. (c) Execution of the policies and plans
143. (a) Lower level Management
144. (d) Authority
145. (d) Span of Control
146. (a) Leadership
147. (c) Laissez-Faire
148. (d) Self realisation
149. (d) Herzberg
150. (a) Planning
151. (c) Goals and Objectives
152. (d) All the above
153. (a) Line
154. (d) All the above
155. (d) All the above
156. (a) Line Organization
157. (c) Functional
158. (a) Line Organization
159. (c) Vertical Co-ordination
160. (c) Line Organization
161. (d) People
162. (a) Proficiency test
163. (d) Both a and c
164. (d) Both a and c
165. (b) Boosting morale
166. (c) Lessez-Fair Leadership
167. (c) Prefer to be directed
168. (c) Herzberg
169. (a) Dunlog
170. (a) Only important
171. (a) Informal communication
172. (d) All the above
173. (a) Departmentation by Process
174. (a) Peter Drucker
175. (d) All the above
176. (b) Recruitment
177. (d) None of these
178. (a) Selecting experienced workers
179. (b) Intelligence Tests
180. (a) Motivation = Valance X Expectancy
181. (a) Performance = Attractiveness X Effort
182. (d) Specific, Measurable, Attainable, Result and Time limit
183. (b) Douglas Mc Gregor
184. (b) Rebort House
185. (c) Maturity
186. (b) Increase
187. (b) Dissatisfaction
188. (a) Collective Bargaining
189. (a) Co-operation
190. (d) All the above.

****

II

MANUFACTURING ANALYSIS, PRODUCTION MANAGEMENT AND MATERIAL MANAGEMENT

1. An organized activity of converting raw materials into useful product is called______

(a) Production Function (b) Production Planning

(c) Production System (d) Production Environment

2. The term Product Assembly refers to ______

(a) The final stage of productions (b) Intermediate stage of production

(c) Initial stage of production (d) All the above

3. In the stage of development in production management attention given to controlling is refers to as

(a) Factory Labour Cost (b) Factory Material Cost

(c) Materials Handing Cost (d) Factory Over Heads

4. The Process of production may occur _______

(a) In series (b) In parallel

(c) In series and parallel (d) None of these

5. The larger the plant is refers to ______

(a) Simpler is the production problem (b) Complex is the production problem

(c) Has no relation with production problem (d) All the above

6. In a Capital Intensive Production System the dominant position is occupied by ______

(a) Labour Policy (b) Material Procurement Policy

(c) Capital Investment Policy (d) Replacement Policy

7. A Developed Economy is associated with ______

(a) Large output per man hour (b) Low output per man hour

(c) Average out put per man hour (d) No effect on output per man hour

8. An Underdeveloped Economy is characterized by ______

(a) Efficient Production System (b) Inefficient Production System

(c) Organized Production System (d) Un Organized Production System

9. In Developed Economics

(a) Cost of machines are low (b) Cost of equipment are low

(c) Cost of labours are high (d) All the above

10. A productions system is said to be efficient if it minimizes the

(a) Resources per unit of production

(b) Resources per unit of marketing the products

(c) Resources per unit of administration expenses

(d) None of these

11. The success production depends on

(a) Sound Production Plan (b) Good Information System

(c) Effective Decision Making Techniques (d) All the above

12. As the number components increases the reliability

(a) Increases (b) Decreases

(c) Remains constant (d) None of these

13. The manufacture of products to meet the specific customers requirement is called ______

(a) Job Production (b) Batch Production

(c) Flow Production (d) Mass Production

14. The manufacture of products concerned with special projects models, prototypes, special machinery or equipment is called______

(a) Continuous Production (b) Batch Production

(c) Job Production (d) Flow Production

15. If machinery setup is used for only a short time and then changed to some other different product, this is known as _____

(a) Job Production (b) Batch Production

(c) Mass Production (d) Flow Production

16. Which of the following example relates to Batch Production?

(a) Large steam turbines (b) Machine tools, glass manufacturing

(c) Mechanized stamping shop (d) Household machinery

17. The job shop manufacturing situation where custom products are fabricated and assembled is ______

(a) A continuous Production System (b) Most Complex Type of Production System

(c) Mass Production System (d) None of these

18. Continuous Flow of Production undertaken by factories is called ______

(a) Two shift basis
(b) Single shift basis
(c) Three shift basis
(d) None of these

19. Intermittent Flow of Production Systems are those where the facilities must be flexible enough to handle a ________

(a) Uniform products
(b) Variety of products and sizes
(c) Both 'a' and 'b'
(d) Unrelated Products

20. In Intermittent Production System, we normally find a

(a) Fixed operations sequence
(b) Variety of operation sequence
(c) Mixed operation sequence
(d) Complex operation sequence

21. A mathematical study of production structure of industries where the different sectors of industries are inter-dependent on each other is known as ______

(a) Value Analysis
(b) Input Output Analysis
(c) Product Analysis
(d) Industrial Analysis

22. The maximum output which can be achieved with a given inputs or say resources with a given state of technology is determined by the help of _______

(a) Productivity
(b) Production Function
(c) Linear Programming
(d) Operation Research

23. If a manufacturing concern, producing 10 items per day with an expenditure of Rs.50, expands its facilities, and then produced 12 items at the expenditure of Rs.55, then its productivity will be said to be ______

(a) Increased
(b) Decreased
(c) Constant
(d) None of these

24. ABC Ltd, with an investment of Rs.50 lakhs, produces garments for exports, has an output of Rs.250 lakhs per year and decided to expand and produced 500 lakhs with an input of Rs400 lakhs, then its productivity will be said to be ______

(a) Increased
(b) Decreased
(c) constant
(d) something else

25. Maximum productivity can be increased through control and effective management of ______

(a) Labour Management
(b) Material Management
(c) Production Management
(d) Management of Finance

26. Sub-Optimizations can take place through short range view of

(a) Maximizing profits
(b) An organizational narrow gauge view
(c) Both 'a' and 'b'
(d) None of these

27. By Comparing an individual's performance to a standard performance indexes can be computed for ______

(a) Whole department
(b) Whole division
(c) Whole plant
(d) All the above

28. Production Plans are attempts to allocate available resources in the most effective way for a given ________.

(a) Forecast of demand (b) Forecast of supply/sales

(c) Forecast of cost (d) Forecast of cost/demand

29. Waste conversion is a part of the __________ and must be included in a conceptual frame work

(a) Marketing process (b) Production process

(c) Both 'a' and 'b' (d) Inventory process

30. Input – Output Analysis is processed through ________

(a) Work Study (b) Transaction Matrix

(c) Value Analysis (d) Product Analysis

31. Input - Output Analysis is used for making decisions pertaining to economic policy at ________

(a) National level (b) Industry level

(c) Factory level (d) All the level

32. If output of one sector of economy is consumed as input raw materials of the other sector of economy then they are said ________

(a) Inter dependent sectors (b) Independent sectors

(c) Mutual benefit sectors (d) Organized sectors

33. ________ refers to either to reduce the number of product lines is the product mix or to reduce the number of products it in product lines

(a) Optimum Product Mix (b) Product Mix

(c) Contraction of Product Mix (d) Place Mix

34. Which of the following is related to Product Line?

(a) Specific product of certain specification

(b) Group of different product items

(c) Composite of all the product offered for sale

(d) None of these

35. A group of different product items, closely related with each other is known as________

(a) Product Item (b) Product Mix

(c) Product Line (d) Consistency of Product Mix

36. Which of the following refers to Width of Product Mix ?

(a) Number of product lines being produced by the producer

(b) Average of number of product items in a product line of producer

(c) Product lines of an enterprises are related with one another

(d) None of these

37. Which of the following relates to Method Study?

(a) To improve methods of productions (b) To assess human effectiveness

(c) To select the work to be measured (d) All the above

38. Which of the following is the basic components of Work Study?

(a) Method Study (b) Work Measurement

(c) Time Study (d) Both 'a' and 'b'

39. Which of the following symbol relates to storage of Process Chart?

(a) ○ (b) □ (c) D (d) ▽

40. _________ is refers to a pictorial representations of the activities that occur in the work method or procedure, in which suitable symbols are used to represent the various activities

(a) Process Chart (b) Simo Chart

(c) Flow Diagram (d) Cyclograph

41. Which of the following techniques is used to Work Measurement?

(a) Time study (b) Pre-Determined Motion Time System

(c) Analytical Estimating (d) All the above

42. ___________ is refers to the application of techniques to establish the time for a qualified worker to carry out specified work at a defined level of performance

(a) Motion Study (b) Method Study

(c) Work Measurement (d) Time Study

43. Time study engineer multiplies actual time with a factor known as _______ to get the average time which a normal worker would take

(a) Retain Factor (b) Leveling Factor

(c) Both a and b (d) Synthetic Rating

44. Performance Rating can be measured by ___________

(a) $\text{Performance Rating} = \dfrac{\text{Observed Performance}}{\text{Normal performance}} \times 100$

(b) $\text{Performance Rating} = \dfrac{\text{Normal performance}}{\text{Observed performance}} \times 100$

(c) $\text{Performance Rating} = \dfrac{\text{Rating Factor}}{\text{Average of Actual Time}} \times 100$

(d) None of these

45. Value Analysis for cost reduction technique was developed by__________

(a) L.H.C. Tippett (b) RIL. Morrow (c) Lorry D. Miles (d) Gordon B. Carson

46. Value can be measured by _______

(a) $\text{Value} = \dfrac{\text{Function}}{\text{Cost}}$

(b) $\text{Value} = \dfrac{\text{Utility}}{\text{Cost}}$

(c) $\text{Value} = \dfrac{\text{Cost}}{\text{Function}}$

(d) Both 'a' and 'b'

47. Use value is also called as ________

(a) Functional Value (b) Esteem Value

(c) Exchange Value (d) Cost Value

48. Which of the following is the aim of Value Analysis?

(a) Simplify the product

(b) Use cheaper and better materials

(c) Modify and improve product design

(d) All the above

49. ________ refers to the process of measuring the qualities of a product or service in terms of established standards

(a) Checking (b) Inspection

(c) Supervision (d) Identification

50. Centralized Inspections implies

(a) Is done at one centralized place

(b) More materials handling is involved

(c) All the items are brought for inspections

(d) All the above

51. ______ refers to the industrial management technique or group of techniques by means of which products of uniform acceptable quality are maintained.

(a) Quality Control (b) Cost Control

(c) Inventory Control (d) Span of Control

52. Acceptable Quality Level (AQL) means

(a) Quality level of a good lot (b) Quality level of a bad lot

(c) Quality level of a moderate lot (d) Quality level of average lot

53. Lot Tolerance Percent Defective (LTPD) means

(a) Quality level of a good lot (b) Quality level of a bad lot

(c) High probability of acceptance (d) Quality level of a moderate lot

54. X Chart is one of the type of ________

(a) Process Chart (b) Control Chart (c) Order Chart (d) None of these

55. Which of the following application relates to P Chart?

(a) Control of individual characteristics

(b) Control of overall number of defects per unit

(c) Control of overall fraction defective of a process

(d) None of the above

56. ________ refers to the process of transforming raw materials into finished products for sale

(a) Production (b) Development

(c) Creation (d) Concept Development

57. In the conversion process, the value added is the difference between ______ and ______

(a) Value added = Value of input – Value of output

(b) Value added = Value of output – Value of input

(c) Value added = Value of raw material – Value of finished good

(d) Value added = Value of WIP - Value of input

58. The Ratio of Productivity refers to

(a) productivity = $\frac{\text{Input}}{\text{Output}}$

(b) Productivity = $\frac{\text{Output}}{\text{Input}}$

(c) Productivity = $\frac{\text{Output of wealth produced}}{\text{Input of resources used}}$

(d) Both 'b' and 'c'

59. __________ refers to the arrangements of facilities in a particular work station

(a) Production System (b) Production Process

(c) Plant Layout (d) Production Environment

60. _________ refers to the upkeep and protection of plant, building, machinery and other fixed assets

(a) Maintenance (b) Plant Layout

(c) Production System (d) None of these

61. _______ refers to the systematic and analytical study of work process and work methods with the objective of increasing efficiency and reducing cost

(a) Method Study (b) Motion Study

(c) Work Study (d) Time Study

62. Which of the following properties is not related to Principles of Materials?

(a) Physical Properties (b) Mechanical Properties

(c) Chemical Properties (d) Service Properties

63. Melting point, specific point, specific gravity are the features of

(a) Chemical properties (b) Manufacturing point of view

(c) Physical properties (d) Mechanical properties

64. Which of the following properties relates to manufacturing point of view?

(a) Castability, Weldability and Brazability (b) Oil, Greases and Petrol

(c) Compressive, Bending and Shear (d) Magnetic properties, Specific gravity

65. Ferrous metals are commonly used as materials in ___________

(a) Manufacturing Industries (b) Hotel and Hospitals

(c) Service Industries (d) Agricultural Industries

66. Which of the following is the example of Non-Ferrous Metals?

(a) Aluminum (b) Copper (c) Tin (d) All the above

67. If cast iron retains the whole carbon, it is known as _______

(a) Chilled Cast Iron (b) White Cast Iron

(c) Alloy Cast (d) Grey Cast Iron

68. Nickel, Chromium, Silicon are the main element of _____

(a) Malleable Cast Iron (b) Alloy Cast Iron

(c) White Cast Iron (d) Chilled Cast Iron

69. Which of the following relates to high carbon of plain carbon steel?

(a) Structural for buildings (b) Boiler plate

(c) Railway rails (d) Steel rolling mills

70. _______ refers to a process of joining similar metals by the application of heat filter

(a) Welding (b) Soldering (c) Brazing (d) None of these

71. _______ refers to the method of joining two or more sheet metals by means of a fusible alloy

(a) Welding (b) Soldering (c) Brazing (d) None of these

72. ______ refers to the process of joining two metals in which a non-ferrous alloy is introduced

(a) Welding (b) Soldering (c) Brazing (d) None of these

73. Welding process is mainly applicable to _____

(a) Aeronautical Industries (b) Electric and Electronic Industries

(c) Fastening the Pipe Fittings (d) Chemical Industries

74. Which of the following relates to the melting point of Brazing?

(a) 2500^{oC} (b) 150.–900^{oC} (c) 650. – 800^{oC} (d) 1200^{oC}

75. _______ refers to the processes of pouring a molten metal into a prepared cavity or mould and allowing it to solidify

(a) Forging (b) Cashing (c) Extruding (d) Sizing

76. Lathe is popularly known as _______

(a) King of Machines (b) Versatile Machine

(c) Miller (d) Both 'a' and 'b'

77. Which of the following is the main operation of Lathes?

(a) Screw cutting (b) Parting (c) Boring (d) All the above

78. Which of the following does not relate to planning machines?

(a) It is meant for big jobs (b) Cutting and return speed are uniform

(c) Work table is stationary (d) Tools are robust

79. Which of the following is the element of Alloy Steel?

(a) Nickel (b) Cobalt (c) Tin (d) Both 'a' and 'b'

80. A Nickel Alloy containing 36% of Nickel is called ________

(a) Invar Steel (b) Stainless Steel (c) Lead (d) Tin

81. Stainless steel are mainly employed for ______

(a) Magnetic materials (b) Nuclear power productions

(c) Electrical machinery (d) Surgical instruments

82. Which of the following is not related to Flow Production System?

(a) The volume of output is made at large scale

(b) Special purpose machines are used

(c) Flow of production is continuous

(d) It is carried on to specific consumer's demand

83. Which of the following is not related to Intermittent Productions?

(a) The flow of production is irregular

(b) Sequence of operations are subject to change

(c) It is cheaper

(d) Special purpose machines are used

84. Electrical, bicycles and automobiles are the examples of________

(a) Process Production (b) Assembly Lines

(c) Mass Production (d) Job Production

85. ________ refers to the manufacturing of a single complete unit with the use of a team of employees

(a) Batch Production (b) Job Production

(c) Process Production (d) Assembly Lines

86. ________ refers to a process by which the physical properties or features of materials are modified with the help of operators and machines

(a) Metal working processes (b) Fabrication processes

(c) Machining process (d) None of these

87. Which of the following is related to Shaper?

(a) Work table reciprocate and the tool is held rigid

(b) It is costlier

(c) It is meant for small jobs

(d) It is meant for big jobs

88. Cutting tools are used to give shape to work shape by cutting away extra material which is called as _______

(a) Chips (b) Scrape (c) Jigs (d) None of these

89. __________ refers to the mooring of a procession of materials and part in and out of machines and the operating of the machines automatically, all without human control

(a) Automations (b) Up gradation

(d) Mechanization (d) Advancement

90. _______ refers to either a place where goods are produced or distributed or where services are provided

(a) Firm (b) Plant (c) Industry (d) Unit

91. A business unit or undertaking which owns the plant, controls and manages it refers to

(a) Firm (b) Unit (c) Plant (d) Both a and b

92. All the firm owning, controlling and managing plants engaged in the production of similar products are collectively known as _______

(a) Plant (b) Industry (c) Organization (d) Concern

93. Input can be measured on the basis of _________

(a) Value of the factors of productions employed

(b) Volume of the factors of production employed

(c) Value of output and size of business unit

(d) Both a and b

94. Which of the following technique is used for choice of equipment?

(a) Differential Yield method (b) Capitalized Cost method

(c) Minimum Annual Cost Method (d) All the above

95. Which of the following methods is used for analysis of replacement of existing machines?

(a) Minimum Annual Cost

(b) MAP (Machinery and Allied Product) Analysis

(c) Both 'a' and 'b'

(d) Differential Yield Method

96. Weber's Deductive Theory of location has identified two important factors viz _______ and _______

(a) Transportation Costs, Labour Costs

(b) Material Costs, Interest on Investments

(c) Administrative Cost, Factory Costs

(d) Works Costs, Labour Costs

97. According to Weber's Deductive Theory, Material Index can be calculated by

(a) Material Index $= \dfrac{\text{Weight of localised Labours}}{\text{Weight of finished products}}$

(b) Material Index $= \dfrac{\text{Weight of localised Materials}}{\text{Weight of transported}}$

(c) Material Index $= \dfrac{\text{Weight of localised materials}}{\text{Weight of finished product}}$

(d) None of these

98. Inductive Analysis of location was developed by _______

(a) Weber (b) Sargant Florence

(c) Machinery and Allied Product Institute (d) Prof. Florence

99. Which of the following is related to location identified by Sargant Florence for Inductive Analysis?

(a) Transportation Cost (b) Location Factor

(c) Co-efficient of Localization (d) Both 'b' and 'c'

100. Which of the following primary factor is affects Location?

(a) Availability of raw materials (b) Site and services

(c) Finance (d) Personal factor

101. Purchasing for profit is the primary objective of ________

(a) Production Management (b) Material Management

(c) Marketing Management (d) Inventory Management

102. ________ refers to the scientific way of determining the requirement of raw materials, components spares and other items that go into meeting production needs

(a) Materials Planning (b) Production Planning

(c) Sales Planning (d) Both a and b

103. Which of the following techniques is used for Material Planning?

(a) Bill of Material Technique

(b) Past Consumption Analysis Technique

(c) Both a and b

(d) Systems Approach

104. ________ refers to the process of systematically defining and describing all items in stock

(a) Identification (b) Classification (c) Codification (d) Grading

105. ________ refers to assigning or giving a code number or symbol to a stores item

(a) Classifications (b) Codifications (c) Grading (d) Identification

106. Which of the following method is related to Codifications?

(a) Kodak System (b) The Brisch System

(c) Numerical Codification (d) All the above

107. Material Handling is the ________

(a) Art (b) Science (c) Both a and b (d) Profession

108. Which of the following is not related to Material Handling?

(a) Movement (b) Time (c) Quantity and Space (d) None of these

109. Safety Stock is also called as________

(a) Minimum Inventory (b) Buffer Stock

(c) Reserve Stock (d) All the above

110. Which of the following family is not related to CPM (Critical Path Method)?

(a) CPA (Critical Path Analysis)

(b) CPS (Critical Path Scheduling)

(c) PEP (Program Evaluation Procedure)

(d) MCM (Minimum Cost Expenditure)

111. Which of the basic factor is related to plant location?

(a) Land and Building (b) Transportations Cost
(c) Labour (d) All the above

112. __________ refers to the phase of production control which rates the work in the order of its priority and then provides for its release to the plant at the proposed time and in the correct sequence

(a) Routing (b) Scheduling (c) Dispatching (d) Expediting

113. Building raw materials, machine and equipments relate to __________

(a) Material functions (b) Production functions
(c) Marketing functions (d) Personnel functions

114. Products are produced according to specializations refers to

(a) Line Layout (b) Process Layout
(c) Stationary Layout (d) Combined Layout

115. Conveyor refers to __________

(a) Fixed Path Equipment (b) Movable Path Equipment
(c) Non-Movable Path Equipment (d) Combined Path Equipment

116. Rating of work relates to __________

(a) Routing (b) Scheduling (c) Dispatching (d) Processes Chart

117. The device used to describe the job pictorially refers to __________

(a) Gantt Chart (b) Order Chart (c) Process Chart (d) Mean Chart

118. Arranging for finance, storage and distribution are functions relating to ______

(a) Material Management (b) Integrated Material Management
(c) Production Management (d) Purchase Management

119. Lead time is one of the problem relating to ______

(a) Procurement of Material (b) Materials Planning
(c) Design and Specification (d) Obsolescence

120. Inventory Control is the function relating to ______

(a) Production Management (b) Material Management
(c) Production and Material Management (d) Marketing Management

121. Gantt Chart is also known as ______

(a) Bar Chart (b) Milestone Chart (c) Program Chart (d) Flow Chart

122. ______________ refers to the represent the planned sequential relationship of work performance

(a) Bar Chart (b) Gantt Chart (c) Progress Chart (d) Flow Chart

123. Flow-Chart was developed by __________

(a) Mr. Henry L. Gantt (b) Gilberths (c) D.R. Fulkerson (d) None of these

124. Logic planning of activities separated from time scheduling refers to

(a) Bar Chart (b) Net Work (c) CPM (d) PERT

125. ____________ refers to a particular instant in time showing the end or beginning of an activity

(a) Event (b) Activity (c) Incident (d) Occurrence

126. ___________ refers to efforts applied over a period of time which has a definite beginning and end

(a) Event (b) Performance (c) Activity (d) Transactions

127. Activity on the arrow system of the network representations is also known as ______

(a) AOA System (b) Arrow Diagram Method

(c) Both a and b d) Activity on the Node System

128. ______ refers to ascertain whether a business enterprise is properly discharging its obligations to the society or not

(a) Social Audit (b) Company Audit (c) Internal Audit (d) External Audit

129. Who is in charge of Stores Department?

(a)Chief Store Keeper (b) Stores Superintendent

(c) Both a and b (d) Production Manager

130. Which of the following is the major responsibilities of store?

(a) Receipt of incoming goods (b) Packing

(c) Store accounting (d) All the above

131. ____ refers to materials raw, in process, finished packaging, spares and others stocked in order to meet an unexpected demand or distribution in the future

(a) Inventory (b) production (c) Stock (d) Both a and c

132. Lubricating oil, soap, machine spare parts are the example of

(a) Productions Inventories (b) MRO Inventories

(c) In – process Inventories (d) Finished goods Inventories

133. Cost of receiving a nd inspecting the materials relates to

(a) Ordering Cost (b) Carrying Costs

(c) Storage Space Costs (d) Inventory Service Costs

134. Which of the following relates to inventory risk costs?

(a) Obsolescence (b) Cost of machine set-up

(c) Insurance on inventory (d) Rent on building

135. Which of the following is not related to storage space cost?

(a) Rent on building (b) Depreciations on building

(c) Cost of maintenance (d) Losses from pilferage

136. ABC Analysis stands for _________

(a) Always Better Control (b) Always Best Control

(c) Accurate Better Control (d) Always Before Control

137. According to ABC classification 'c' indicates________

(a) High in value and low in quantity

(b) High in quantity and low in value

(c) More or less equal in quantity and in value

(d) None of these

138. Which of the following is the basis of VED classifications inventories?

(a) Consumption value (b) Unit value

(c) Criticality of inventories (d) Qualities

139. Which of the following relates to FSN Analysis?

(a) High, Medium and Low

(b) Always Better Control

(c) Vital, Essential and Desirable

(d) Fast Moving, Slow Moving and Non-Moving

140. Two-Bin technique is adopted to control________

(a) 'A' Group Inventories (b) 'B' Groups Inventories

(c) 'C' Group Inventories (d) All the above

141. Just in Time is also known as________

(a) ZIPS (Zero Inventory Productions System)

(b) MAN(Materials As Needed)

(c) NOT (Nick of Time)

(d) All the above

142. Overall Inventory Turn Over Ratio can be calculated by

(a) Overall Inventory Turn over Ratio $= \dfrac{\text{Cost of good sold}}{\text{Average Inventory at cost}}$

(b) Overall Inventory Turnover Ratio $= \dfrac{\text{Sales}}{\text{Average inventory.}}$

(c) Overall Inventory Turnover Ratio $= \dfrac{\text{Sales}}{\text{Total Inventory}}$

(d) None of these

143. Raw Materials Inventory Turnover Ratio can be calculated by

(a) Raw materials Inventory Turnover Ratio $= \dfrac{\text{Cost of goods sold}}{\text{Average inventory at cost}}$

(b) Raw Materials Inventory turnover ratio $= \dfrac{\text{Annual consumptions of raw materials}}{\text{Average raw materials inventory}}$

(c) Raw materials inventory Turnover Ratio $= \dfrac{\text{Sales}}{\text{Average raw material inventory}}$

(d) None of these

144. Which of the following is used to measure Finished Goods Inventory Turnover Ratio?

(a) Cost of goods sold and average finished goods inventory at cost

(b) Cost of goods sold and average inventory at cost

(c) Finished goods inventory and sale of finished goods

(d) None of these

145. Work – in – Progress Inventory Turnover Ratio can be measured by

(a) $\text{W.I.P Turnover Ratio} = \dfrac{\text{Cost of Manufacture}}{\text{Average WIP inventory at cost}}$

(b) $\text{W.I.P Turnover Ratio} = \dfrac{\text{Sales}}{\text{Total WIP}}$

(c) $\text{W.I.P Turnover Ratio} = \dfrac{\text{Cost of goods sold}}{\text{Average finished goods}}$

(d) None of these

ANSWERS

1. (c) Production System
2. (b) Intermediate stage of production
3. (a) Factory Labour Cost
4. (c) In series and parallel
5. (c) Has no relation with production problem
6. (d) Replacement Policy
7. (a) Large output per man hour
8. (a) Efficient Production System
9. (d) All the above
10. (a) Resources per unit of production
11. (d) All the above
12. (b) Decreases
13. (a) Job production
14. (a) Continuous Production
15. (a) Job Production
16. (a) Large steam turbines
17. (b) Most Complex type of Production System
18. (c) Three shift basis
19. (b) Variety of products and sizes
20. (a) Fixed operation sequence
21. (b) Input Output Analysis
22. (b) Production Function
23. (c) Constant
24. (c) Constant
25. (b) Material Management
26. (c) Both 'a' and 'b'
27. (a) All the above
28. (a) Forecast of demand
29. (b) Production process
30. (b) Transaction Matrix
31. (d) All the level
32. (a) Inter dependent sectors
33. (c) Contraction of Product Mix
34. (b) Group of different product items
35. (c) Product line
36. (a) Number of product lines being produced by the producer
37. (a) To improve methods of production
38. (d) Both 'a' and 'b'
39. (d) ∇
40. (a) Process Chart

41. (d) All the above
42. (c) Work Measurement
43. (c) Both 'a' and 'b'
44. (a) $\text{Performance Rating} = \frac{\text{Observed performance}}{\text{Normal performance}} \times 100$
45. (c) Lorry D. Miles
46. (d) Both 'a' and 'b'
47. (a) Functional Value
48. (d) All the above
49. (b) Inspection
50 (d) All the above
51. (a) Quality Control
52. (a) Quality level of a good lot
53. (b) Quality level of a bad lot
54. (b) Control Chart
55. (c) Control of overall fraction defective of a process
56. (a) Production
57. (b) Value added = Value of output – Value of input
58 (d) Both 'b' and 'c'
59. (c) Plant Layout
60. (a) Maintenance
61. (a) Method Study
62. (d) Service properties
63. (c) Physical properties
64. (a) Castability, Weldability and Brazability
65. (a) Manufacturing Industries
66. (d) All the above
67. (b) White cast iron
68. (b) Alloy cast iron
69. (c) Railway rails
70. (a) Welding
71. (b) Soldering
72. (c) Brazing
73. (a) Aeronautical industries
74. (c) $650^{oC} - 800^{oC}$
75. (b) Casting
76. (d) Both 'a' and 'b'
77. (d) All the above
78. (c) Work table is stationary
79. (d) Both 'a' and 'b'
80. (a) Invar Steel
81. (b) Nuclear power production
82. (d) It is carried on to specific consumer's demand
83. (d) Special purpose machine are used
84. (c) Mass Production
85. (b) Job Production
86. (b) Fabrication Processes
87. (c) It is meant for small jobs
88. (a) Chips
89. (a) Automation
90. (b) Plant
91 (d) Both 'a' and 'b'
92. (b) Industry
93. (d) Both 'a' and 'b'
94. (d) All the above
95. (c) Both 'a' and 'b'
96. (a) Transportation Costs, Labour Costs
97. (a) $\text{Material Index} = \frac{\text{Weight of localised Labours}}{\text{Weight of finished products}}$
98. (b) Sargant Florence
99. (d) Both 'a' and 'b'
100. (a) Availability of raw materials
101. (b) Material Management
102. (d) Both 'a' and 'b'
103. (c) Both 'a' and 'c'
104. (a) Identification
105. (b) Codification
106. (d) All the above
107. (c) Both 'a' and 'b'
108. (d) None of the these
109. (d) All the above
110. (c) PEP [Program Evaluation Procedure]

111. (d) All the above
112. (b) Scheduling
113. (b) Production Function
114. (a) Line Layout
115. (b) Movable Path Equipment
116. (b) Scheduling
117. (c) Processes Chart
118. (b) Integrated Material Management
119. (a) Procurement of Material
120. (c) Production and Material Management
121. (a) Bar Chart
122. (d) Flow Chart
123. (b) Gilberths
124. (b) Network
125. (a) Event
126. (c) Activity
127. (c) Both 'a' and 'b'
128. (a) Social Audit
129. (c) Both 'a' and 'b'
130. (d) All the above
131. (d) Both 'a' and 'b'
132. (b) MRO Inventories
133. (a) Ordering Costs
134. (c) Insurance on Inventory
135. (d) Losses from pilferage
136. (a) Always Better Control
137. (b) High in quantity and low in value
138. (c). Criticality of Inventories
139. (d) Fast moving, Slow moving and Non-moving
140. (c) 'C' Group inventories
141. (d) All the above
142. (a) Overall Inventory Turn Over Ratio $= \frac{\text{Cost of Goods Sold}}{\text{Average Inventory at cost}}$
143. (b) Raw Materials Inventory Turnover Ratio $= \frac{\text{Annual consumptions of raw materials}}{\text{Average raw materials inventory}}$
144. (a) Cost of goods sold and average finished goods inventory at cost
145. (a) W.I.P Turnover Ratio $= \frac{\text{Cost of Manufacture}}{\text{Average WIP inventory at cost}}$

****

III

MARKETING MANAGEMENT AND SALES PROMOTION

1. __________ refers to any body of persons who are in intimate business relation and carry on any extensive transaction in any commodity

(a) Market (b) Organization (c) Body Corporate (d) Institution

2. __________ is the performance of business activities designed to plan, price, promote and distribute want satisfying product and services to present and potential customers

(a) Buying (b) Marketing (c) Manufacturing (d) Selling

3. The main features of Modern Marketing is

(a) Marketing is Consumer – Oriented

(b) Marketing is Production Oriented

(c) Marketing is Demand Oriented

(d) Marketing is Competition Oriented

4. Micro – Marketing describes________

(a) Equalising and distribution functions

(b) Marketing comprises a wide range of activities

(c) Centralised exchange function

(d) All the above

5. ____________ refers to a consumer orientation backed by integrated marketing aimed at generating customer satisfaction as the key to satisfying organizational goals

(a) Social Concept (b) Selling Concept

(c) Marketing Concept (d) Management Concept

6. A situation which may come about as a result of temporary shortage occasioned by short–term excess demand for a company's products is called as ________

(a) De Marketing (b) Social Marketing

(c) Remarketing (d) Over Marketing

7. ________ refers to focus all scientific, social, ethical and managerial experience on marketing.

(a) Over Marketing (b) De Marketing

(c) Social Marketing (d) Meta Marketing

8. ________ refers to an interacting set of institutions activities and flows designed to facilitate exchange transactions between organizations and its market

(a) Marketing System (b) Marketing Process

(c) Marketing Functions (d) Marketing Objectives

9. The product, the price structure, the promotional activities and the distributions system are the four inputs refers to

(a) Promotional Mix (b) Product Mix

(c) Marketing Mix (d) Place Mix

10. ________ refers to external factors and forces that affect the company's ability to develop and maintain successful transactions and relationships with its target customers

(a) Market Segment (b) Marketing Mix

(c) Marketing Environment (d) Marketing System

11. ________ has the task of influencing the level, timing and composition of demand is a way that win help the organization achieve its objectives

(a) Marketing Management (b) Financial Management

(c) Production Management (d) Personnel Management

12. "Find wants and fill them" is a theme described in

(a) Selling Concept (b) Marketing Concept

(c) Product Concept (d) Production Concept

13. ________ refers to a person's feelings of pleasure or disappointment resulting from comparing a products perceived performance in relation to his or her expectations.

(a) Perception (b) Attitude (c) Involvement (d) Satisfaction

14. An organization-wide approach to continuously improving the quality of all organization's processes, products and services are described as ________

(a) Total Quality Management (TQM) (b) Total Inventory Management

(c) Frequency Marketing Programmes (d) CPM

15. Modern Marketing concept lays greater importance on the freedom of the

(a) Producer (b) Seller (c) Advertiser (d) Consumer

16. ________ means consists of analyzing marketing opportunities developed marketing strategies, and managing the marketing effort

(a) Marketing Strategies (b) Marketing Functions

(c) Marketing Process (d) Marketing Opportunity

17 ________Consists of people, equipment and procedures to gather, sort, analyze, evaluate, and distribute needed, timely, and accurate information to marketing decision markers.

(a) Data Processing System (b) Marketing Information System (MIS)

(c) Reporting to Management (d) Business Communication

18. ___________ is a set of procedures and sources used by managers to obtain their everyday information about pertinent development in marketing environment

(a) Sales Reporting System (b) Electronic Data Interchange

(c) Internal Records System (d) Marketing Intelligence System

19. _____________ are relatively homogenous and enduring divisions in a society, which are hierarchically ordered and whose members share similar values, interest and behavior

(a) Social Classes (b) Personal Factors

(c) Reference Groups (d) Psychological Factors

20. Groups having a direct influence on a person are called as ________

(a) Social Groups (b) Membership Groups

(c) Informal Groups (d) Formal Groups

21. A Person's distinguishing psychological characteristics that lead to relatively consistent and enduring responses to his or her environment is called

(a) Motivation (b) Lifestyle (c) Personality (d) Occupations

22. _______ is the process by which an individual select organizes and interprets information inputs to create a meaningful picture of the world

(a) Perception (b) Personality (d) Motivation (d) Belief

23. ______ involves changes in an individual's behavior arising from experience

(a) Drive (b) Experience (c) Motives (d) Learning

24. Descriptive thought that a person holds about something is refers to_______

(a) Belief (b) Attitudes (c) Perception (d) Wishes

25. A person's enduring favorable or unfavorable evaluation of object or idea is ________

(a) Personality (b) Attitudes (c) Drive (d) Perception

26. __________ is the decision – making process by which formal organizations establish the need for purchased products and services and identify evaluate and choose among alternative brands and suppliers

(a) Individual Buying (b) Group Buying

(c) Organizational Buying (d) Buying Motives

27. The need hierarchy Theory was developed by

(a) Maslow .H (b) Peter F. Drucker

(c) Taylor (d) Herzberg

28. "Mass Marketing" refers to the seller who engages in the______

(a) Mass Productions (b) Mass Promotions

(c) Mass Distributions (d) Mass Competition

29. _______ consists of a large identifiable group with in a market.

(a) Market Segment (b) Preference Segment

(c) Target Market (d) Counter Marketing

30. Grouping of buyers or segmenting the market is described as _________

(a) Marketing System (b) Market Segmentation

(c) Marketing Management (d) Marketing Functions

31. Age of person is a ___________

(a) Demographic variables (b) Geographic variables

(c) Socio-Economic variables (d) Behavioral variables

32. ______ means only a single product is produced and offered to the entire market

(a) Market Segmentation (b) Concentrated Marketing

(c) Market Aggregation (d) Stimulational Marketing

33. _________ is suitable for introducing a new product

(a) Concentrated Marketing (b) Industrial Marketing

(c) Target Marketing (d) Synchro Marketing

34. ___________ refers to a group of customers at whom the organization specially intends to aim its market effort

(a) Market Positioning (b) Marketing Segmentation

(c) Marketing Aggregation (d) Target Marketing

35. User status, benefits, loyalty status etc are the variables of___________

(a) Behavioral variables (b) Geographic variables

(c) Socio-Economic variables (d) Political variables

36. Which of the following is a Geographic variable?

(a) Family size (b) Social (c) Cities (d) Occasions

37. __________ refers to a set of objectives, policies and rules that guide over time firm's marketing efforts

(a) Marketing Strategy (b) Marketing System

(c) Marketing Function (d) Market Segmentation

38. ________ refers to the level at which the products primary characteristics operate

(a) Product Feature (b) Product Differentiation

(c) Durability (d) Performance Quality

39. __________ refers to a measure of the products expected operating life under natural and/or stressful conditions

(a) Product Durability (b) Product Feature

(c) Product Attributes (d) Product Policies

40. _________ describes the products looks and feel to the buyer

(a) Product Reliability (b) Product Design

(c) Product Durability (d) Product Style

41. ________ refers to the act of designing the company's offering and images

(a) Product Positioning (b) Product Strategies

(c) Product Modifications (d) Product Differentiations

42. ________ concerned with defining the type, volume and timing of the product a company offers for sale

(a) Performing Policy (b) Product Policy

(c) Price Policy (d) Product Mix

43. Cigarettes, newspapers and magazines are examples of

(a) Convenience goods (b) Industrial goods

(c) Specialty goods (d) Shopping goods

44. Product line and product mix are the important areas covered by ________

(a) Promotion Policy (b) Distribution Policy

(c) Product Policy (d) Price Policy

45. Introduction, growth, _____ and ______are the four stages of product life cycle

(a) Maturity, Saturation (b) Maturity, Decline

(c) Decline, Maturity (d) None of these

46. ________ refers to the full list of all products offered for sale by a company

(a) Product Line (b) Product Mix

(c) Product Items (d) Product Policies

47. Product Mix is also termed as ________

(a) Product Assortment (b) Product Attributes

(c) Product Dimensions (d) Product Strategies

48. Length, Width, Depth and Consistency are the four dimensions of ________

(a) Product Line (b) Product Item

(c) Product Mix (d) Marketing Mix

49. Index search is a method referring to ________

(a) New Product Development (b) Business Analysis

(c) Market Testing (d) Commercialization

50. Product deficiencies is one of the reason for ________

(a) Product diversification (b) New product development

(c) Failure of a product (d) All the above

51. Name, Term, Symbol, Design and the like refer to ________

(a) Brand Name (b) Brand (c) Brand Mark (d) Brand Equity

52. Which of the following relates to Brand Name?

(a) Term (b) Words (c) Letters (d) Both 'b' and 'c'

53. A set of assets and liabilities linked to a brand is termed as ________

(a) Brand Mark (b) Brand Name

(c) Brand Equity (d) Brand Loyalty

54. A brand or a part of brand that is given legal protections is called as _____

(a) Trade Mark (b) Brand Equity

(c) Brand Name (d) Brand Valuation

55. _________ is described as the embracing functions of package selection, manufacturing, filling and handling

(a) Trade Mark (b) Packaging (c) Labeling (d) Branding

56. House hold buying is required for ________

(a) Consumer Package (b) Bulk Package

(c) Industrial Package (d) Dual Use Package

57. Bulk package is useful for _________

(a) Consumer goods (b) Large quantity of industrial goods

(c) Durable consumer goods (d) Agricultural goods

58. A.I.D.A.S. formula is applicable to ________

(a) Buy or Make decisions (b) Price fixations

(c) Packaging decisions (d) Branding

59. ________ gives the information about the product

(a) Labeling (b) Trade Mark (c) Band Loyalty (d) Packaging

60. __________ is refers to the exchange value of product or service in terms of money

(a) profit (b) Price (c) Sales (d) Cost

61. Cost of the product is one of the decisive factors relating to_________

(a) Product decisions (b) Promotion decisions

(c) Pricing decisions (d) Profit decisions

62. _________ refers to a price in just under a round number

(a) Odd Pricing (b) Customary Pricing

(c) Dual Pricing (d) Cost Plus Pricing

63. Prestige pricing is applicable to __________

(a) Consumer Goods (b) Industrial Goods

(c) Essential Goods (d) Luxury Goods

64. Penetration pricing describes __________

(a) Product penetrate into markets to hold a position

(b) Adopting low prices in the initial stages

(c) Both 'a' and 'b'

(d) None of these

65. Skimming pricing is otherwise called as __________

(a) Skim – the Cream Pricing (b) Sealed Bid Pricing

(c) Odd Pricing (d) Negotiated Pricing

66. ____________ refers to sell the same product at two or more different prices

(a) Monopoly Pricing (b) Dual Pricing

(c) Expected Pricing (d) Zone Pricing

67. Cost – Plus Pricing is also known as ________

(a) Discriminatory Pricing (b) Pricing lining
(c) Mark up Pricing (d) Expected Pricing

68. Target pricing is also termed as ________

(a) Cost Oriented Pricing (b) Break Even Pricing
(c) Cost Plus Pricing (d) Demand Oriented Pricing

69. ________ is connecting link between personal selling and advertising

(a) Copy Testing (b) Media (c) Sales Promotion (d) Publicity

70. Sales Promotion is a sales tool to be used as ________

(a) Short term sales stimulus (b) Medium term sales stimulus
(c) Long term sales stimulus (d) All the above

71. Sales Promotional activities may be ________

(a) Consumer Promotion (b) Trade Promotions
(c) Sales Force Promotions (d) All the above

72. Sampling and couponing are the effective tools for

(a) Trade Promotions (b) Consumer Promotions
(c) Sales Force Promotions (d) None of these

73. Which one of the following method relates to Trade Promotions?

(a) Sales force contests (b) Demonstrations
(c) Buy back allowance (d) Money refund offers

74. Which of the following method is not Sales Force Promotions?

(a) Bonus to Sales Force (b) Sales Force Contest
(c) Sales Meeting (d) Merchandise Allowances

75. Promotional activities is also termed as ________

(a) Promotional Mix (b) Product Mix
(c) Marketing Mix (d) Place Mix

76. ________ emphasizes personal selling

(a) Pull Mix (b) Push Mix (c) Product Mix (d) Place Mix

77. Mass impersonal sales efforts are given the greatest importance in.

(a) Product Mix (b) Push Mix
(c) Pull Mix (d) Marketing Mix

78. Oral persuasion in a conversations with one or more prospective purchasers for the purpose of making sales is called as ________

(a) Advertising (b) Personal Selling
(c) Sales Promotions (d) Publicity

79. Any paid form of non-personal persuasion and promotions of ideas or services by an identified sponsor is called as ________

(a) Advertising (b) Sales Promotions
(c) Personal Selling (d) Sales Force Promotion

80. __________ is the science of creating in the mind of a prospect a desire that only possession of your product will satisfy

(a) Sales Promotion (b) Salesmanship

(c) Personal Selling (d) Advertising

81. Advertising can be interpreted as ______

(a) "Ad and verto" (b) "Ad" means "towards"

(c) "Verto" means "I turn" (d) All the above

82. Which one of the following is an element of Advertising?

(a) Non-personal Communications (b) Personal Communications

(c) Both 'a' and 'b' (d) Informal Communications

83. Commercial Advertising is referred to ____________

(a) Advertising of a product for commercial

(b) Advertising for a particular product

(c) Stimulate the demand for a general product

(d) All the above

84. __________is referred to advertising of a particular product

(a) Trade Advertising (b) Professional Advertising

(c) Product and Institutional Advertising (d) Farm Advertising

85. ________ refers to the reading matter in an advertisement

(a) Advertisement Manuals (b) Advertisement Copy

(c) Media of Advertisement (d) Advertising Budget

86. A.I.D.A is described as

(a) Attitude, Involvement, Desire and Attractions

(b) Attentions, Important, Desire and Actions

(c) Attentions, Interest, Desire and Actions

(d) Ability, Interest, Desire and Attentions

87. ________ refers to through which the advertiser convey his message to audience

(a) Advertising Media (b) Advertising Budget

(c) Advertising Copy (d) Advertising Agencies

88. Cards, sales letter, folder are the forms relating to

(a) Indirect Advertising (b) Direct Advertising

(c) Outdoor Advertising (d) Film Advertising

89. New papers and magazines are the media used in

(a) Direct Advertising (b) Outdoor Advertising

(c) Indirect Adverting (d) Selective Advertising

90. ________ refers to the display of advertisement in the form of posters, painted displays

(a) Direct Advertising (b) Indoor Advertising

(c) Outdoor Advertising (d) Film Advertising

91. Point of purchase advertising is used in the form of ________

(a) Window Display (b) Painted Display

(c) Calendars (d) Brochures

92. The specialist who undertakes the promotion of the advertising programme is known as ________

(a) Advertising Budget (b) Advertising Agency

(c) Advertising Media (d) Advertising Copy

93. Which of the following method is used to deciding Advertising Budget?

(a) Market Share Approach (b) Task and Objective Method

(c) Concurrent Test Method (d) Both 'a' and 'b'

94. Which of the formula of cost per contract is used in evaluating media alternatives?

(a) $\text{CPM} = \dfrac{\text{Cost of single advertisement}}{\text{Audience size (in thousand)}} \times 100$

(b) $\text{CPM} = \dfrac{\text{Cost of group advertisement}}{\text{Audience size (in thousand)}} \times 100$

(c) $\text{CPM} = \dfrac{\text{Cost of multiple advertisement}}{\text{Audience size (in thousand)}} \times 100$

(d) None of these

95. ________ is used to measure the effectiveness before the advertisement is placed

(a) Split Run Test (b) Readability Studies

(c) Recall Test (d) None of these

96. Which of the following method relates to post testing to measure the effectiveness of advertisement?

(a) Attitude Test (b) Eye Movement Analysis

(c) Tachistoscope Tests (d) Simple Retrocession Analysis

97. Post Test is used to measure the ________

(a) Communications effect on advertisement

(b) Sales effect on effectiveness of advertisement

(c) Readers recognition on advertisement

(d) All the above

98. Who remarked that "we are not the boss ; the consumer is ; what the consumer wants the consumer gets"?

(a) H. Fayol (b) Philp Kotler

(c) Bead well, W.J. Stanton (d) H. Koraner

99. Personal selling relates to ________

(a) Impersonal activities (b) Mass communications

(c) Useof written, oral and visual message (d) Face to face contract with buyer

100. Creative sales man is one who

(a) Emphasizes the creations of demand of the product

(b) Specializes in selling intangible products

(c) Specializes in selling drug products

(d) Supplement for activities of wholesalers and retailers

101. Indoor Salesmen is also termed as ________

(a) Staple sales man (b) Counter salesman

(c) Wholesalers salesman (d) Detail salesman

102. Which of the following principles relates to Consumerism?

(a) Protected against the marketing of goods

(b) Protected against fraudulent activities

(c) Protected the right of consumers

(d) All the above

103. "Consumer Bill of Rights" refers to ________

(a) Right to safety (b) Right to consume

(c) Right to purchase (d) Right to claim

104. The doctrine of 'Caveat Emptor' is pertaining to

(a) Consumer (b) Manufacturer (c) Government (d) Traders

105. Consumer Guidance Society of India (CGSI) was established in ________

(a) 1962 (b) 1966 (c) 1968 (d) 1990

106. Set of moral principles and values with regard to marketing process is termed as ______

(a) Marketing Morality (b) Marketing Ethics

(c) Consumer protections (d) Marketing Principles

107. _____' let the seller beware 'against the old concept of Caveat Emptor'

(a) Consumerism (b) Moral Idealism

(c) Intuitionism (d) Utilitarianism

108. Dry cleaners, laundries, beauty parlors the kind of

(a) Food services (b) Car services

(c) Transport services (d) Personal care services

109. Any activity, benefits or satisfactions which are offered for sales are

(a) Industrial Goods (b) Capital Goods

(c) Services (d) Agricultural Goods

110. Services can be determined by ________

(a) Cost Based Pricing (b) Demand and Supply Based Pricing

(c) Expected Pricing (d) Monopoly Pricing

111. Which of the following concept is related to services?
(a) Tangible nature (b) Intangible nature
(c) Both a and b (d) Visible

112. State Trade Corporations (S.T.C.) was started in the year ______
(a) 1955 (b) 1956 (c) 1957 (d) 1958

113. Sale and Agreement to sell are ______
(a) Subject matter (b) General contract
(c) Sale of contract (d) Personal contract

114. A channel is a ______ of marketing
(a) Live organ (b) Dead organ
(c) Sterile organ (d) Lifeless organ

115. Conventional channels are ______ channels
(a) Individual (b) Institutional (c) Private (d) Government

116. Which of the following relates to Non-Conventional channels?
(a) Vertical (b) Horizontal (c) Both a and b (d) Concave Convex

117. Direct channel is the ______ channel
(a) Shortest (b) Longest (d) Medium (d) All the above

118. Middlemen can be ______ and ______
(a) Merchant, Agent (b) Principal, Agent
(c) Owner, worker (d) Producer, principle

119. Unit Store is a form of small scale ______
(a) Wholesaler (b) Retailer (c) Dealer (d) Agent

120. Super Market is a form of ______ retailing
(a) Small scale (b) Large scale (c) Medium scale (d) All the above

121. Chain Stores mostly deal in one line and on ______ terms
(a) COD (b) CC (c) Cash (d) Credit

122. Who are the following person relates to Merchant Middlemen?
(a) Wholesalers (b) Retailers (c) Broker (d) Both a and b

123. Broker is a ______
(a) Merchant Middlemen (b) Converter
(c) Agent Middlemen (d) Drop- Shopper

124. Sales promotions measures are suitable to attain ______ term goals
(a) Short (b) Medium (c) Long (d) All the above

125. Sales Promotions ______ costs for dealers
(a) Adds (b) Maintains (c) Cuts (d) Increase

126. Setting a low initial price to as many buyers and possible is called ______
(a) Competitive Pricing (b) Unfair Trade Pricing
(c) Penetrative Pricing (d) Price Lining

127. The selling of different qualities of a product at different prices is known as ______

(a) Leader Pricing (b) Price Lining
(c) Variety Trading (d) Consumer Matching

128. Price deal are a form of ______

(a) Consumer promotions (b) Dealers promotions
(c) Sales force promotions (d) Both a and b

129. Off the pack premiums are a form of ______

(a) Consumer Promotions (b) Dealer Promotions
(c) Sales Force Promotions (d) Trade Promotions

130. Which of the following method of pricing relates to Target Return Pricing?

(a) Cost Based (b) Demand Based
(c) Cost and Demand Based (d) Competitions Based

131. Which of the following method of pricing relates to Going Rate Pricing?

(a) Cost Based Method (b) Demand Based Method
(c) Cost and Demand Based (d) Competition Based

132. Non-Variable Pricing is also called as ______

(a) Cost Oriented Price Policy (b) Competition Oriented Price Policy
(c) One Price Policy (d) Demand Oriented Price Policy

133. Zonal pricing results in ______ prices for different areas

(a) Demand oriented (b) Uniform (c) Varied (d) Mixed

134. Service is a ______ product

(a) Tangible (b) Intangible (c) Invisible (d) None of these

135. Red, orange and yellow goods fit in ______ classification of products

(a) Traditional (b) Modern
(c) Ultra Modern (d) Non-Traditional

136. The concept of Product Mix is not ______

(a) Constant (b) Stagnant (c) Changing (d) Flexible

137. Trading up is the act of ______ high priced prestigious products to existing product line

(a) Reducing (b) Adding
(c) Maintaining (d) None of the above

138. Product Life Cycle concept was convinced and popularized by

(a) Mr. D.J. Luck (b) C.R. Wassan (c) T. Levitt (d) D.T. Collat

139. A strategy of moving form 300cc motorbike to 150 and 100cc is a case refers to

(a)Trading Up (b) Trading Down
(c) Trading on Line (d) None of these

140. Sales Manager is also called as ______

(a) Sales Executive (b) Market Manager
(c) Marketing Executive (d) All the above

141. Sound judgment is a ________ quality of a Sales Manager

(a) Physical (b) Mental (c) Behavioral (d) Observation

142. Recruitment of salesmen is ________ process

(a) Positive (b) Negative (c) Proactive (d) Reactive

143. Training is a process of ________

(a) Learning (b) Recruitment (c) Fiddling (d) Placement

144. Sound health is ________ quality of a Sales Manager

(a) Mental (b) Behavioral (c) Physical (d) All the above

145. Which of the following is a medium of Press Advertising?

(a) Window Display (b) Packages

(c) Exhibition (d) Trade Directories

146. Selling a product at the going market rate is know as

(a) Leader Pricing (b) Competitive Pricing

(c) Price Lining (d) Follow the Leader Pricing

147. Price is equal to consumer ________

(a) Demands (b) Expectations

(c) Commands (d) Requirement

148. Price is determinant of ________

(a) Profit (b) Loss (c) Cost (d) All the above

149. Market Potential is related to

(a) a Company (b) Competitors (c) an Industry (d) a Subsidiary

150. Marketing Mix is a ________ factor influencing pricing decisions

(a) External (b) Internal

(c) Both a and b (d) International

151. Rolls Royce Automobile Company follows ________

(a) Differentiated Marketing (b) Concentrated Marketing

(c) Social Marketing (d) Modern Marketing

152. Opinion Leader is the ________ determinant of consumer

(a) Economic (b) Sociological (c) Psychological (d) Geographical

153. Family is a ______ determinant of consumer behavioral

(a) Sociological (b) Psychological

(c) Economic (d) Demographic

154. Personality is a ________ determinant of consumer behavioral

(a) Demographic (b) Economic

(c) Sociological (d) psychological

155. Consumer Behavior is the process of responding to a ________

(a) Questions (b) Problem (c) Stimuli (d) Like or Dislike

156. AGMARK was introduced in India during ________

(a) 1939 (b) 1938 (c) 1936 (d) 1948

157. Indian Standards Institution Certifications Marks Act was passed in the year ______

(a) 1952 (b) 1954 (c) 1964 (d) 1965

158. Agricultural Produce (Grading and Marketing) Act was passed in during ______

(a) 1937 (b) 1939 (c) 1938 (d) 1940

159. A standard is referred to ________

(a) Norm (b) Tool (c) Model (d) Method

160. The concept of Marketing Mix was introduced by ________

(a) N.H. Borden (b) Philip kotler (c) Marthy (d) Peter Drucker

161. Consumer wants and needs are ________

(a) Different (b) Same
(c) Constant (d) Synonymous

162. Product Mix is the focus of marketing and ________ efforts

(a) Making (b) Producing (c) Innovation (d) Manufacturing

163. Product Line is a group of ________

(a) Closely related products (b) Closely unrelated products
(c) Entirely different products (d) None of these

164. Which of the following relates to Labels?

(a) To identify the product
(b) To aware the quality of product
(c) To differentiate from competitive product
(d) All the above

165. Which of the following is relates to Place Mix?

(a) Transportations (b) Warehousing
(c) Channels of distributions (d) Storage

166. Price is the ________ of a product expressed in terms of ________

(a) Quantity, kind (b) Value, money
(c) Cost, quantity (d) Value, units

167. Advertising is an ______ effort to sell the products

(a) Indirect (b) Direct (d) Independent (d) All the above

168. General Motors of America follows ________ Marketing Approach

(a) Concentrated (b) Modern (c) Differentiated (d) Meta

169. Language relates to________ dimensions

(a) Political (b) Social (c) Cultural (d) Economical

170. India presents a case of unity in ________

(a) Diversity (b) Adversity (c) Advances (d) Plurality

171. One of the rights of unpaid seller is ________

(a) Right to consume (b) Right of lien
(c) Right of might (d) None of these

172. MRTP Act of 1969 aims aroud controlling ______ and ______practices

(a) Monopolistic, Unfair (b) Unrestricted, Normal
(c) Restrictive, Free Fair (d) Fairly, Restored

173. Price discrimination is one of the finest examples of ________

(a) Restrictive Trade Practice (b) Monopolistic Trade Practice
(c) Unfair Trade Practice (d) None of these

174. In evaluating public interest ________ gate ways are followed

(a) Four (b) Six (c) Eight (d) Eleven

175. According to Peter Drucker, the purpose of business is to create a

(a) Customer (b) Debtor (c)Investor (d) Producer

176. Indian Sale of Goods Act was passed in ______ which is Replica of British Act

(a) 1928 (b) 1930 (c) 1968 (d) 1970

177. One of the implied warrantee is that goods are ________any encumbrance

(a) Free subject (b) Exempt existing
(c) Both (a) and (b) (d) None of these

178. "Let the buyer be aware" is refers to ________

(a) Daveat Emptor (b) Caveat Emptor
(c) Laveat Emptor (d) All the above

179. Sales contest is a form of ________

(a) Dealers Promotions (b) Consumer Promotions
(c) Sales – Force Promotions (d) Trade Promotion

180. A.A.A.A. is refers to

(a) Advertising Agencies Associations of America
(b) Associations of Advertisers Agencies of Africa
(c) Advertising Agencies Associations of Atlanta
(d) Always All out at All Lines

181. Always Better Control is refers to

(a) ABC Analysis (b) ACB Analysis
(c) EOQ Analysis (d) T Q M Analysis

182. I.A.A. refers to

(a) Institute of Associate with Advertisers
(b) Institute of Associations of Advertises
(c) International Associations of Advertises
(d) Indian Association of Advertisers

183. Check – list – Test is one of the _______ Testing Method of Advertising

(a) Pre (b) Post (c) Concurrent (d) None of these

184. Which of the following method relates to consumer devices used to measure Advertising?

(a) Pre Test (b) Post Test (c) Concurrent (d) None of these

185. Split – run test is one of the _______ method Used to measure the effectiveness of advertising?

(a) Pre test (b) Post test (c) Concurrent (d) None of these

186. The word 'retailer' means cut again in _________ language

(a) Spanish (b) German (c) Italian (d) French

187. Consumer Protection Act provides _______ Quasi Judicial Arrangement

(a) Three tier (b) Two tier (c) Four tier (d) Five tier

188. Which of the following does not relate to the medium of Outdoor Advertising?

(a) Sky writings (b) Cinema (c) Wall writings (d) Hand Bills

189. The fundamental cause of consumer movement in any country is consumer ________

(a) Discretions (b) Obedience

(c) Dissonance (d) Acceptance

190. A _________ is a specification used in providing certain basic qualities, like Shape, Size, to the goods for their use

(a) Measurement (b) Standard (c) Quality (d) Quantity

191. The first Step in the Marketing Function is

(a) Marketing (b) Assembling (c) Selling (d) Buying

192. The greatest cause of failure of Consumerism is

(a) Consumers are organized (b) Consumers are scattered

(c) Consumers are unorganized (d) Consumer are singled out

193. Consumer Protection Act 1986 provides the _______ as the machinery for redressing consumer grievances

(a) District Forum (b) State Commission

(c) National Commission (d) All the above

194. Economic factors relate to _________ dimensions of consumers

(a) Psychological (b) Social (c) Cultural (d) Economical

195. ________ helps to move the goods or services to the place of final consumption

(a) Storage (b) Transport (c) Finance (d) Insurance

196. Habits and Custom are referred to ________ dimensions of consumers

(a) Social (b) Political (c) Ecological (d) Cultural

197. Consumerism is a _____

(a) Political force (b) Economical force (c) Social force (d) Legal force

198. Consumer Protections Act India came into existence during _____

(a) 1985 (b) 1986 (c) 1987 (d) 1988

199. Consumer Protection is the revolutions started during ____

(a) 1962 in America (b) 1963 in England

(c) 1964 in France (d) 1965 in Germany

200. John F. Kenedy described consumers as a force ____

(a) Against attrocities by political community

(b) Against attrocities by business community

(c) Against attrocities by religious organizations

(d) All the above

201. Consumer Movement started in India during ____

(a) 1930 (b) 1940 (c)1920 (d)1910

202. National Commission is like a Supreme Court cases deal with

(a) Involving amount more than 10 lakhs

(b) Involving amount less than 10 lakhs

(c) Involving amount more than 20 lakshs

(d) Involving amount less than 20 lakhs

203. Self regulations is the best on the part of ____

(a) Professionals and Exporters (b) Consumers and Political

(c) Consumers and Business community (d) All the above

204. Popular products being sold at below cost to attract customers is called ____

(a) Penetrative Pricing (b) Leader Pricing

(c) Cost Pricing (d) Dual Pricing

205. Which of the following element in the Marketing Mix is subject to legal control?

(a) Product (b) Promotion (c) Price (d) Distribution

206. Storage creates ____ utility

(a) Time (b) Place (c) Capital (d) Form

207. Central Warehousing Corporations was set up in ____

(a) 1956 (b) 1958 (c) 1957 (d) 1960

208. The term Brand is refers to ____

(a) Identifications (b) Communications

(c) Promotional tool (d) All the above

209. Trade Mark is a Name or Mark which should be ____

(a) Registered (b) Legalized (c) Franchised (d) Both a and b

210. The failure of new product can often be traced to

(a) Consumer protection (b) Mismanagement

(c) Market trends (d) Marketing weakness

211. Modern Marketing focuses on the

(a) Business Environment (b) Consumer Satisfaction

(c) Business Ethics (d) Profit Making

212. Integrated Marketing Communications implies ______

(a) Does not require a good communications system

(b) Does not produce good results in the long run

(c) Makes the task of marketing a product easier

(d) None of these

213. Communication requires ____

(a) Clarity of ideas (b) Correctiveness of the message

(c) Courtesy (d) All the above

214. Sales Promotions is aims at

(a) Maintaining good relations with the salesman

(b) Preparing sales budget

(c) Increasing sales volume

(d) Improving the quality of products

215. Which of the following relates to habitual buying behavioral?

(a) Consumer have low involvement (b) Consumer have high involvement

(c) Brand differences are significant (d) Little differences in the brands

216. Which of the following is not related to Outdoor Advertising?

(a) Neon sings (b) Sky – writing

(c) Sand which men (d) Catalogues

217. "Value for money for years" is the slogan of ______

(a) Ceat (b) VIMIAL (c) BAJAJ (d) North Star

218. One of the causes of low profile of Indian advertising industry is due to ______

(a) Consumer illiteracy (b) Company policies

(c) Govt. Policies (d) High cost

219. A good advertisement is one which is characterized by ______

(a) Brief (b) Clear (c) Apt (d) All the above

220. When the consumers are highly involved in a purchase and aware of significant differences among brands refers to

(a) Variety seeking buying behavioral

(b) Habitual buying behavioral

(c) Complex buying behavioral

(d) Dissonance reducing buying behavioral

ANSWERS

1. (a) Market
2. (b) Marketing
3. (a) Marketing is Consumer – Oriented
4. (b) Marketing comprises a wide range of activities
5. (a) Social Concept
6. (a) De Marketing
7. (d) Meta Marketing
8. (a) Marketing System
9. (c) Marketing Mix
10. (c) Marketing Environment
11. (a) Marketing Management
12. (b) Marketing Concept
13. (d) Satisfaction
14. (a) Total Quality Management (TQM)
15. (d) Consumer
16. (c) Marketing Process
17. (b) Marketing Information System (MIS)
18. (d) Marketing Intelligence System
19. (a) Social Classes
20. (b) Membership Groups
21. (c) Personality
22. (a) Perception
23. (d) Learning
24. (a) Belief
25. (a) Attitudes
26. (c) Organizational Buying
27. (a) Maslow .H
28. (d) All the above
29. (a) Market Segment
30. (b) Market Segmentation
31. (a) Demographic variables
32. (c) Market Aggregation
33. (a) Concentrated Marketing
34. (d) Target Marketing
35. (a) Behavioral
36. (c) Cities
37. (a) Marketing Strategy
38. (d) Performance Quality
39. (a) Product Durability
40. (d) Product Style
41. (a) Product Positioning
42. (b) Product Policy
43. (a) Convenience Goods
44. (c) Product Policy
45. (b) Maturity, Decline
46. (b) Product Mix
47. (a) Product Assortment
48. (c) Product Mix
49. (a) New Product Development
50. (d) All the above
51. (b) Brand
52. (d) Both 'b' and 'c'
53. (c) Brand Equity
54. (a) Trade Mark
55. (b) Packaging
56. (a) Consumer Package
57. (b) Large quantity of industrial goods
58. (c) Packaging
59. (a) Labeling
60. (b) Price
61. (c) Pricing Decisions
62. (a) Odd Pricing
63. (d) Luxury Goods
64. (c) Both 'a' and 'b'
65. (a) Skim - the Cream Pricing
66. (b) Dual Pricing
67. (c) Mark Up Pricing
68. (a) Cost Oriented Pricing
69. (c) Sales Promotion
70. (a) Short term sales stimulus
71. (d) All the above
72. (b) Consumer Promotion
73. (c) Buy Back Allowance
74. (d) Merchandise Allowances
75. (a) Promotional Mix
76. (b) Push Mix
77. (c) Pull Mix
78. (b) Personal Selling
79. (a) Advertising
80. (b) Salesmanship
81. (d) All the above

82. (a) Non- Personal Communications
83. (a) Advertising of a product for commercial
84. (c) Product and institutional advertising
85. (b) Advertisement Copy
86. (c) Attention, Interest, Desire and Action
87. (a) Advertising Media
88. (b) Direct Advertising
89. (c) Indirect Advertising
90. (c) Outdoor Advertising
91. (a) Window Display
92. (b) Advertising Agency
93. (d) Both 'a' and 'b'
94. (a) CPM= $\frac{\text{Cost of single advertisement}}{\text{Audience size (in thousand)}}$ x100
95. (b) Readability
96. (a) Attitude Test
97. (d) All the above
98. (b) Philip Kotler
99. (d) Face to fact contract with buyer
100. (a) Emphasizes the creation of demand of the product
101. (b) Counter Sales Man
102. (d) All the above
103. (a) Right to safety
104. (a) Consumer
105. (b) 1966
106. (b) Marketing Ethics
107. (a) Consumerism
108. (d) Personal care services
109. (c) Services
110. (a) Cost Based Pricing
111. (b) Intangible nature
112. (b) 1956
113. (c) Sale of contract
114. (a) Live organ
115. (a) Individual
116. (c) Both a and b
117. (b) Longest
118. (a) Merchant, Agent
119. (b) Retailer
120. (b) Large scale
121. (c) Cash
122. (d) Both 'a' and 'b'
123. (c) Agent Middlemen
124. (c) Long
125. (c) Cuts
126. (c) Penetrative Pricing
127. (b) Price Lining
128. (d) Both 'a' and 'b'
129. (a) Consumer Promotion
130. (a) Cost Based
131. (c) Competition Based
132. (c) One Price Policy
133. (b) Uniform
134. (b) Intangible
135. (a) Traditional
136. (b) Stagnant
137. (b) Adding
138. (c) T. Levitt
139. (b) Trading Down
140. (d) All the above
141. (b) Mental
142. (a) Positive
143. (a) Learning
144. (c) Physical
145. (d) Trade Directories
146. (b) Competitive Pricing
147. (b) Expectations
148. (d) All the above
149. (c) an Industry
150. (b) Internal
151. (b) Concentrated Marketing
152. (b) Sociological
153. (a) Sociological
154. (d) Psychological
155. (c) Stimuli
156. (b) 1938
157. (a) 1952
158. (a) 1937
159. (c) Model
160. (a) N.H. Borden
161. (a) Different
162. (a) Making

163. (a) Closely related products
164. (d) All the above
165. (a) Transportations
166. (b) Value, Money
167. (a) Indirect
168. (c) Differentiated
169. (c) Cultural
170. (a) Diversity
171. (b) Right of lien
172. (a) Monopolistic and Unfair
173. (c) Unfair Trade Practice
174. (d) Eleven
175. (a) Customer
176. (b) 1930
177. (a) Free
178. (b) Caveat Emptor
179. (c) Sales – force promotions
180. (a) Advertising Agencies, Association of America
181. (a) ABC Analysis
182. (c) International Association of Advertises
183. (a) Pre
184. (a) Pre – Test
185. (a) Post – Test
186. (d) French
187. (a) Three tier
188. (b) Cinema
189. (c) Disonance
190. (b) Standard
191. (d) Buying
192. (d) Consumers are singled out
193. (d) All the above
194. (d) Economical
195. (b) Transport
196. (d) Cultural
197. (c) Social force
198. (b) 1986
199. (a) 1962 in America
200. (b) Against atrocities by business community
201. (c) 1920
202. (a) Involving amount more than 10 lakhs
203. (c) Consumers and Business Community
204. (b) Leader Pricing
205. (c) Price
206. (a) Time
207. (c) 1957
208. (d) All the above
209. (b) Legalized
210. (d) Marketing weaknesses
211. (b) Consumer Satisfaction
212. (c) Makes the task of marketing a product easier
213. (d) All the above
214. (C) Increasing sales volume
215. (a) Consumer have low involvement
216. (d) Catalogues
217. (c) BAJAJ
218. (a) Consumer illiteracy
219. (d) All the above
220. (c) Complex Buying Behavior

*****

IV

RESEARCH METHODOLOGY AND MARKETING RESEARCH

1. ______ is a systematic gathering, recording and analyzing of data about problems relating the marketing of goods and services
   (a) Marketing Research (b) Social Research
   (c) Technical Research (d) Production Research
2. **'Price' is one of the four P's of ______**
   (a) Product Mix (b) Promotions Mix
   (c) Marketing Mix (d) Market Characteristics
3. **Future market trends is one of the important characteristics of**
   (a) Market (b) Buyer Behavior
   (c) Competition (d) General Environment
4. **Multiple – Regression and Attitude Measurement Instrument techniques used in marketing research during**
   (a) 1920 – 30 (b) 1940-50
   (c) 1960 – 70 (d) 1950 – 60
5. **Who said "Business is the satisfaction of customers"**
   (a) Peter Drucker (b) Zaltman and Burger
   (c) H. Fayol (d) C. Kinnear
6. **Research on analysis of sales potentials is covered under**
   (a) Research on Product (b) Research on Market
   (c) Research on Promotions (d) Research on Sales Forecasting

7. The study of product Line Research is covered under

(a) Research on pricing
(b) Research on product and services
(c) Research on promotions
(d) Research on Buyer motives

8. Assign equal probabilities to each competitive actions is referred by________

(a) Laplace (b) L.J. Sarage (c) Wald (d) Bayesian

9. The concept of Coefficient of Optimism Procedure was developed by

(a) Bayesian (b) Laplace (c) Hurwicz Criterion (d) Wald

10. Persimism Criterion or Maxim in Choice was introduced by

(a) Hurwicz
(b) Ressell L. Ackoff
(c) Wald
(d) Bayesian

11. ________ is particularly useful scheme for structuring the research decision

(a) Bayesian Decisions Theory
(b) H.V. Raberts Approach
(c) L.J. Savage's Minimax Regret Criterion
(d) None of these

12. The formal marketing research project can be viewed as a series of steps called as ________

(a) Research Design
(b) Research Process
(c) Research Problem
(d) Research Report

13. ________ is purely and simply the framework or plan for a study that guides the collection and analysis of the data

(a) Research Design
(b) Research Process
(c) Statistical Design
(d) Research Analysis

14. ________ is used to establish priorities in studying the competing explanations of phenomenon

(a) Descriptive Study
(b) Exploratory Study
(c) Casual Study
(d) Case Study

15. ________ is typically concerned with determining frequency with which something occurs or how two variables vary together.

(a) Case Study
(b) Descriptive Study
(c) Panel Analysis
(d) Scientific Analysis

16. Longitudinal analysis relates to

(a) Panel Research
(b) Time Series Analysis
(c) Trend Analysis
(d) Case Study

17. ________ is to measures the type of the image people have formed about a company, product and its brand

(a) Panel Research
(b) Corporate Research
(c) Image Research
(d) Survey Research

18. Omnibus Surveys aims to

(a) Reduce the cost of conducting surveys

(b) Limit number of questions

(c) Handle complex questions

(d) All the above

19. Study on various stages of distributions network is covered under

(a) Audit Research (b) Retail Research (c) Trade Research (d) Panel Research

20. Sales determined in Retail Audit is

(a) Sales = First stock + Deliveries between visits – Second stock

(b) Sales = Deliveries between visits + Second stock – First stock

(c) Sales = Second stock + First stock – Deliveries between visits

(d) None of these

21. The actual variables chosen to measure the subjects response are known as ______

(a) Independent variable (b) Dependent variable

(c) Quantitative variable (d) Qualitative variable

22. Variables manipulated in an experiment refers to

(a) Extraneous variables (b) Dependent variables

(c) Both a and b (d) Independent Variables

23. Data which are collected from government source refers to

(a) Primary Data (b) Secondary Data

(c) Both a and b (d) Qualitative Data

24. Mailed Questionnaires is a technique which is used for generating

(a) Primary Data (b) Secondary Data

(c) Both a and b (d) Quantitative Data

25. Data which are collected for earlier research work and are applicable to present study under taken is known as

(a) Observation (b) Primary Data

(c) Secondary Data (d) None of these

26. Sources of data from abstracts, indices, and directories refers to

(a) Experiments (b) Observations and Personal Interviews

(c) Primary Data (d) Secondary Data

27. Age, sex, material status and education are the demographic variables related to

(a) Primary Data (b) Secondary Data

(c) Both a and b (d) Historical Data

28. Conclusive Research is designed to

(a) Evaluation of alternative course of action

(b) Determining the frequency of occurrence

(c) Determining the marketing variables are associated

(d) None of these

29. ________ means data collected specifically for purposes of the research needs at hand

(a) Secondary Data (b) Primary Data

(c) External Secondary Data (d) Historical Data

30. _______ is an individuals enduring perceptual, knowledge – based, evaluative and actions oriented processes will respect to an object

(a) Behavior (b) Personality (c) Learning (d) Attitude

31. An individual anticipated or planned future behavior refers to

(a) Intentions (b) Motivations (b) Behavior (d) Awareness

32. Need, want, drive, an urge, wish, desire, etc are variables relating to

(a) Behavior (b) Motivations (c) Intentions (d) Perception

33. _______ is to a formal list of questions to be answered in the survey

(a) Questionnaire (b) Schedule (c) Manual Report (d) Observations

34. Which of the following is Survey Technique?

(a) Personal Interview (b) Telephone Survey

(c) Mail Survey (d) All the above

35. Questionnaire refers to

(a) Highly Structured and Standardized

(b) Mostly Unstructured

(c) Questions are not Standardized

(d) Highly unstructured and standardized

36. The term 'Interview Schedule' refers to

(a) Self administered process by the respondent

(b) list of questions that will be discussed and recorded by the interviewer

(c) Highly structured

(d) Highly standardized

37. _______ is a technique of Attitude Measurement

(a) Checklists (b) Closed – End Questions

(c) Rating Scale (d) Open – End Questions

38. Multi – Dimensional Scaling (MDS) is also termed as

(a) Disaggregate Method (b) Aggregative Scaling Method

(c) Stapel Scale Method (d) None of these

39. Likert's Summated Scale is similar to ________

(a) Guttman Scale (b) Q – Sort Technique

(c) Thurstone Differential Scale (d) Rank Order Rating Scales

40 ________ is to determine whether a Cumulative and Unidimensional Scale is being achieved

(a) Guttman Scale Technique (b) Likert's Summated Scale Technique

(c) Semantic Differential Technique (d) None of these

41. Thurstone Differential is also called as ______

(a) Semantic Differential (b) Thurstone's Equal Appearing Intervals

(c) Paired Comparison (d) Ratio Scales

42. Collecting data about each and every unit of the population is called as ______

(a) Census Method (b) Sampling Method

(c) Systematic Sampling (d) Convenience Sampling

43. Where only a few units of populations under study are considered for analysis is called as ________

(a) Census method (b) Statistic

(c) Sampling method (d) Ratio Analysis

44. ______means a summary description of a measure in the defined population

(a) Statistic (b) Parameter (c) Sample Size (d) Sample Design

45. ______ means each member of the populations has a known and equal chance of being selected

(a) Judgement Sampling (b) Simple Random Sampling

(c) Systematic Sampling (d) Non Probability Sampling

46. The universe divided into strata on the basis of measurable characteristics refers to

(a) Cluster Sampling (b) Systematic Sampling

(c) Stratified Sampling (d) Judgment Sampling

47. _______refers to the basis of the distribution of the defined population across control characteristics

(a) Quota Samples (b) Convenience Samples

(c) Simple Random Samples (d) None of these

48. Judgment samples is selected on the basis of ________

(a) Distribution of the defined populations

(b) Expert opinion of the researcher

(c) Convenience of the researcher

(d) None of these

49. _______ is a summary description of a measure in the selected sample

(a) Parameter (b) Sample Error (c) Statistic (d) Sample Size

50. The ratio of sample size 'n' to population size 'N' is called ______

(a) Sample Size (b) Sample Error (c) Sample Design (d) Sampling Fraction

51. A sample statistic whose expected value equals the populations parameter is called ______

(a) Un Biased Statistic (b) Absolute Precision

(c) Standard Deviations (d) Relative Precision

52. ________ refers to provide summary measures of the data contained in the sample

(a) Statistic (b) Descriptive Statistics

(c) Descriptions of the Sample (d) Inferential Statistics

53. The mean and _______ are the relevant descriptive measures of central tendency

(a) Dispersions (b) Mode

(c) Standard Deviations (d) Median

54. _______ is the relevant descriptive measures of central tendency for ordinal data

(a) Median (b) Mode (c) Index (d) Chi – Square Test

55. __________ is a statement that a populations parameter takes on a particular value or set of values

(a) Alternative Hypothesis (b) Null Hypothesis

(c) Both a and b (d) None of these

56. A Null Hypothesis should be _________

(a) Rejected (b) Accepted

(c) Rejected or Accepted (d) None of these

57. _________ is the appropriate inferential test about means for interval data when standard deviation is unknown

(a) 't' – Test (b) Z - Test (c) F – Test (d) X^2 – Test

58. _________ is the appropriate inferential test about means for interval data

(a) T – Test (b) X^2 – Test (c) F – Test (d) Z – Test

59. __________ is the appropriate inferential test for the distributions of subjects across a nominal variable

(a) Chi – Square Test (b) Z – Test (c) t – Test (d) F-Test

60. 1 – B is the probability of rejecting a false null hypothesis is called as _________

(a) Univariate Data Analysis (b) Power of the Test

(c) Chi – Square Test (d) None of these

61. _______ refers to involves analyzing two variables at a time

(a) Regression Analysis (b) Q – Factor Analysis

(c) Bivariate Anlysis (d) Correlation Analysis

62. _______ is to measure of the degree to which two interval variables are linearly associated

(a) Linear Correlations (r) (b) Simple Regressions

(c) Coefficient of Correlations (d) Multiple Regression

63. _________ shows how the independent variable is related to the dependent variable

(a) Coefficient Correlations (b) Simple Regressions

(c) Chi – Square Test (d) t – Test

64. Yc = a + bX is the equation is refers to

(a) Chi – Square Test (b) Linear Correlations

(c) Simple Regression (d) t – Test

65. _________ is suitable to evaluates the null hypothesis when two nominal variables are independent

(a) t – Test (b) Z – Test (c) Simple Regression (d) Chi – Square Test

66. Which of the following method is relates to Interdependence Method?

(a) Factor Analysis (b) Cluster Analysis

(c) Multidimensional Scaling (d) All the above

67. ________ takes Correlations Matrix as input

(a) Factor Analysis (b) Discriminate Analysis

(c) Cluster Analysis (d) None of these

68. Applications of _______ include data reductions, structure identification, scaling and data transformation

(a) Multidimensional Scaling (b) Cluster Analysis

(c) Factor Analysis (d) None of the above

69. _______ input is a matrix of associations between variables or objects

(a) Factor Analysis (b) Cluster Analysis

(c) Regressions Analysis (d) Analysis of Variance

70. ______ is used to measure the perception of brand similarities and preferences in marketing

(a) Correlations (b) Simple Regressions

(c) Chi – Square Test (d) Multidimensional Scaling

71. ____________ is used to measure the relationship between one intervally scaled dependent variable and a set of intervally scaled independent variables

(a) Multiple Regression (b) Simple Regressions

(c) Correlations (d) Correlation Matrix

72. Applications of ________ is used with one nominally scaled dependent variable and a set of intervally scaled independent variables

(a) Simple Regression (b) Analysis of Variance

(c) Multiple Regression (d) Discriminant Analysis

73. Application of ______ is used with one ordinally scaled dependent variable and set of nominally scaled independent of variable

(a) Canonical Correlations (b) Simple Regressions

(c) Conjoint Measurement (d) Multivariate Analysis

74. Applications of _____ is used with one intervally scale dependent variable and a set of nominally scaled independent variable

(a) Analysis of Variance (b) Canonical Correlation

(c) Multiple Regressions (d) Multiple Correlation

75. _______ is suitable for the calculations of different variances

(a) CRD Measures (b) RBD Design Measures

(c) ANOVA (d) FD Measures

76. _______ is the difference between an individual score and the treatment group mean to which the score belongs

(a) Go Error (b) Drop Error

(c) Experimental Error (d) None of these

77. Presentations of the research finding to a specific audience for a specific purpose is called as ______

(a) Management Information System (b) Research Report

(c) Management of Exceptions (d) Management By Objectives

78. The presentations of Report can be ______

(a) Written (b) Oral (c) Both 'a' and 'b' (d) Informal

79. In estimating future demand a firm may use ______ methods

(a) Qualitative Methods (b) Time series extrapolation

(c) Causal Methods (d) All the above

80. Which of the following is relates to qualitative method of Forecasting?

(a) Executive Opinion (b) Sales Force Method

(c) Consumer Surveys (d) All the above

81. Time – Series methods of forecasting is well suited for

(a) Short Term Forecast (b) Medium Term Forecast

(b) Long Term Forecast (d) None of these

82. Which of the following relates to Timer series methods of forecasting?

(a) Moving Average Method (b) Exponential Smoothing Method

(c) Both a and b (d) Simple Correlation Analysis

83. Research Procedure is used in ______ are repertory grid and focus group interviews

(a) New product idea generations (b) Concept development

(c) Business Analysis (d) Test Marketing

84. Research procedure used in concept development and testing are focused in ____

(a) Paired Comparison Rating (b) Conjoint Analysis

(c) Usage Test (d) All the above

85. Test marketing is frequently used as ______

(a) Business Analysis (b) Managerial Control Function

(c) Predictive Research Function (d) All the above

86. Which of the following is the major applications areas of Advertising Research?

(a) Product appeals (b) Media selections

(c) Copy Testing (d) All the above

87. Media Research focuses its attention on ______

(a) Media vehicle distributions (b) Media vehicle audience

(c) Both a and b (d) Media selection

88. Copy Testing Research is dealt with ______

(a) Advertising perception (b) Advertising exposure

(c) Advertising communication (d) All the above

89. ______ is suitable to measures the circulations of print media and the penetration level of Broadcast media

(a) Media Selection Research (b) Product Appeal Research

(c) Copy Testing Research (d) None of these

90. Which of the following method is used to measure the effectiveness of advertising?

(a) Survey Method (b) Copy Testing

(c) Media Selections Research (d) All the above

91. _______ is used to measure the communications effect of an advertisement before it is released in media

(a) Post – Test (b) Pre – Test (c) Recognition Test (d) Recall Test

92. Which of the following test relates to Pre-Testing?

(a) Consumer Jury and Portfolio Test

(b) Recognition Test and Recall Test

(c) Inquiry Test and Physiological Test

(d) Both a and c

93. Post - Testing of Advertising Research is also termed as

(a) Pre Publications Test (b) Post Publication Test

(c) Before Test (d) None of these

94. Which of the following test relates to Post-Test techniques in Advertising Research?

(a) Recognition Test (b) Inquiry

(c) Consumer Jury Test (d) Portfolio Test

95. Penetrations, Comprehension, Recall, Believability (P.C.R.B) method of Advertisement Research was developed by

(a) Taylor (b) Crisp (c) Jury (d) Oliver

96. Which of the following aspect relate to research on Sales Forecasting?

(a) Research on Market (b) Research on Product

(c) Research on Price (d) Research on Promotions

97. Primary data are collected through _______

(a) Books (b) Government Records

(c) Journals (d) Questionnaire Method

98. Product Research deals with the analysis of

(a) Demand and Supply (b) Product Line

(c) Advertisement Effectiveness (d) Physical Distribution

99. A. system of frame work or plan for a study that guides the collections and analysis of the date refers to _______

(a) Sampling (b) Data Collections

(c) Research Design (d) Group Discussion

100. The investigator questions the respondents in a face to face meeting refers to

(a) Telepnone Survey (b) Personal Interview

(c) Mail Survey (d) None of these

101. Advertisement aims at increasing the ______

(a) Sales (b) Demand (c) Profit (d) All the above

102. Interview Schedule is mostly ______

(a) Structured (b) Unstructured (c) Standard (d) None of these

103. A report prepared on the basis of audience on general back ground and interest is called______

(a) Popular Report (b) Technical Report
(c) Mixed Report (d) None of these

104. Product Research deals with the problems facing the ______

(a) Product planning (b) Market planning
(c) Organizational planning (d) Administrative planning

105. The term Product is a complex of ______

(a) Tangible attributes (b) Intangible attributes
(c) Both a and b (d) All the above

106. Which of the following steps relates to New Product Development?

(a) Generating Ideas (b) Business Analysis
(c) Concept Development and Testing (d) All the above

107. ________ is carried out to find consumers attitude towards a product through or product concept

(a) Analysis Testing (b) Performance Testing
(c) Consumer Testing (d) Association Testing

108. _______ is used to know what images come to respondents mind after bearing about the present brand name

(a) Association Test (b) Learning Test
(c) Memory Test (d) Preference Tests

109. ______ is used to know which one of several names are preferred and on what basis

(a) Concept Test (b) Preference Test
(c) Memory Test (d) Analysis Test

110. Which of the following test is used to measure the concept development?

(a) Analysis Test (b) Performance Test
(c) Association Test (d) Both a and b

111. Which of the following test is used to measure the package design?

(a) Visual Test (b) Dealer Test
(c) Engineering Test (d) All the above

112. High rate of Trail rate and Repurchase rate indicate________

(a) Drop the product (b) Commercialize the product
(c) Redesign the product (d) Increase Sales Promotion

113. Low Rate of Trail Rate and Repurchase Rate indicate ________

(a) Drop the product (b) Increase Advertisement
(c) Commercialize the product (d) Increase Sales Promotion

114. Copy Testing is also termed as ________

(a) Advertising Research (b) Advertising Message Research

(c) Product Appeal Research (d) Media Selection Research

115. ____________ is suitable for an application of Marketing research aimed at the measurement of advertising effectiveness

(a) Advertising Research (b) Media Research

(c) Product Appeal Research (d) Sales Promotion Research

116. Copy Testing used to measure the ____________

(a) Communication effect of the advertisement

(b) Sales effect of the advertisement

(c) Ability to influence the product sales

(d) All the above

117. ____________ is used to find out whether readers have read the advertisement and up to what extent the given brand has resented in their minds.

(a) Penetration Test (b) Progress Tests

(C) Recall Tests (d) P.C.R.B. Method

118. ____________ is used to measure the attitudes of the consumer toward products brand in question and sales results.

(a) Triple Association Tests (b) Progress Tests

(c) Penetration Tests (d) Recognition Tests

119. Starch Advertisement Readership Rating was developed by ________

(a) Daniel Starch (b) K.L.McGown

(c) David J.Luck (d) High G.Walse, Donald A.Taylor

120. Magazines is one of the example of ____________.

(a) Broadcast Media (b) Print Media (c) Publicity (d) Advertisement

121. Which of the following method is used to measure the radio and TV audience size and characteristics?

(a) Roster-Recall Method (b) Coincidental Method

(c) Diary Method (d) All the above

122. ____________ refers to the reaction of the mind to either a mental or physical stimulus.

(a) Attitude (b) Assumptions (c) Sensations (d) Images

123. Which of the following method is used, when number of advertisement to be evaluated are more than six in number?

(a) Order of Merit (b) Paired Comparison

(c) Consumer Jury Test (d) P.C.R.B. Method

124. According to Paired Comparison Method the number of advertisements can be evaluated with help of the following formula________

(a) Number of Comparisons = n(n-1)/2

(b) Number of Comparisons = n(n-10)/2

(c) Number of Comparisons = n(n-5)/2

(d) None of these

125. ___________ is used to measure the physiological reactions in respondents due to advertisement.

(a) Laboratory Tests (b) Order of Merit
(c) Inquiries (d) Simulated Sales Tests

126. Which of the following devices relates to laboratory test to measure the physiological reactions in respondents due to advertisements?

(a) Eye Camera (b) Perceptoscope
(c) Psychogalvanometer (d) All the above

127. ___________ is used to expose the consumer to alternative copies of the advertisement through the point-of purchase displays or direct mail

(a) Consumer Jury Test (b) Inquiries
(c) Simulated Sales Test (d) Association Test

128. Motive is also termed as ___________

(a) Need (b) Want (c) Drive and urge (d) All the above

129. ___________ refers to the mental pictures that are formed as a result of stimuli.

(a) Assumption (b) Sensation
(c) Image (d) Frames of reference

130. Which of the following techniques is adopted in Motivation Research?

(a) Non-Disguised-Structured Techniques
(b) Non-Disguised-Non-Structured Techniques
(c) Disguised-Non-Structured Techniques
(d) All the above

131. Non-disguised-non-structured techniques is also called as ___________

(a) Depth Interviews Technique
(b) Qualitative Interviews Technique
(c) Clinical Interviews Technique
(d) All the above

132. Disguised-Non-Structured techniques is also referred to as

(a) Non-Directive Approach (b) Projective Techniques
(c) Focused Interviews (d) Camera-Action Interviews

133. Which of the following techniques relates to Projective techniques?

(a) Word Association Tests (b) Sentence Completion Tests
(c) Story Completion Test (d) All the above.

134. Which of the following area is covered in Sales Control Research?

(a) Sales Forecasting
(b) Market Potential and Market Share Analysis
(c) Determination of Market Characteristics
(d) All the above

135. Jury Executive Opinion Method is used to measure___________.

(a) Sales Forecasting (b) Sales Analysis
(c) Market Potential (d) Market Characteristics.

ANSWER

1. (a) Marketing Research
2. (c) Marketing Mix
3. (a) Market
4. (d) 1950-60
5. (a) Peter Drucker
6. (b) Research on Market
7. (b) Research on Product and Services
8. (a) Laplace
9. (c) Hurwicz
10. (c) Wald
11. (a) Bayesian Decision Theory
12. (b) Research Process.
13. (a) Research Design
14. (b) Exploratory Study
15. (b) Descriptive Study
16. (a) Panel Research
17. (c) Image Research
18. (a) Reduces the cost of conducting surveys
19. (a) Trade Research
20. (a) Sales - First stock + Deliveries between visits - Second stock
21. (b) Dependent variable
22. (d) Independent variable
23. (b) Secondary Data
24. (a) Primary Data
25. (c) Secondary Data
26. (d) Secondary Data
27. (a) Primary Data
28. (a) Evaluation of alternative course of action
29. (b) Primary Data
30. (d) Attitude
31. (a) Intentions
32. (b) Motivation
33. (a) Questionnaire
34. (d) All the above
35. (a) Highly Structured and Standardized
36. (b) List of questions that will be discussed and recorded by the interviewer
37. (c) Rating Scale
38. (a) Disaggregative Method
39. (c) Thurstone Differential Scale.
40. (a) Guttman Scale Technique.
41. (b) Thurstone's Equal Appearing Intervals
42. (a) Census Method
43. (c) Sampling Method
44. (b) Parameter
45. (b) Simple Random Sampling
46. (c) Stratified
47. (a) Quota Samples
48. (b) Expert Opinion of the researcher
49. (c) Statistic
50. (d) Sampling Fraction
51. (a) Unbiased Statistic
52. (b) Descriptive Statistics
53. (c) Standard Deviation
54. (a) Median
55. (b) Null Hypothesis
56. (a) Rejected
57. (a) 't' test
58. (d) z-test
59. (a) Chi-Square Test
60. (b) Power of the Test
61. (c) Bivariate Anaylysis
62. (a) Linear Correlation (r)
63. (b) Simple Regression
64. (c) Simple Regression
65. (d) Chi-Square Test
66. (d) All the above
67. (a) Factor Analysis
68. (c) Factor Analysis
69. (b) Cluster Analysis
70. (d) Multi Dimensional Scaling
71. (a) Multiple Regression
72. (d) Discriminant Analysis
73. (c) Conjoint Measurement
74. (a) Analysis of Variance
75. (c) ANOVA
76. (c) Experimental Error

77. (b) Research Report
78. (c) Both 'a' and 'b'
79. (d) All the above
80. (d) All the above
81. (a) Short Term Forecast
82. (c) Both 'a' and 'b'
83. (a) New Product Idea Generation
84. (d) All the above
85. (d) All the above
86. (d) All the above
87. (c) Both 'a' and 'b'
88. (d) All the above
89. (a) Media Selection Research
90. (b) Copy Testing
91. (b) Pre-Test
92. (d) Both 'a' and 'c'
93. (b) Post Publication Test
94. (a) Recognition Test
95. (b) Crisp
96. (a) Research on Market
97. (d) Questionnaire Method
98. (b) Product-Line
99. (c) Research Design
100. (b) Personal Interview
101. (d) All the above
102. 9(b) Unstructured
103. (a) Popular Report
104. (a) Product Planning
105. (c) Both 'a' and 'b'
106. (d) All the above
107. (c) Consumer Testing
108. (a) Association Test
109. (b) Preference Test
110. (d) Both 'a' and 'b'
111. (d) All the above
112. (b) Commercialize the product
113. (a) Drop the product
114. (b) Advertising Message Research
115. (a) Advertising Research
116. (d) All the above
117. (a) Penetration Test
118. (b) Progress Tests
119. (a) Daniel Starch
120. (b) Print Media
121. (d) All the above
122. (c) Sensations
123. (b) Paired Comparison
124. (a) Number of Comparisons = n(n-1)/2
125. (a) Laboratory Tests
126 (d) All the above
127. (c) Simulated Sales Test
128. (d) All the above
129. (c) Images
130. (d) All the above
131. (d) All the above
132. (b) Projective Techniques
133. (d) All the above
134. (d) All the above
135. (a) Sales Forecasting

****

V

EXPORT MANAGEMENT, INTERNATIONAL MARKETING AND EXPORT PROMOTION

1. _____________ refers to managing marketing activities abroad and dealing with related activities.
   (a) Export Management (b) Export Marketing
   (c) Foreign Trade (d) International Marketing
2. Which of the following main activities is Export Management?
   (a) Execution of.export orders
   (b) Involves functions such as planning, organizing, staffing etc
   (c) Identification of export product for the export market
   (d) Both 'a' and 'b'
3. Which of the following product is not Traditional Exports?
   (a) Tea (b) Coffee (c) Sugar (d) Textiles
4. Which of the following product is related to Traditional Export?
   (a) Engineering goods (b) Iron ore (c) Clothing (d) Cashew
5. MNCS standards for
   (a) Multinational Corporation (b) Multinational Countries
   (c) Multinational Contracts (d) Multinational Marketing
6. Which of the following country is not relating to Trade Blocks?
   (a) EEC (b) LAFIA (c) ASEAN (d) NATO
7. Which of the following broad area is covered under scope of Export Management?
   (a) Export Formation and procedures (b) Export Pricing
   (c) Export Services (d) All the above

8. Export Management is a____________

(a) Team Effort (b) Profession (c) Art (d) Science

9. Export manager is ______________

(a) Like any other Manager (b) Specialized in Export Marketing

(b) Leader of the Exporting Firm (d) All the above

10. Switzerland is the example of ____________

(a) Most Developed Countries (b) Developed Countries

(c) Under Developed Countries (d) Developing Countries

11. Which of the following relates to benefits of export?

(a) Optimum utilization of resources (b) Technological advancement

(c) World peace (d) All the above

12. "Export or Perish" is a national slogan raised by _________

(a) Prime minister Pandit Jawaherlal Nehru

(b) Prime minister Mrs. Indra Gandhi

(c) Prime minister Mr. Rajive Gandhi

(d) Prime minister Mr. Narashima Rao

13. ________ refers to customs duties and taxes levied on import of goods from abroad.

(a) Tariff Barriers (b) Non – Tariff Barriers

(c) Import Quotas (d) Export Quotas

14. _________ relates to quantitative restrictions imposed on import of goods

(a) Tariff Barriers (b) Non-Tariff Barriers

(c) Import Quotas (d) Customs Duties

15. Which of the following is not relating to Tariff Barriers?

(a) Specific Duties (b) Advalorem Duties

(c) Import Licensing (d) Countervailing Duties

16. Which of the following is not relating to Non-Tariff Barriers?

(a) Quotas (b) Import Licensing

(c) Consular Formalities (d) Antidumping Duties

17. Which of the following relates to Tariff Barriers?

(a) to increase in price of imported goods

(b) it discourages imports through quantitative restrictions

(c) Both 'a' and 'b'

(d) None of these

18. Which of the following is the impact of Tariff Barriers?

(a) It may not affect the demand (b) It may not affect the export

(c) It may increase the price (d) All the above

19. Which of the following is not relating to Non-Tariff Barriers?

(a) It takes long time for implementation

(b) It restricts imports in quantitative terms

(c) Provides direct protection to home industries

(e) It is not easy to withdraw one imposed

20. Which of the following is not relating to Import Quotas?

(a) Unilateral Quota (b) Bilateral Quota

(c) Mixed Quota (d) Double or Single column tariff

21. Which effects relates to Import Quotas?

(a) Import quotas do not provide revenue to the government

(b) Quantitative restrictions imposed on the goods to be imported from abroad

(c) Both 'a' and 'b'

(d) Do not restrict the imports quickly and directly.

22. Which of the following is not relating to Tariff?

(a) Revenue Tariff (b) Protective Tariff

(c) Anti Dumping Tariff (d) Tariff Quotas

23. When a fixed percent of value of a commodity is charged as tariff it is known as

(a) ADValorem Duty (b) Specific Duty

(c) Anti Dumping Duty (d) Countervailing Duties

24. When a fixed sum of money is levied as tariff, keeping in view the weight and other physical aspects of the commodity it is known as________

(a) AdValorem Duty (b) Specific Duty

(c) Anti Dumping Duty (d) None of these

25. Which of the following is not relating to ADValorem Duty?

(a) It takes only value of goods.

(b) Duties varies from makes and models

(c) Can be imposed on all type of goods

(d) Easy to administer.

26. Which of the following is not relating to Specific Duty?

(a) It takes quantity and quality of goods

(b) Flat rate of duty is charged

(c) Easy to administer

(d) More popular and used by all countries

27. CCC refers to ____________

(a) Customs Co-operations Council

(b) Customer Co-operation Council

(c) Customs Co-operation Corporation

(d) Customs Council for Co-operation

28. When two countries make agreement for mutual trade and Commercial benefits their agreement is called__________

(a) Multilateral Trade Agreement (b) Bilateral Trade Agreement

(c) General Agreement (d) Mutual Trade Agreement

29. When more than two countries enter into trading agreement for the common benefit, the agreement is called________

(a) Multilateral Trade Agreement (b) Bilateral Trade Agreement

(c) General Agreement (d) Mutual Trade Agreement

30. Countries in the World had adopted a policy which is called__________

(a) General Policy (b) Democratic Policy

(c) Protectionist Policy (d) Consumerist Policy

31. GATT came into existence in ________, in a conference held at _______ under the 23 signatory countries agreement.

(a) 1948,Geneva (b) 1947, Newyork (c) 1947, Geneva (d) 1946, London

32. Which of the following is an objectives of GATT?

(a) To remove tariff and Non-tariff barrier of International trade

(b) To make the world trade free

(c) To serve the interests of developing countries

(d) Both 'a' and 'b'

33. Which of the following is not relating to UNCTAD?

(a) Its membership is wider than GATT

(b) To serve the interest of developing countries

(c) Generalized system of Preference

(d) To remove trade barrier

34. Which is the special feature of GATT?

(a) Most favored Nation

(b) Generalized system of preference

(c) One of the permanent organs of United Nations

(d) None of these

35. Which is the main policies of UNCTAD?

(a) To remove trade barrier for the benefit of all countries

(b) To promote world trade particularly developing countries

(c) Most favored nations

(d) Replaced by WTO

36. EEC was established in _________ at ________

(a) 1958, Brussels (b) 1948, Mascow (c) 1947, Newyork (d) 1957, London

37. Which of the following country is not a member of EEC?

(a) France (b) Belgium (c) Italy (d) Poland

38. COMECON was established under the active leadership of ________

(a) France (b) USA (c) USSR (d) India

39. Which one of the following country is the largest trading partner of EEC?

(a) West Germany (b) India (c) China (d) Hongkong

40. Which one of the following country is not a member of COMECON?

(a) Russia (b) Poland (c) Cuba (d) England

41. LAFTA stands for ________

(a) Latin American Free Trade Association

(b) Latin American Foreign Trade Association

(c) Latin Association of Foreign Trade Agreement

(d) Latin American Fashion Trade Association

42. EFTA stands for ________

(a) European Foreign Trade Association

(b) European Free Trade Association

(c) European Foreign Trade Agreement

(d) European Free Trade Agreement

43. Which one of the following is not a founder member of EFTA?

(a) Denmark (b) Norway (c) Sweeden (d) Peru

44. "Outer Seven against Inner Six" refers to

(a) LAFTA (b) EFTA (c) COMECON (d) EEC

45. ASEAN stands for ________

(a) Association of South East Asian Nations

(b) Association of South Europe and Asian Nations

(c) Association of South East African Nations

(d) Association of South European Atlantic Nations

46. ASEAN was established at ________ in ________

(a) Geneva, 1967 (b) Bangkok, 1967 (c) Mexico, 1967 (d) Rome, 1957

47. "Fortress of America" refers to

(a) ASEAN (b) EFTA (c) NAFTA (d) EEC

48. NAFTA stands for ________

(a) North American Free Trade Agreement

(b) North American Free Trade Association

(c) North African Foreign Trade Association

(d) North American Foreign Trade Agreement

49. Which one of the following is not a founder member of NAFTA?

(a) United States of America (b) Canada

(c) Saudi Arabia (d) Mexico

50. SAARC stands for ________

(a) South African Association of Regional Co-operation

(b) South Asian Association of Regional Co-operation

(c) South Asian Association of Regional Council

(d) South Asian Agreement of Regional Council

51. Which of the following country is a member of SAARC?

(a) India (b) Pakistan (c) Bhutan (d) Kenya

52. OPEC stands for ________

(a) Organization of Petroleum Exporting Countries

(b) Organization of Economic Co-operation

(c) Organization of Economic Community Development

(d) Organization of Petroleum Export Council

53. ________ is basically a manufacturer but also takes interest in exporting his products abroad

(a) Merchant- Exporter (b) Manufacturer- Exporter

(c) Export Houses (d) Trading Houses

54. ________ is essentially a middleman in export marketing and looks exclusively after exporting goods abroad.

(a) Merchant- Exporter (b) Manufacturer- Exporter

(c) Entrepreneur Merchant- Exporter (d) Trading Houses

55. Which of the following is not relating to Manufacturer Exporter?

(a) Gets profit out of his own export

(b) Requires huge capital for the business

(c) Marketing abroad is the main aspect of business

(d) Acts as a seller in foreign markets

56. Which of the following relates to Merchant-Exporter?

(a) Gets commission out of his export transactions

(b) Requires limited capital

(c) Specializes in export marketing

(d) All the above

57. Which of the following intermediaries is not relating to Manufacturer Exporters?

(a) Super Star Trading Houses (b) Trading Houses

(c) Merchant Exporters (d) None of these

58. Indian Trade Promotion Organization was formed in ________

(a) 1952 (b) 1992 (c) 1972 (d) 1962

59. Which of the following is used to tap foreign marketing for exports?

(a) Trade Delegates (b) Trade Fair and Exhibition

(c) Foreign Offices (d) All the above

60. Export-Import policy is also called as ________

(a) Export Policy (b) EXIM Policy

(c) Foreign Trade Policy (d) Export Marketing Policy

61. Which of the following is the main objectives EXIM Policy?

(a) Encouraging foreign trade

(b) Improving export performance

(c) Creating favorable balance of the payment position

(d) All the above

62. The basic structure of EXIM policy (1985-88) was based on the recommendation of

(a) Mudaliar Committee (b) Export Promotions Committee

(c) Abid Hussain Committee (d) All the above

63. EXIM Policy of 1992-97 was announced by________

(a) Mr. V.P. Singh (b) Mr. P. Chidambaram

(c) Mr. N.D. Tiwari (d) Mr. Manmohan Singh

64. Which of the following is the salient features of EXIM Policy of 1985-88?

(a) Import of 53 items was decanalized

(b) 201 items of industrial machinery included in OGL

(c) The Export-Import Pass Book Scheme was introduced

(d) All the above

65. OGL Stands for__________

(a) Open General License List

(b) List of Capital Goods

(c) List of Industrial Goods

(d) Open General List

66. Star Trading Houses is one of special features of ________

(a) Export-Import Policy (1990-93)

(b) Export-Import Policy (1988-91)

(c) Export-Import Policy (1985-88)

(d) Export-Import Policy (1992-97)

67. ______ involves fixing the price of export product or service which the exporter intends to sell in the overseas markets.

(a) Cost Price (b) Export Pricing

(c) Import Pricing (d) Sales Price

68. Which of the following factor is considered for pricing decisions?

(a) Cost (b) Demand (c) Competition (d) All the above

69. Which one of the following is referred to Full Cost Approach export price? Export Price =

(a) Average fixed cost – Average variable cost + Desirable profit

(b) Average fixed cost – Average variable cost + Desirable profit

(c) Average fixed cost + Average variable cost – Desirable profit

(d) Average fixed cost – Average variable cost – Desirable profit

70. Which is the Marginal Cost Approach export price? Export price =

(a) Cost of Production + Fixed Cost – Variable Cost

(b) Cost of Production – Fixed Cost + Variable Cost

(c) Cost of Production – Fixed Cost – Marginal Cost

(d) Cost of Production – Fixed Cost + Average Variable Cost

71. When the seller takes upon himself the responsibility of sending the goods to the sea port and also of loading, it is called _______

(a) Free on Rail Price (b) Free Along Ship Price

(c) Free on Board Price (d) On the Spot Price

72. ________ includes all the expenses up to the shipment of the goods from the port of shipper, the importer has to receive all the delivery of the goods in his country.

(a) Cost and Freight Price (b) Cost, Insurance and Freight Price

(c) Franco Price (d) Ex-Ship Price

73. While calculating _______the cost of marine insurance premium is borne by the importer.

(a) Free Along Ship Price (b) Free On Board Price

(c) Cost and Freight Price (d) Loco Price

74. ________ is referred to all the possible expenses in transit are to be borne by the seller, and the seller has to supply goods at the factory of the buyer.

(a) Franco Price (b) Ex-Ship Price

(c) LOCO Price (d) At Station Price

75. __________ is referred to high in the initial period and goes on reducing a gradual manner

(a) Penetration Price (b) Skimming Price

(c) FOB (d) Cost, Insurance and Freight Price

76. ______ is referred to low at the initial period and goes on increasing in a gradual Manner.

(a) Cost and Freight Price (b) Penetration Price

(c) Skimming Price (d) Marginal Cost Price

77. Which of the following is not relating to Skimming Price?

(a) To collect huge profit within short period of time

(b) Is convenient in the case of fashion goods

(c) Is a short term policy

(d) Initial low price is used

78. Which of the following is not relating to Penetration Price?

(a) Initial low price is used

(b) Is a long term pricing policy

(c) To capture the available market in a gradual manner

(d) Heavy advertising and promotional expenditure necessary

79. ________ is an export incentive and is given on the FOB value of goods exported with a view to enabling the exporter to charge low price in the same proportion in the foreign market.

(a) Duty Drawback (b) Cash Assistance (c) Credit Assistance (d) All the above

80. ____________ is paid on the imported raw materials used for manufacturing goods to be exported in due course.

(a) Duty Drawback (b) Cash Assistance
(c) Credit Assistance (d) Gurantee Facilities

81. Cash assistance claims are to be submitted to the _________ for approval

(a) Directorate of Duty Drawback (Customs)
(b) Controller of Import and Export
(c) Commissioner of Central Board of Taxes
(d) Director of Central Board of Direct Taxes

82. Duty Drawback claims are to be submitted to the ______________.

(a) Director Central Board of Direct Taxes
(b) Controller of Import and Export
(c) Directorate of Duty Drawback
(d) None of these

83. Which of the following is not relating to Total Cost Price?

(a) Inclusive of all costs
(b) Done in Domestic Marketing
(c) Operating in Monopolistic Market
(d) Operating in Competitive Marketing

84. Pre-Shipment Credit is also called as ____________.

(a) Packing Credit (b) Pre-Shipment Finance
(c) Both 'a' and 'b' (d) Security Overdraft

85. Post-Shipment is provided to meet the _________ requirements

(a) Working Capital (b) Long Term Capital
(c) Both 'a' and 'b' (d) Medium Term Capital

86. Which of the following documentary evidence is required for Pre-Shipment Finance?

(a) Confirmed export order (b) Letter of Credit
(c) Relevant policy issued by ECGC (d) All the above

87. Which of the following method is not included in Pre-Shipment Finance?

(a) Cash Packing Credit Loan (b) Against Hypothecation
(c) Advance Red LC (d) Advance Against Bill Under Collection

88. Normal period of Packing Credit is _________.

(a) 90 days (b) 120 days (c) 180 days (d) 200 days

89. Which of the following relates to Pre-Shipment Finance?

(a) Extended Credit Packing Loan (b) Packing Credit Loan

(c) Secured Shipping Loan (d) All the above

90. Finance assistance extended to the exporter prior to shipment of goods from India is called as ________

(a) Post-Shipment Finance (b) Pre-Shipment Finance

(c) Working Capital Assistance (d) None of these

91. Who are the following is the beneficiary of Pre-Shipment Finance?

(a) Indian Exporters (b) Suppliers of Export Goods

(c) Both 'a' and 'b' (d) Overseas Buyers

92. Which is the main purpose of Pre-Shipment Finance?

(a) It is sanctioned for procuring and manufacturing the goods meant for exports

(b) Sanctioned for packing and warehousing the goods for exports

(c) Shipping the goods meant for exports

(d) All the above.

93. ________ is referred to provided after the actual shipment of goods from India

(a) Post-Shipment Finance (b) Pre-Shipment Finance

(c) Finance for Term Loan (d) Both 'a' and 'b'

94. Who are the following is a beneficiary of Post-Shipment Finance?

(a) Overseas Buyers (b) Overseas Financial Institutions

(c) Governments (d) All the above

95. Which is the main purpose of Post-Shipment Finance?

(a) It is sanctioned for manufacturing the goods for exports

(b) It is sanctioned for processing the goods for exports

(c) It is sanctioned during the period between shipment of goods

(d) It is sanctioned for finished goods for sale

96. ECGC stands for________

(a) Export Credit Guarantee Corporation of India Ltd

(b) Export Guarantee Credit Corporation of India

(c) Export Credit Guarantee Commission

(d) Export Credit Guarantee Council

97. Export Import Bank (EXIM Bank) of India was established ________

(a) 1992 (b) 1972 (c) 1982 (d) 1962

98. The ECGC is under the control of ________

(a) Ministry of Finance (b) Ministry of Commerce

(c) Ministry of External Affairs (d) Ministry of Industry

99. Which of the following forms relate to Post-Shipment Finance?

(a) Negotiation of Bills drawn under LC

(b) Purchase/Discounting of Bills

(c)Overdraft against Bills under collection

(d) All the above

100. Which is the headquarter of EXIM Bank?

(a) New Delhi (b) Calcutta (c) Bombay (d) Bangalore

101. Which of the following guarantees relate to ECGC?

(a) Packing Credit Guarantee

(b) Export Production Finance Guarantee

(c) Export Finance Guarantee and Export Performance Guarantee

(d) All the above

102. Which of the following risk is covered by ECGC?

(a) Buyer's failure to accept goods

(b) Buyer's protected default to pay for goods accepted by him

(c) Insolvency of the buyer

(d) All the above

103. ECGC is provides safeguard banks in India against losses arising out of risks of confirmation of LC is refers to

(a) Transfer Guarantee (b) Export Performance Guarantee

(c) Export Finance Guarantee (d) Packing Credit Guarantee

104. Importer-Exporter (IEC) Code Number issued by ________

(a) RBI (b) Income Tax Authorities

(c) ECGC (d) Chief Controller of Imports and Exports

105. Income Tax Number is allocated to the exporter on the basis of ________

(a) IEC (b) CNX Form

(c) ECGC (d) Registrar of Companies

106. Which of the following forms is issued by the Export Promotion Council?

(a) Application for Registration

(b) Application for Membership

(c) Registration Cum Membership Certificates

(d) All the above

107. IIFT Stands for ________

(a) Indian Institute of Foreign Trade (b) Institute of Indian's Foreign Trade

(c) Indian Institute of Fashion Trade (d) International Institute of Foreign Trade

108. The Chamber of Commerce is authorized to issue an important document known as ________ to the members

(a) Certificate of Quality (b) Certificate of Origin

(c) Certificate of Goodwill (d) Certificate of Membership

109. All shipping and customs formalities and the actual loading of the goods on board the ship, is done by a specialist called as ________

(a) Packing Agent (b) Ship Master

(c) Forwarding Agents (d) Exchange Dealer

110. Which of the following function is performed by the Forwarding Agents?

(a) Negotiations of Shipping Contracts

(b) Execute Customs formalities

(c) Marine Insurance Policy and Loading of Goods

(d) All the above

111. The exporter approaches the shipping company, presents the Mate's Receipt and in exchange receives a document known as ________

(a) Certificate Origin (b) Bill of Lading

(c) Consular Invoice (d) Shipping Bills

112. In those countries where Advalorem duties are charged, it is in the interest of the importer to present to the customs authorities of the importing country the document called________ is order to save time and trouble while taking delivery of the goods.

(a) Letter of Indemnity (b) Certificate of Origin

(c) Consular Invoice (d) Securing Payment

113. In order to prove that the imported goods belong originally to the exporting country with whom the trade agreement has been entered into, the importer has to present to customs authorities the certificate called ________

(a) Bill of Lading (b) Letter Indemnity

(c) Consular Invoice (d) Certificate of Origin

114. Which of the following document is submitted for obtaining excise duty rebate?

(a) GP-1 (b) AR-4 (c) PLA BOOK (d) All the above

115. Which colour relates to Triplicate Copies of Form AR-4?

(a) Pink (b)White (c) Buff (d) Green

116. Which of the following is the main purpose of Shipping Bill?

(a) Granting Permission for Shipment

(b) For obtaining excise duty rebate

(c) For obtaining formal approval from customs authorities

(d) None of these

117. For export, Carting Order is issued by ________

(a) Income Tax Authorities (b) Customs Authorities

(c) Port Trust Authorities (d) Forwarding Agents.

118. As soon as the goods are loaded on board the ship, the Captain or Master of the ship furnishes a document called as ________

(a) Let Ship Order (b) Mate's Receipt (c) Carting Order (d) Shipping Bill

119. The exporter to obtain permanent Account Number is allotted by ________

(a) Income Tax Authorities (b) Customs Authorities

(c) Export Promotion Councils (d) Prot Trust Authorities

120. Which of the following document is not required by Exporter to claim cash compensatory?

(a) Copy of Commercial Invoice (b) Bank Certificate

(c) Copy of Shipping Bill (d) Original Copy of Gate Pass

121. The exporter could apply for DBK after the customs officer has given Let Export Order

(a) 50 days (b) 60 days (c) 30 days (d) 40 days

122. Which of the following documents is required to claim Central Excise Rebate?

(a) Application in Form 'C' is Triplicate

(b) Duplicate copy of AR-4/AR-4A

(c) Copy of Bill of Lading and Original Copy of Gate Pass

(d) All the above

123. The Exporter, should apply REP with in a period of ______ from the date of export

(a) 2 months (b) 4 months (c) 3 months (d) 6 months

124. Which of the following documents is not required to exporter to claim REP?

(a) Statement of Exports (b) Bank Certificate

(c) List of Items Imported and Shipping Bill (d) Duplicate Copy of AR-4/AR-4A

125. Which of the following export document is not a principal documents?

(a) Packing Credit (b) Bill of Lading

(c) Combined Transport Document (d) Porforma Invoice

126. Which of the following export document is Auxiliary documents?

(a) Proforma Invoice (b) Shipping Order

(c) Both 'a' and 'b' (d) Bill of Lading

127. Bill of Exchange is one of the export document which relates to ______

(a) Principal Documents (b) Auxiliary Documents

(c) Regulatory Documents (d) None of these

128. Exports Aligned Documents are prepared on the basis of ______

(a) Export Promotion Councils (b) United Nations Layout

(c) World Trade Organization (d) International Trade Promotion Councils

129. Which of the following export document is not Regulatory Documents?

(a) AR-4/AR4A (b) Bill of Export

(c) Export Application/Dock Chellan (d) Mate's Receipt

130. Which one of the export document is relate to goods?

(a) Invoice (b) Mate Receipt (c) Letter of Credit (d) GR Forms

131. Which of the following document does not relate to shipment?

(a) Mate Receipt (b) Ship Bill (c) Cart Ticket (d) Bill of Exchange

132. Which one of the following document is related to payment?

(a) Bill of Lading (b) Bill of Exchange (c) Form C (d) GR Forms

133. Air Way Bill is one of the document relating to ______

(a) Goods (b) Shipment

(c) Payment (d) Foreign Exchange Regulation

134. Which of the following document relates to Exchange Regulations?

(a) GR Forms (b) PP Forms (c) CNX Forms (d) All the above

135. AR-4/AR-4A form is one of the export document relating to _______

(a) Goods (b) Excisable Goods

(c) Shipment (d) Foreign Exchange Regulations

136. Improter's Bank undertakes guarantees for payment on behalf of the importer based on

(a) Letter of Credit (b) Bill of Exchange

(c) Bill of Lading (d) Bank Certificate for Payment

137. The party to a Letter of Credit is

(a) Opener (b) Beneficiary of Opening Bank

(c) Negotiating Bank (d) All the above

138. Which of the following bills are drawn and accepted by commercial firms or companies?

(a) Documentary Bills (b) Short Bills

(c) Long Bills (d) Trade Bills

139. _________ cannot be withdrawn by the importer or opening bank without prior permission and intimation of exporter.

(a) Revocable Letter of Credit (b) Irrevocable Letter of Credit

(c) Clean Letter of Credit (d) Confirmed Letter of Credit

140. Which of the following is not relating to Clean Letter of Credit?

(a) Does not make any condition for making payment

(b) Does not making conditions for acceptance of Bill of exchange

(c) It can be withdrawn by the importer

(d) It can not be withdrawn by the importer

141. A letter of credit which can be easily transferable by exporter with its rights in favour of any person is called as _______

(a) Revolving Letter of Credit (b) Non-Assignable Letter of Credit

(c) Assignable Letter of Credit (d) Clean Letter of Credit

142. When the export transaction between the same parties is of regular and continuous feature, this letter of credit is called as_______

(a) Assignable Letter of Credit (b) Revolving Letter of Credit

(c) Confirmed Letter of Credit (d) Irrevocable Letter of Credit

143. Sometime the importer may insist upon shipping document to be negotiated through a specified bank only. Any Letter of Credit making such restrictions is called _______

(a) Restricted Letter of Credit (b) Traveling Letter of Credit

(c) Omnibus Letter of Credit (d) Revolving Letter of Credit

144. Which of the following relates to Commercial Invoice?

(a) It is a main document in export sale

(b) It is prepared by the export

(c) Its basic purpose is to inform the importer about the amount due from him.

(d) All the above

145. Which of the following country does not require a document of Consular Invoice for export trade?

(a) Philippines (b) Australia (c) New Zealand (d) USA

146. Consular Invoice is a Certificate issued by ________

(a) Chamber of Commerce

(b) Export Promotion Council

(c) Commodity Boards

(d) Trade Consulate of the Importer's country stationed in the Exporter's country

147. Which of the following is not related to Mate's Receipt?

(a) Is a receipt issued by the Master of the vessel

(b) It is a prima facie evidence of goods

(c) Is not a negotiable document

(d) Is a receipt for the payment of freight for the carriage of goods.

148. ________ refers to official receipt issued by the shipping company for the good loaded in the ship.

(a) Mate's Receipt (b) Bill of lading (c) Shipping Bill (d) Consular Invoice

149. The export procedure begins with the ________

(a) Indent (b) Commercial Invoice

(c) Shipping Bill (d) Bill of Lading

150. Exports exceeding imports indicates the balance of trade to be

(a) Unfavorable (b) Favorable

(c) Neither favorable nor unfavorable (d) None of these

151. Imports exceeding exports indicate the balance of trade to be

(a) Favorable (b) Unfavorable

(c) Most Unfavorable (d) Neither favorable nor unfavorable

152. International trade must exist because of a variety of

(a) Political factors (b) Economic factors

(c) Differences in available material resources (d) All of the above

153. Markout the organization that can sanction exchange for the import of goods

(a) RBI (b) Export Promotion Councils

(c) Ministry of External Affairs (d) Controller of Import and Export

154. Which of the following relates to Loco Price?

(a) Only cost of goods sold

(b) Cost of goods + Normal profit

(c) Cost of goods and Freight expenses

(d) Cost of goods and Insurance

155. Which of the following price quotations is exclusive of railway freight?

(a) CIF (b) C2F (c) LOCO (d) FAS

156. Which of the following relates to the entire ship being hired?

(a) Bill of Entry (b) Letter of Credit (c) Shipping Order (d) Charter Party

157. An importer wishing to reexport the goods is required to prepare a ______

(a) Shipping Order (b) Bill of Lading (c) Shipping Bill (d) Charter Party

158. The Bill of Entry is required to be prepared for

(a) Goods for domestic use

(b) Goods that are exempted from custom duties

(c) Bonded goods

(d) All the above

159. The STC (State Trading Corporation) was established in India ______

(a) By a Special Act of the Parliament

(b) Under the Companies Act, as a Private Limited Company

(c) Under the Companies Act, as a Public Limited Company

(d) None of these

160. Cashew Corporation is a Subsidiary wholly owned by ______

(a) MMTC (b) RBI (c) EXIM (d) STC

161. IDBI was established in India during ______

(a) 1948 (b) 1949 (c) 1964 (d) 1954

162. Airway Bill refers to______

(a) Receipt of the goods meant for dispatch

(b) Acts as a Customs Declaration Form

(c) It represents a Freight-Bill

(d) All the above

163. Which of the following colour does not relate to AR-4 Form?

(a) Original-Red (b) Duplicate-Buff

(c) Triplicate-Pink (d) Quadruplicate-Green

164. Open Account is also termed as ______.

(a) Documentary Bill (b) Trade Credit

(c) Bank Credit (d) Cash Against Documents

165. Indian Institute of Packaging (IIP) was set up in the year______

(a) 1967 (b) 1976 (c) 1966 (d) 1986

166. Federation of Indian Export Organizations (FIEO) relates to

(a) Training Institutions (b) Trading /Service Corporations

(c) Commodity Organizations (d) Financial Institutions

167. Which of the following organization is meant for the support of small scale industries?

(a) National Small Industries Corporation (b) National Textile Corporation

(c) Commodity Boards (d) Export Promotion Councils

168. Indian Institute of Foreign Trade (IIFT) was established________

(a) Under the Export Act of 1964

(b) Under the Societies Registration Act in 1963

(c) Under the Companies Act

(d) Under the Factories Act

169. Export Promotion Council was established in India________

(a) By a Special Act of Parliament

(b) Under the Companies Act as a Non-Profit making Limited Companies

(c) Under the Societies Registration Act

(d) Under the Companies Act, as a public Limited Company

170. Coffee Board was set up in India during __________.

(a) 1942 (b) 1952 (c) 1962 (d) 1972

171. Tea Board (1965) was set up in India

(a) Under the Factories Act of Parliament

(b) Under the Special Act of Parliament

(c) Under the Companies Act

(d) Under the Tea Act of 1955

172. Where is the headquarter of Tea Board in India?

(a) Bombay (b) New Delhi (c) Calcutta (d) Bangalore

173. Rubber Board was setup in India in__________

(a) 1946 (b) 1947 (c) 1957 (d) 1967

174. Coir Board was setup in India in__________

(a) 1953 (b) 1963 (c) 1973 (d) 1983

175. Where is the headquarter of Indian Institute of Packaging?

(a) Madras (b) Bombay (c) New Delhi (d) Calcutta

176. Indian Council of Arbitration (ICA) was set of in India during__________

(a) 1955 (b)1975 (c) 1965 (d) 1985

177. Indian Council of Arbitration was established________

(a) Under the Societies Registration Act.

(b) Under the Special Act of Parliament

(c) Under the Factories Act

(d) Under the Companies Act

178. Export Inspection Council was established in India in__________

(a) 1953 (b) 1963 (c) 1973 (d) 1983

179. Which of the following is relates to Indian Institute of packaging?

(a) To Upgrade packaging standards

(b) To provide testing facilities in packaging

(c) To Organize consultancy services for the industry

(d) All the above

180. Which of the main objective of Export Promotion Councils?

(a) To Upgrade packaging standards

(b) To Upgrade quality standards

(c) To Under take export promotion activities

(d) To Settle disputes between exporters and imports

181. To protect exporters against payment risk is the main objective of ________.

(a) Indian Institute of Foreign Trade

(b) Indian Institute of Packaging

(c) Export Credit and Guarantee Corporation

(d) Export Inspection Council

182. To provide training facilities is the main objective of __________.

(a) Indian Institute of Foreign Trade

(b) Export Promotion Councils

(c) Export Inspection Councils

(d) Indian Council of Arbitration

183. The Kandla Free Trade Zone (KFTZ) was setup in India for the first time by______.

(a) Prime Minister Indira Gandhi

(b) Shri Lal Bahadur Shastri

(c) Prime Minister Rajive Gandhi

(d) Shri V.V. Giri

184. Santacruz Electronics Export Processing Zone (1974) was setup in India under

(a) Minister of Commerce

(b) Minister of Information and Telecommunication

(c) Ministry of Industry

(d) Ministry of Foreign Affairs

185. Trade Fair Authority of India was established in India __________.

(a) Under the Indian Companies Act 1956

(b) Under the Indian Factories Act 1942

(c) Under the Indian Societies Registration Act

(d) Under the Special Act of Parliament

186. Where is World Trade Centers Association located?

(a) Geneva (b) Newyork (c) London (d) Paris

187. MMTC Stands for ________.

(a) The Minerals and Mechanical Trading Corporation of India

(b) The Minerals and Metals Transport Corporation of India

(c) The Minerals and Metals Trading Corporation of India Ltd

(d) The Metals and Minerals Transport Corporation

188. State Trading Corporation is a ___________

(a) Public Sector Agency (b) Private Sector Agency
(c) Both 'a' and 'b' (d) Quasi Government Agency

189. Which of the following organization promotes Export Trade?

(a) STC (b) ECGC (c) MMTC (d) All the above

190. Primage refers to a payment made for

(a) Insurance (b) Packing the goods
(c) Loading the goods (d) Unloading the goods

191. State the number of copies prepared for a bill of lading is

(a) Two (b) Three (c) Four (d) Five

192. How many copies are prepared for a Bill of Entry?

(a) One (b) Two (c) Three (d) Four

193. Prior to Jan.15, 1964, the ECGC functioned as

(a) Export Insurance Company (b) Export Risks Insurance
(c) Export Corporation (d) Export Risks Insurance Corporation

194. Entrepot Trade refers to ___________

(a) Imports (b) Goods exported for re-import
(c) Foreign Trade (d) Goods imported for re-export

195. Who should produce a Letter of Credit?

(a) The Shipping Company (b) The Custom Authorities
(c) Exporter (d) Importer

196. Which of the following is a Non-Traditional Product?

(a) Tea (b) Cashew (c) Coffee (d) Consumer durables

197. Trade Deficit exists when ________

(a) Import > Export (b) Export > Import (c) Import = Export (d) Import <> Export

198. The area where the Government provides infrastructure facilities such as land, water, electricity and construction is refers to

(a) Export House (b) Trade House
(c) Free Trade Zone (d) Export Processing Zone

199. The agency, which canalizes exports and imports of a lot of items is called ______

(a) Indian Institute of Foreign Trade
(b) State Trading Corporation of India
(c) Federation of Indian Export Organization
(d) Zonal Export and Import Advisory Committee

200. EXIM Bank extends its finance to ___________.

(a) Short Term Exports (b) Medium Term Exports
(c) Long Term Exports (d) Medium and Long Term Exports

201. The bank, which establishes letter of credit on behalf of the opener is called ______

(a) Opening Bank (b) Negotiating Bank
(c) Beneficiary Bank (d) Endorsing Bank

202. The clause, which protects the exporter for non-fulfillment of contract due to war is called______

(a) Escalation Clause (b) Force Majeure Clause
(c) Commercial Clause (d) Coverage Clause

203. The risk, which is not covered by the ECGC is called________

(a) Insolvency of budget
(b) Cancellation of export license
(c) War between buyer's country and India
(d) Dispute about quality

204. Cash assistance is referred to as ____________

(a) Cash Compensatory Support (b) Cash Credit
(c) Cash Discount (d) Duty Draw Back

205. Open General License refers to

(a) A Category of Import License (b) A Category of Export License
(c) A Category of Shipment License (d) A Category of Trading License

206. FTZ Stands for________

(a) Free Trade Zone (b) Free Trading Zone
(c) Fixed Trade Zone (d) Foreign Trading Zone

207. The institution, which offers specialized services for promotion of export of non-traditional items is referred to

(a) Export House (b) Trading House
(c) Commodity Board (d) Export Promotional Council

208. The document, which carries legal title to the goods shipped on board is called ______

(a) Bill of Lading (b) Ship Order
(c) Mate Receipt (d) Shipping Bill

209. The document required by the RBI as exchange control document is called______

(a) AR-4 Form (b) GR-1 Form
(c) Certificate of Origin (d) Letter of Credit

210. The risk, covered by the standard policy of the ECGC is known as__

(a) Escalation Clause (b) Force Majeure Claue
(c) Commercial Clause (d) Coverage Clause

ANSWER

1. (a) Export Management
2. (d) Both 'a' and 'b'
3. (c) Sugar
4. (d) Cashew
5. (a) Multinational Corporation
6. (d) NATO
7. (d) All The above
8. (b) Profession
9. (d) All the above
10. (a) Most Developed Countries
11. (d) All the above
12. (a) Prime Minister Pandit Jawaharlal Nehru
13. (a) Tariff Barriers
14. (b) Non-Tariff Barriers
15. (c) Import Licensing
16. (d) Anti Dumping Duties
17. (a) To increase in price of imported goods
18. (d) All the above
19. (d) It is not easy to withdraw one imposed
20. (d) Double (or) Single Column Tariff
21. (c) Both 'a' and 'b'
22. (d) Tariff Quota
23. (a) Advalorem Duty
24. (a) Specific Duty
25. (d) Easy to administer
26. (d) More popular and used by all countries
27. (a) Customs Co-operation Council
28. (b) Bilateral Trade Agreement
29. (a) Multilateral Trade Agreement
30. (c) Protectionist Policy
31. (c) 1947 Geneva
32. (d) Both 'a' and 'b'
33. (d) To remove trade barrier
34. (b) Generalized System of Preference
35. (b) To promote world trade particularly developing countries
36. (a) 1958, Brussels
37. (d) Poland
38. (c) USSR
39. (b) India
40. (d) England
41. (a) Latin American Free Trade Association
42. (b) European Free Trade Association
43. (d) Peru
44. (b) EFTA
45. (a) Association of South East Asian Nations
46. (b) Bangkok, 1967
47. (c) NAFTA
48. (a) North American Free Trade Agreement
49. (c) Soudi Arabia
50. (b) South Asian Association of Regional Co-operation
51. (d) Kenya.
52. (a) Organization of Petroleum Exporting Countries
53. (b) Manufacturer-Exporter.
54. (a) Merchant-Exporter
55. (c) Marketing abroad is the main aspect of business
56. (d) All the above
57. (d) None of these
58. (b) 1992
59. (d) All the above
60. (b) EXMIN Policy
61. (d) All the above
62. (c) Abid Hussain Committee
63. (b) Mr. P.Chidambaram.
64. (d) All the above
65. (a) Open General License List
66. (a) Export-Import Policy (1990-93)
67. (b) Export Pricing
68. (d) All the above
69. (a) Average fixed cost + Average Variable Cost + Desirable profit
70. (b) Cost of production-Fixed cost + Variable cost

71. (c) Free on Board Price
72. (b) Cost, Insurance and freight Price
73. (c) Cost and Freight Price
74. (a) Franco Price
75. (b) Skimming Price
76. (b) Penetration Price
77. (d) Initial low price is used
78. (d) Heavy advertising and promotional expenditure necessary
79. (d) Cash Assistance
80. (a) Duty Drawback
81. (b) Controller of Import and Export
82. (c) Directorate of Duty Drawback
83. (d) Operating in competitive marketing
84. (c) Both 'a' and 'b'
85. (a) Working capital
86. (d) All the above
87. (d) Advance Against Bill under Collection
88. (c) 180 days
89. (d) All the above
90. (b) Pre Shipment Finance
91. (c) Both 'a' and 'b'
92. (d) All the above
93. (a) Post – Shipment Finance
94. (d) All the above
95. (c) It is sanctioned during the period between shipment of goods
96. (a) Export Credit Guarantee Corporation of India Ltd.
97. (c) 1982
98. (b) Ministry of Commerce
99. (d) All the above
100. (c) Bombay
101. (d) All the above
102. (d) All the above
103. (a) Transfer Guarantee
104. (d) Chief Controller of Imports and Exports
105. (b) CNX Form
106. (d) All the above
107. (a) Indian Institute of Foreign Trade
108. (b) Certificate of Origin
109. (c) Forwarding Agents
110. (d) All the above
111. (b) Bill of Lading
112. (c) Consular Invoice
113. (d) Certificate of Origin
114. (d) All the above
115. (a) Pink
116. (a) Granting Permission for Shipment
117. (c) Port Trust Authority
118. (b) Mate's Receipt
119. (a) Income Tax Authorities
120. (d) Original Copy of Gate Pass
121. (b) 60 days
122. (d) All the above
123. (c) 3 months
124. (d) Duplicate copy of AR-4/AR4A.
125. (d) Proforma Invoice
126. (C) Both 'a' and 'b'
127. (a) Principal Documents
128. (b) United Nations Layout
129. (d) Mate's Receipt
130. (a) Invoice
131. (d) Bill of Exchange
132. (b) Bill of Exchange
133. (b) Shipment
134. (d) All the above
135. (b) Excisable Goods
136. (a) Letter of Credit
137. (d) All the above
138. (a) Documentary Bills
139. (b) Irrevocable letter of credit
140. (c) It can be withdrawn by the importer
141. (c) Assignable Letter of Credit
142. (b) Revolving Letter of Credit
143. (a) Restricted Letter of Credit
144. (d) All the above
145. (d) USA
146. (d) Trade Consulate of the Importer's country stationed in the exporter's country
147. (d) Is a receipt for the payment of freight for the carriage of goods
148. (b) Bill of Lading

149. (a) Indent
150. (a) Unfavorable
151. (b) Unfavorable
152. (d) All the above
153. (a) RBI
154. (b) Cost of goods + Normal profit
155. (c) LOCO
156. (d) Charter Party
157. (c) Shipping Bill
158. (d) All the above
159. (b) Under the Companies Act, as a Private Limited Company
160. (d) STC
161. (c) 1964
162. (d) All the above
163. (a) Original-Red
164. (b) Trade Credit
165. (c) 1966
166. (c) Commodity Organizations
167. (a) National Small Industries Corporation
168. (b) Under the Societies Registration Act in 1963
169. (a) By a Special Act of Parliament
170. (a) 1942
171. (d) Under the Tea Act of 1955
172. (c) Calcutta
173. (b) 1947
174. (a) 1953
175. (b) Bombay
176. (c) 1965
177. (a) Under the Society Registration Act
178. (b) 1963
179. (d) All the above
180. (c) To under take export promotion activities
181. (c) Export Credit and Gurantee Corporation
182. (a) Indian Institute of Foreign Trade
183. (b) Shri. Lal Bahadur Shastri
184. (a) Ministry of Commerce
185. (a) Under the Indian Companies Act 1956
186. (b) Newyork
187. (c) The Minerals and Metals Trading Corporation of India Ltd
188. (a) Public Sector Agency
189. (d) All the above
190. (c) Loading the goods
191. (d) Five
192. (c) Three
193. (d) Export Risks Insurance Corporation
194. (d) Goods imported for re-export
195. (d) Importer
196. (d) Consumer durables
197. (a) Import > Export
198. (c) Free Trade Zone
199. (b) State Trading Corporation of India
200. (d) Medium and long term exports
201. (a) Opening Bank
202. (b) Force Majeure Clause
203. (d) Disbute about quality
204. (a) Cash Compensatory Support
205. (a) A category of Import License
206. (d) Fixed Trading Zone
207. (a) Export House
208. (a) Bill of Lading
209. (b) GR-1 Form
210. (a) Escalation Clause

*****

VI

HUMAN RESOURCES AND PERSONNEL MANAGEMENT

1. **Organisational interest is uppermost in ________**
   (a) Human Resource Management
   (b) Personnel Management
   (c) International Labour Force Management
   (d) Labour Management
2. **Human Resource Management is also known as ________**
   (a) Personal Management (b) Man Power Managment
   (c) Staff Management (d) All the above
3. **Which of the following objectives relates to Human Resource Management?**
   (a) Societal objectives (b) Production objectives
   (c) Personnel objectives (d) Both 'a' and 'c'
4. **________ refers to a plan of action**
   (a) Objective (b) Policy (c) Principle (d) Strategy
5. **____________ is the fundamental truth established by research, investigation and analysis**
   (a) Policy (b) Guide (c) Principles (d) Objectives
6. **Human Resource Planning is also termed as ______**
   (a) Man Power Planning (b) Personnel Planning
   (c) Employment Planning (d) All the above

7. Forecast of personnel needs and supplies relate to

(a) Human Resource Planning (b) Sales Promotion Force Planning

(c) Production Planning (d) All the above

8. ________ refers to a method for forecasting personnel needs.

(a) Work Study Technique (b) Dalphi Technique

(c) Ratio Trend Analysis (d) All the above

9. Absenteeism can be calculated by

(a) $\frac{\text{Number of Separations during one year}}{\text{Average Number of employees during the year}} \times 100$

(b) $\frac{\text{Number of Additions during the year}}{\text{Average number of employees during the year}} \times 100$

(c) $\frac{\text{Number of person – Days lost}}{\text{Average number of persons X Number of working days}} \times 100$

(d) None of the above

10. The audit of Non -Managers is called as ________

(a) Skills Inventories (b) Management Inventories

(c) Inventories of Stock (d) Unskill Inventories

11. ________ is refered the process of collecting job-related data

(a) Job Analysis (b) Performance Appraisal

(c) Labour Turnover (d) All the above

12. The Application of Job Analysis is useful for ________

(a) Preparing Job Description (b) Job Specification

(c) Human Resource Planning (d) All the above

13. ________ refers to the lists of human qualities and qualification necessary to do the job.

(a) Job Description (b) Job Specification

(c) Job Evaluation (d) Performance Apparisal

14. ________ refers to the lists of job title, duties, machines, working conditions surrounding a job and the like

(a) Job Specification (b) Job Evaluation (c) Job Description (d) Job Analysis

15. A logical sequence to job analysis relates to ________

(a) Job Design (b) Job Rotation (c) Job Enlargement (d) Job Enrichment

16. ________ is described as the movement of employees from Job to job

(a) Job Enlargement (b) Job Rotation (c) Job design (d) None of these

17. ________ is otherwise termed as "adding zero to zero"

(a) Job Enlargement (b) Job Design (c) Job Enrichment (d) Job Rotation

18. Job Enrichment is related to

(a) Substituting one zero for another zero (b) Adding zero to zero
(c) Job Intrinsic Factor (d) None of these

19. Vertical Job Enrichment describes______

(a) More responsibility (b) More variety of tasks
(c) More responsibility and autonomy (d) None of these

20. Horizontal Job Enrichment relates to ______

(a) More variety of tasks (b) More growth opportunitiers
(c) Both a and b (d) More responsibility and autonomy

21. ______ refers to the process of finding and attracting capable of applicants for employment.

(a) Recuritment (b) Training (c) Posting (d) Promotion

22. Job Analysis is performed on any of the following occasion ______

(a) When new job is created (b) Adoption of new technology
(c) On a set time cycle (d) All the above

23. The enriched name for Personnel Management is

(a) People Management (b) Human Resource Management
(c) Welfare Management (d) Industrial Management

24. Uniform dress code is

(a) Military Rule (b) Personal Policy (c) Adevertisement (d) Beauty

25. ______ is concerned with picking the right candidates from the pool of applicants.

(a) Selection (b) Recruitment (c) Searching (d) Screening

26. ______ refers to measure ability of employees

(a) Personality Test (b) Achievement Test
(c) Thematic Appreciation Test (d) Interest Test

27. Psychological test is a tool for

(a) Selection (b) Transfer (c) Punishment (d) Trade Union

28. GMAT refers to ______

(a) General Management Ability Test (b) General Managers Attitude Test
(c) General Management Aptitude Test (d) None of these

29. Aptitude Test is suitable to measure ______

(a) Fitness of an individual (b) Individual's activity preferences
(c) Handwriting of an individual (d) Individual achievements

30. ______ refers to measure physical fitness of a candidate

(a) Drug Test (b) Graphology Test (c) Medical Test (d) Aptitude Test

31. TAT refers to

(a) Thematic Aptitude Test (b) Thematic Ability Test
(c) Thematic Appreception Test (d). Thematic Attitude Test

32. _______ refers to the assignment of a new employee to his or her job.

(a) Orientation (b) Placement (c) Confirmation (d) Induction

33. Training and Developement can be determind by

(a) Training and Development = Standard Performance - Actual Performance

(b) Training and Development = Actual Performance - Standard Performance

(c) Training and Development = Both a and b

(d) Training and Development = None of the above

34. Which of the following relates to Training?

(a) Theoretical Orientation (b) General Concepts

(c) Class Room learning (d) Application oriented

35. _________ is described as imparting specific skills

(a) Development (b) Training (c) Education (d) Distinction

36. _________ refers to the process of theoretical learning in classrooms

(a) Distinction (b) Development (c) Education (d) Training

37. On the Job Training is mostly given for ________

(a) Supervisors (b) Managers

(c) Unskilled and Semi-skilled workers (d) Top Executives

38. Simultation Technique is one of the Training Method used in________

(a) Furniture Industry (b) Chemical Industry

(c) Textile Industry (d) Aeronautical Industry

39. _________ refers to Training which is not part of everyday job activity.

(a) On the Job Training (b) Off-the Job Training

(c) Training-Centre Training (d) Class Room Training

40. Attending educational course by an employee is

(a) Degree Orientation (b) Off-the Job Training

(c) Social Responsibility (d) Industrial Rule

41. Role-Playing is also called as _________

(a) role-reversal (b) Socio-drama (c) Psychodrama (d) All the above

42. _________ refers to a vertical move in rank and responsibility

(a) Demotion (b) Transfer (c) Promotion (d) Separation

43. __________refers a Horizontal Movement of an employee from one job to an other.

(a) Transfer (b) Separation (c) Demotion (d) Addition

44. Termination by the employer of the services of workmen for any reason is known as _________

(a) Resignation (b) Surpression (c) Retrenchment (d) Dismissal

45. Which of the following does not relate to Lay-Off?

(a) Indefinite separation of the employee (b) Inability of an employer

(c) Financial slump (d) Upward Advancement of an employee

46. **The rate of change in the working staff of a concern during a definite period is called as __________**

(a) Labour Turnover (b) Absenteeism (c) Retrenchment (d) Lay-Off

47. **The systematic evaluation of the individual's performance on the job called as ______**

(a) Performance Appraisal (b) Job Evaluation
(c) Job Description (d) Job Analysis

48. **Which of the following does not reltaes to Performance Appraisal Process?**

(a) Objectives of Performance Appraisal (b) Establish Job Expectations
(c) Design an Appraisal Programme (d) Organisational Climate Indices

49. **Which of the following relates to Rater?**

(a) Immediate Supervisors (b) Subordinates
(c) Peers (d) All the above

50. **Behaviourally Anchored Rating Scales is also called as ______**

(a) Behavioural Expectation Scales (b) BARS
(c) Field Review Method (d) Both 'a' and 'b'

51. **Confidential Records are maintained mostly in _________**

(a) Government Departments (b) Private Departments
(c) Educational Institutions (d) Industry and Companies

52. **Management By Objectives (MBO) concept was conceived by_______**

(a) L.J. Lindley (b) B.O. Wheeler (c) Y.K. Bhushan (d) Peter F. Drucker

53. **Section 2 (KKK) of the Industrial Disputes Act 1947 is relates to _______**

(a) Transfers (b) Promotions (c) Lay-Off (d) Demotion

54. **Voluntary Retirement Scheme is also called as _________**

(a) Golden Hand Shake Plan (b) Handsome Compensation Plan
(c) Voluntary Retrenchment Scheme (d) None of these

55. **Where the termination of employment is initiated by the employer is known as**

(a) Transfer (b) Demotion (c) Dismissal (d) Seperation

56. **Which of the following relates to Wage?**

(a) Monthly rate of pay (b) Payment for labours services
(c) Paid in addition to salaries (d) Incentives

57. **Paid holidays, car and furnished house are the benefits relate to ______**

(a) Perquisities (b) Wages (c) Salaries (d) Fringe Benefits

58. **Which of the following is not relates to Non-Monetary Benefits?**

(a) Accident relief (b) Recognition of merit
(c) Status (d) Reponsibilities

59. **Which of the following relates to Fringe Benefits ?**

(a) Paid holidays (b) Stock option schems
(c) Canteen and uniform (d) Company Car

60. __________ is base on not only bare sustenance of life but also cover efficiency of the worker.

(a) Fair Wage (b) Time Rate Method

(c) Minimum Wage Method (d) None of the above

61. Wage which is above the minimum wage but below the living wage is relates to

(a) Fair Wage Method (b) Need Based Wage Method

(c) Living Wage Method (d) Minimum Wage Method

62. Under Straight-Piece-Work method, Wage is calculated by _______

(a) Total earnings = Total Output x Rate per unit

(b) Total earnings = Hours Worked x Rate per unit

(c) Total earnings = Standard Time x Rate per hour

(d) Total earnings = Hours Worked x Guranteed Rate

63. Which of the following relates to Taylor's Difffernetial Piece Rate System?

(a) For each job, Standard time is stipulated

(b) Lower piece rate is for the output below the standard

(c) Higher piece rate is for the output above the standard

(d) All the above

64. Which of the following is not to Merrick Differential Piece Rate System?

(a) Up to 83 % : Ordinary Piece rate

(b) 83 % to 90 % : 100 % of Ordinary piece rate (Guranteed rate)

(c) 83 % to 100 % : 110 % of Ordinary piece rate

(d) Above 100 % : 120 % of Ordinary piece rate.

65. Which of the following is Gantt Task and Bonus Scheme?

(a) Combined with Time, Piece Rate and Bonus

(b) Day wages are guranteed

(c) Standard are set and bonus is paid

(d) All the above.

66. Halsey Premimum Plan is also known as _______

(a) Split Bonus Plan (b) Fifty - Fifty Plan

(c) Merrick Plan (d) Both 'a' and 'b'

67. According to Halsey-Weir Scheme, Worker gets a bonus of ______ of the time saved.

(a) 50 % of Time Saved (b) 30% of Time Saved

(c) 48% of Time Saved (d) 40% of Time Saved

68. According to Barth Scheme wages can be calculated by _______

(a) Earnings = Hours worked X Rate per hour

(b) Earnings = Guranteed wages + Bonous (50% of Time Saved)

(c) Earnings = Rate per unit X Units produced

(d) Earnings = Rate per hour X Standard hours X Actual hours worked

69. Stock options are ______ offered to executives

(a) Short term benefits (b) Bonus

(c) Long term benefits (c) Medium term benefits

70. Which of the following is Wage and Salary Administration?

(a) Ability to pay (b) Cost of living

(c) Supply and demand of labour (d) All the above

71. V room's Theory of Motivation relates to ________

(a) Equity (b) Expectancy Model

(c) Performance and Satisfaction (d) Reinforcement

72. Equity Theory of Motivation was developed by ______

(a) Adams (b) V rooms (c) Porter & Lawler (d) Alderfer

73. Which of the following is Porter & Lawler's Theory of Motivation?

(a) Expectancy Model (b) Reinforcement Model

(c) Performance Satisfaction Model (d) TW. Factor Model

74. Which of the following is Maslow's Need Hierarchy Model?

(a) Physiological Needs (b) Safety Needs

(c) Belonginess and Love Needs (d) All the above

75. Two - Factor Theory of Motivation was developed by ______

(a) Maslow (b) Herzberg (c) Alderfer (d) V room

76. Hygiene Factors and Motivators are related to ______ of motivation

(a) Alderfer's ERG Theory (b) MCcleland Achivement Theory

(c) Herzberg Two Factory Theory (d) V room's Expectancy Theory

77. Which of the following is MC clelland's Achivement Motivation Theory?

(a) Power (b) Afiliation (c) Achivements (d) All the above

78. H.V room's Expectancy Theory of Motivation is also called as ______

(a) Instrumentality Theory (b) Path - Goal Theory

(c) Valence - Instrumentality Theory (d) All the above

79. Expectancy Theory of Motivation describes ______

(a) Motivation x Instrumentality x Valence

(b) Motivation x Instrumentality x Expectancy

(c) Valence x Instrumentality x Expectancy

(d) None of these

80. Adam's Equity Theory of Motivation is also called as ______

(a) Social Comparision Theory (b) Inequity Theory

(c) Both a and b (d) None of these

81. Which of the following need is the greatest significance of MC Clelland's Achivement Motivation Theory?

(a) Need for Power (b) Need for Affiliation

(c) Need for Achievement (d) None for Essentials

82. _______ means to a process governing choices made by persons or lower organisms among alternative forms of voluntary activity.

(a) Personality (b) Motivation (c) Learning (d) Perception

83. Which of the folowing is Contemporary Theory of Motivation?

(a) Content Theories (b) Process Theories

(c) Reinforcement Theories (d) All the above

84. Which of the following is not Content Theories of Motivation?

(a) Maslow's Need Hierarchy Theory (b) Alderfer's ERG Theory

(c) Herzberg's Two-Factor Theory (d) Adam's Equity Theory

85. Which of the following is Process Theories of Motivation?

(a) Vroom's Expectancy Model

(b) Adam's Equity Theory

(c) Porter & Lawler's Performance Satisfaction Theory

(d) Alderfers ERG Theory

86. A personal plan must incorporate information on _____

(a) Personnel philosophy (b) Promotion policy

(c) Recruitment (d) All the above

87. _______ is the important element of Elton Mayo's Human Relations Model of Motivation

(a) Social Needs (b) Individual Needs (c) Safety Needs (d) Achievement Needs

88. Content Theories of Motivation is very much help ful to ______

(a) Understanding Job Satisfaction (b) Understanding Work Behaviour

(c) Understanding Individual Needs (d) All the above

89. Maslow's Need Hierarchy divide human needs into ______ levels

(a) 6 (b) 5 (c) 4 (d) 7

90. Which of the following is the basic level of Maslow's Need Hierarchy?

(a) Safety Needs (b) Self Esteem

(c) Self Actualisation (d) Physiological Needs

91. Food, Drink, Sex and Oxygen are the examples of_______

(a) Physiological Needs (b) Belonging and Love Needs

(c) Safety Needs (d) Self Esteem Needs

92. Safety Needs exert influence beyond _ _____

(a) Young (b) Old (c) Childhood (d) Adulet

93. Job Security, Unionisation and Safe working conditions are the examples of

(a) Self Esteem Needs (b) Belonging and Love Needs

(c) Physiological Needs (d) Safety Needs

94. Belonging and Love Needs arise when _______ and ________ needs are Satisfied.

(a) Safety, Self Esteem (b) Physiological, Safety

(c) Safety, Self Actualisation (d) None of these

95. Which of the following does not relate to Self Esteem Needs?
(a) Recognition (b) Professional friendship
(c) Dependence on adults (d) Protection

96. Which of the following relates to self-Actualisation Needs?
(a) Excelling Oneself in One's Job (b) Advancing an important idea
(c) Successfully managing a unit (d) All the above

97. ______ is referred to part of management process which is primarily concerned with human constituents of an organisation
(a) Personnel Managent (b) Personnel Development
(c) Personnel Administration (d) Organisation Development

98. Which of the following relates to operative function's of Personnel Management?
(a) Procurement and Development
(b) Compensation and Integration
(c) Maintenance, records, research and audit
(d) All the above

99. Which of the following Source relates to internal sources of recruitment?
(a) Employment Agencies (b) Employment Exchanges
(c) Field Trips (d) None of these

100. ________ is a face to face, observational and personnel appraisal method of evaluating the applicant where the interviewer who is higher in status is in a dominant role.
(a) Selection (b) Interview (c) Group Discussion (d) Personal Opinion

101. If more than one person interviews an applicant at the same time then it is called___.
(a) Systematic Depth Interview (b) Group Interview
(c) The Stress Interview (d) Panel or Board Interview

102. Which of the following is Psychological Test?
(a) Knowledge Test (b) Ability Test (c) Physical Test (d) Aptitude Test

103. Alderfer's ERG theory stands for ______
(a) Existence, Relatedness and Growth (b) Existence, Recognition and Growth
(c) Existence, Responsibility and Growth (d) None of these

104. Achievement Motivation Theory was developed by _______
(a) David C. MC Clelland (b) Alderfer
(c) Herzberg (d) Peterson

105. Morale refers to ______
(a) Esprit de corps
(b) A feeling of enthusiasm
(c) Zeal and confidence in individual or groups
(d) All the above

106. Which of the following factors does not influence of employees Morale?
(a) Food and physical welfare
(b) Desire for achievement and getting over difficulties
(c) Desire for safety, variety and novelty
(d) Sex

107. When employee Attitudes are favourable to the total situation of a group and to the attainment of its objectives it is______

(a) High Morale (b) Good Morale (c) Low Morale (d) Both 'a' and 'b'

108. Which of the following methods relates to Morale?

(a) Observation (b) Attitude or Morale Surveys

(c) Company Records and Counselling (d) All the above

109. ________ refers to the process of passing information and understand from one person to another

(a) Communication (b) Advertisement (c) Interaction (d) Correspondence

110. Upward Comunication particularly refers to

(a) Operational information (b) Achivement of integrated activities

(c) Performance of information (d) None of these

111. Oral Communication is also termed as ______

(a) Face to Face Communication (b) One to One Communication

(c) Both a and b (d) Formal Communication

112. Under Straight Chain Pattern, informal messages are

(a) Top Secrete (b) disclosed by one person to many other

(c) Accidentally Communicated (d) Communicated his close circles

113. Vertical Communication is also known as ______

(a) Upward Communication (b) Downward Communication

(c) Inter-Scalar Communication (d) All the above

114. Transmission of ideas or information from executives to the subordinates is ______

(a) Upward Communication (b) Downward Communication

(c) Lateral Communication (d) Intra - Scalar Communication

115. Communication among equal ranks

(a) Upward Communication (b) Horizontal Communication

(c) Extra - Organisational Communication (d) Organisational Communication

116. ________ means organbisationally useful behaviour by one member of an organisational family toward another member to members of that same organisational family.

(a) Leader (b) Leadership (c) Boss (d) Administer

117. Which of the following relates to Symbolic Leader?

(a) He has prestige but no power (b) Gets things done through others

(c) He has power on a supernatural basis (d) None of these

118. "Geting things done through others" is the main functions of

(a) Symbolic Leader (b) Administrative Leader

(c) Charismatic Leader (d) Situational Leader

119. Which of the following power is not identified by French and Raven?

(a) Coercive Power, Reward Power (b) Legitimate Power

(c) Expert and Referent Power (d) Incremental Influential Power

120. Coercive Power is ______

(a) Powers based on primarily on Organisational factors

(b) Derived from the position of a Superior in the organisational hierarchy

(c) Based upon individual factors

(d) Based upon some personal traits

121. When a leader enjoys power derived from the position of a superior in the organisational hierarchy, it is ______

(a) Coercive Power (b) Legitimate Power

(c) Reward Power (d) Referent Power

122. Initiator - Contributor relates to

(a) Group Task Roles (b) Group Building and Maintenance Role

(c) Individual Role (d) Individual Task Roles

123. Aggressor and Blocker relate to ______

(a) Group Task Roles (b) Individual Role

(c) Group Building and Maintenance Role (d) None of these

124. A leader who is directive and expect obedience is

(a) Bureaucrat (b) Autocrat (c) Expert (d) Diplomat

125. A leader who is concerned only with his own field of specialiation is

(a) Bureaucrat (b) Autocrat (c) Expert (d) Quarter - Back

126. Which of the folowing is the Diplomatic Leadership?

(a) Who is directive and expert obedience

(b) Who is opportunistic and exploits people

(c) Who is concerned only with his own field of specialisation

(d) Who is generally sought by a business organisation

127. ______ refers to the way in which the leader influences followers

(a) Leadership (b) Leadership Style

(c) Leadership Qualities (d) None of these

128. Which of the following leadership style relates Howthone Studies?

(a) Old, Authoritarian Style (b) Participative Style Leader

(c) Supervisory Style (d) Democratic Style

129. The Lippitt and White Study Analysed the impact of ______

(a) Autocratic, Democrataic and Laissez Faire Style

(b) Participative Style of Leadership

(c) Supervisory Style of Leadership

(d) Achivement Oriented Style of Leadership

130. Which of the following is Authoritarian Leadership?

(a) Work Centered (b) Leader Centered

(c) Centeralises Managerial Authority (d) Both 'a' and 'b'

131. Subordinates exercising high degree of both responsibility and freedom relates to

(a) Laisez Faire Leadership (b) Participative Leadership

(b) Bureaucrataive Leadership (d) Export Leadership

132. Free-Rein or Laisez Faire Leadership is _______.

(a) No leadership at all (b) Absence of direct leadership

(c) Centralises managerial authority (d) Both 'a' and 'b'

133. _____ characterised by a high degree of reliance on rules, regulations and procedures to which both leader and his subordinates subscribe.

(a) Expert Leadership (b) Manipulative Leadership

(c) Bureaucratic Leadership (d) Group Centred Leadership

134. Which of the following leadership is relates to Militry?

(a) Autocratic (b)Benevolent Autocratic X Leader

(c) Democratic Leadership (d) Free - Rein.

135. Which of the following leadership relates to Service Industries?

(a) Autocratic (b)Democratic (c) Rules - Centered (d) Expert

136. Managerial Grid Style of Leadership was developed by ________

(a) Blakes and Mouton (b) Ridden

(c) Thomas Carlyle (d) Likert

137. 3D Leadership Style was developed by _________

(a) Rensis Likert (b) Blakes Mounton (c) Ridden (d) Likert

138. "Leaders are born, not made" is described by _______

(a) The Trait Oriented Approach (b) The Situational Approach

(c) The Functional Approach (d) The Interactionistic Approach

139. _______ emphasises on "the study of a leader as a person rather a study of the group

(a) The trait oriented approach (b) The situational approach

(c) The functional approach (d) The Interactionistic approach

140. Which of the following concepts Managrial Grid was developed by Blacke and Mounton?

(a) Concern for production and concern for people

(b) Boss- centred and Subordinate centred

(c) Job- centred and Employee- centred

(d) Consideration and initiating structure

141. Consideration and initiating structure are the core concepts of ______

(a) Sipportive Theory of Leadership (b) Fielder's Theory of Leadership

(c) Two-Dimensional Theory of Leadership (d) Managerial Grid

142. Leader - Member Relation, Task Structure and Position Power are the core concepts of _______

(a) Fielder's Theory of Leadership (b) Managerial Grid

(c) Two - Dimensional Theory of Leadership (d) Supportive Theory of Leadership

143. Which of the following does not relate to Industrial Dispute ?

(a) Strikes (b) Hunger Strikes
(c) Bandhs and lockouts (d) All the above

144. Paired comparison is a method of

(a) Performance Appraisal (b) Development
(c) Security (d) Convenience Handling

145. ______ refers to mandatory settlement of industrial disputes by labour courts or industrial tribunals under the Industrial Disputes Act.

(a) Adjudication (b) Negotiation (c) Arbitration (d) Settlement

146. Industrial Dispute Act was enacted in ______

(a) 1942 (b) 1947 (c) 1946 (d) 1948

147. "Justice delayed is justice denied" is a slogan raised by ______

(a) Jawaharlal Nehru (b) Ambadkar (c) V.V Giri (d) Sardar Patel

148. Trade Union Act was enacted in ______

(a) 1936 (b) 1946 (c) 1926 (d) 1956

149. "Unity is Strength" is the important principle relating to ______

(a) Trade Unionism (b) Charter of Freedom of Labour
(c) Industrial Relations Programme (d) Industrial Peace

150. Which of the folowing principle is relating to Trade Unionism?

(a) Unity is Strength (b) Equal pay for equal work
(c) Security of Service (d) All the above

151. The first Trade Union was founded by ______

(a) Mr. N.K. Lohanda (b) N.M. Joshi
(c) B.T. Randive (d) P. Raganan

152. The name of the first Trade Union is ______

(a) Amalgamated Society of Railway Servants
(b) Bombay Mill Hands Association
(c) The Printers Union of Calcutta
(d) Madras and Calcutta Postal Union

153. Kamgar Hitwardhak Sabha Trade Union was founded in ______

(a) 1890 (b) 1905 (c) 1910 (d) 1907

154. Indian Trade Union Congress was set up in ______

(a) 1942 (b) 1947 (c) 1946 (d) 1945

155. AITUC stands for ______

(a) All India Trade Union Congress (b) All India Trade Union Federation
(c) National Trade Union Federation (d) Indian National Trade Union Congress

156. INTUC, AITUC and HMS combined and joined with employees representatives was formed ______

(a) Centre of Indian Trade Union (b) United Council of Trade Unions
(c) Confederation of Free Trade Unions (d) National Apex Body

157. INTUC is affiliated to ______

(a) Communist Party of India (b) Congress Party of India
(c) Jantha Party of India (d) Bharathia Jantha Party

158. Communist Party of India is closely associated with ______

(a) INTUC (b) AITUC (c) HMS (d) CITU

159. Which of the following concept was developed by Roger's Theory of Personality?

(a) Self Concept (b) Organism
(c) Development of Self (d) All the above

160. ______ refers to relatively permanent change in behaviour that occurs as a result of experience or reinforced practice.

(a) Personality (b) Learning (c) Perception (d) Group Dynamics

161. Which of the following relates to learning process?

(a) Classical Conditioning (b) Operant Conditioning
(c) Observational learning (d) All the above

162. Operant Conditioning is a learning process was developed by ______

(a) Ivan Pavlor Physiologist (b) Skinnerian Psychology
(c) W.H. Freeman (d) Robert A. Baron

163. Suspending an employee is a

(a) Punishment (b) An action
(c) Judgement (d) An unwanted action

164. Learning that takes place in the class room is ______

(a) Observational Learning (b) Cognitive Learning
(c) Classical Conditioning (d) Operant Conditioning

165. Which of the folowing Component is not relating to Attitude?

(a) Affective (b) Cognitive (c) Overt (d) Motive

166. The Affective Component of Attitude refers to ______

(a) emotions associated with an attitude object
(b) beliefs of a person about an attitude object
(c) the way one intends to behave a particular attitude object
(d) None of the above

167. According Sigmund Freud unconscious is guided by ______

(a) Reasoned Reality Principles (b) Hedonistic principles of pleasure
(c) Freidiam Therapentic techniques (d) None of these

168. Superego is also called as ______

(a) Ago - idel (b) Libido (c) Psychic Energy (d) None of these

169. According to Sigmund Freud, the 'ego' refers to ______

(a) the pleasure seeking element (b) the compromising element
(c) the noble and idealistic element (d) None of these

170. Which of the following theory is Type Theories?

(a) Sheldon's Physiognomy Theory
(b) Carl Jung's Extravert and Introvert Theory
(c) Both a and b
(d) Intrapsychic Theory

171. Extrovert - Introvert Theory of Personality was developed by ________

(a) Cattle (b) Sheldon (c) Sigmund Frend (d) Carl Jung

172. Which of the following dimension does not relate to Carl Jung's Extrovert - Introvert Theory of Personality?

(a) Thinking (b) Feeling
(c) Learning (d) Sensation and Intuition

173. According to ______ personality can be defined as an enduring attribute of a person that appears constantly in a variety of situations

(a) Trait Theories (b) Carl Jung's Extrovert - Introvert Theories
(c) Sheldon's Physiognomy Theory (d) None of these

174. ______ refers to an occurance which interfers with the orderly progress of work in an industrial establishment.

(a) Injury (b) Accident (c) Sickness (d) Disablement

175. Which of the following refers to causes of Accidents?

(a) Improper guarded equipment (b) Inadequate safety devices
(c) Poor house - keeping (d) All the above

176. Accident Frequency Rate can be calculated by

(a) Accident Freqency Rate = Number of disability work injuries x 1000000
x Total number of Man-hours worked

(b) Accident Frequency Rate = Number of disabiling work injuries x 100000
x Total Number of Man-hours worked

(c) Accident Frequency Rate = Number of disabiling work injuries x 1000
x Total Number of Man-hours worked

(d) None of these

177. Which of the following formula of Severity Rate used to gather accident information?

(a) Severity Rate = Number of Mandays lost x 1000000 x Total number of man hours worked
(b) Severity Rate = Number of Mandays lost x 10000 x Total number of man hours worked
(c) Severity Rate = Number of mandays lost x 1000 x Total number of man hours worked
(d) None of these

178. According Simonds and Grimaldi, a fulltime Safety Director should be appointed for each ______ employees in a factory

(a) 1500 (b) 1000 (c) 2000 (d) 2500

179. According Factories Act, a Safety Officer can be appointed in a factory where more than ______ workers employed

(a) 1000 (b) 1500 (c) 2000 (d) 2500

180. Accident prevention of three E's stands for ________

(a) Engineering, Education and Enforcement

(b) Earning, Education and Environment

(c) Engineering, Education and Environment

(d) Equipment, Education and Environment

181. 'Model Code' formulated by ICO 1948 relates to

(a) Safety Regulations (b) Security Regulation

(c) Health Regulation (d) Grievance Procedure

182. Which of the folowing Commission or Committee relates to Industrial Health?

(a) Royal Commission on Labour (1931) (b) Labour Investigation Committee (1946)

(c) Labour Welfare Committee (1969) (d) All the above

183. According Factories Act 1948, which one of the following disease does not relate to Occupa tional Diseases?

(a) Anthrax (b) Chrome Poisoning

(c) Toxic Anaemia (d) All the above

184. Occupational diseases are the result of ______

(a) Physical Conditions (b) Presence of Industrial poisonous

(c) Non-poisonous dust in the atmosphere (d) All the above

185. Which of the following method relates to Settlement of Disputes?

(a) Collective Bargaining (b) Conciliation

(c) Adjudication (d) All the above

186. Which of the following is not relates to Collective Bargaining?

(a) Preparation for negotiation's (b) Indentifying bargaining Issues

(c) Reaching the agreement (d) Employer deal with the workers directly

187. Achelors, Clubs, teenagers relate to ______

(a) Interest Groups (b) Frendship Groups

(c) Membership Groups (d) Reference Groups

188. ______ consists of people with low skills who lack unity and power and are usually discountented

(a) Apathetic Groups (b) Erratic Groups

(c) Vocational Groups (d) Instructional Groups

189. Airline Pilot relates to ______

(a) Erratic Groups (b) Strategic Groups

(c) Conservative Groups (d) Apathentic Groups

190. Giving Gratuity is

(a) Retrenchment (b) Warning

(c) A retirement punishment (d) Collective Bargaining

191. ______ refers to the sum total, aggregate or constellation of properties or qualities.

(a) Personality (b) Perception (c) Leadership (d) Attitudes

192. Heredity and Brain are the variables relating to ______

(a) Family and Social Factors (b) Biological Factors

(c) Cultural Factors (d) Situational Factors

193. The contribution of family and social group in combination with the culture is known as ______

(a) Socialization (b) Civilaization (c) Communalization (d) None of these

194. Itrapsychine Theory was developed by ______

(a) William Sheldon (b) Carl Jung (c) Sigmund Freud (d) Karen Horney

195. According to Freud the human mind is composed of ______

(a) Preconscious (b) Conscious (c) Unconscious (d) All the above

196. The Centre of Indian Trade Union (CITU) was established in ______

(a) 1952 (b) 1942 (c) 1962 (d) 1972

197. Hindu Mazdoor Sabha (HMS)'s poitical inspiration is drawn from

(a) Bharathia Janatha Party (b) National Congress Party

(c) Praja Socialist Party (d) Swatantra Party

198. Group Dynamics relates to

(a) Role Palaying (b) Brain Storming

(c) Buzz Groups and Leadership Groups (d) All the above

199. Industrial relations is related to

(a) Punishment (b) Labour Turnover

(c) Workers Participation (d) Industrial Welfare

200. ______ is refers to deliberately created with structural associations and are formed to accomplish specific goals and carry specific tasks.

(a) Formal Groups (b) Informal Groups

(c) Apathentic Groups (d) None of these

201. Which of the following characteristics relates to Small Group?

(a) Common motives conducive to group interaction

(b) Standardisation of norms and values

(c) A group structure with hierarchical status system

(d) All the above

202. Which of the following relates to Interest Groups?

(a) New Comb's Balance Theory (b) Exchange Theory

(c) Cluster Approach (d) None of these

203. Interpersonal Conflicts develop due to ______

(a) Personal differences (b) Emotional problems

(c) Supervisor's role ambiguos (d) None of these

204. Man -to- Man rating system is used for evaluating ________

(a) Military Personnel (b) Technical Personnel
(c) Professional Personnel (d) Administrative Personnel

205. OB Mod. stands for

(a) Organisational Behaviour Modification (b) Organisational Behaviour Model
(c) Organisational Behaviour Marginal (d) Obserational Behaviour Model

206. The Overt Component of attitude is also known as ________

(a) Behavioural Component (b) Conative Component
(c) Cognitive Component (d) Both a and b

207. Which of the following attitude function is identified by Katz?

(a) Adjustment Function (b) Ego-Defensive Function
(c) Value - Expressive Function (d) All the above

208. Which of the following scale is used to measure Attitudes?

(a) Thurstone's Scale (b) Likert's Scale and Guttman's Scale
(c) Bogardus's Social Distance Scale (d) All the above

209. Likert's Scale of Attitude is also called as ________

(a) Summed - Rating Measure (b) Scale Discrimination
(c) Cumulative Scaling Techniques (d) None of these

210. Labour Turnover is high, means

(a) More number of employees move out of the organization
(b) Salary is high
(c) More number of employees retire
(d) Employees are happy

211. Vertical Movement of an employee is

(a) Transfer (b) Promotion (c) Demotion (d) Punishement

212. By Job Evaluation ________ becomes consistent

(a) Recuritment Policy (b) Promotion Policy
(c) Exist Policy (d) Wage Policy

213. For Performance Appraisal ______ is an effective technique

(a) T Q M (b) M B O (c) C P M (d) Work samples

214. The appraisal should be done by ________

(a) Top Management (b) Immediate Supervisor
(c) Advisor (d) Union Leader

215. Activities involved in introducing a new employee is

(a) Placement (b) Induction (c) Interviewing (d) Counseling

216. Promotion based on ______ stimulates employee to improve their performance

(a) Seniority (b) Merit (c) Age (d) Physical condition

217. Golden offerings is aimed at encouraging

(a) Productivity (b) Stability of staff (c) Larly Retirement (d) Employee Safety

Answers

1. (b) Personnel Management
2. (d) All the above
3. (d) Both 'a' and 'c'
4. (b) Policy
5. (c) Principles
6. (d) All the above
7. (a) Human Resource Planning
8. (d) All the above
9. (c) $\frac{\text{No. of persons - Days lost}}{\text{Average no. of persons x No. of working days}}$ x 100
10. (a) Skills Inventories
11. (a) Job Analysis
12. (d) All the above
13. (b) Job Specification
14. (c) Job Description
15. (a) Job Design
16. (b) Job Rotation
17. (a) Job Enlargement
18. (c) Job Intrinsic Factor
19. (c) More responsibility and autonomy
20. (c) Both a and b
21. (a) Recuritment
22. (d) All the above
23. (b) Human Resource Management
24. (a) Military Rule
25. (a) Selection
26. (b) Achievement Test
27. (a) Selection
28. (c) General Management Aptitude Test
29. (a) Fitness of an individual
30. (c) Medical Test
31. (c) Thematic Apperception Test
32. (b) Placement
33. (a) Training and Development = Standard Performance - Actual Performance
34. (d) Application Oriented
35. (b) Training
36. (c) Education
37. (c) Unskilled and Semi-skilled workers
38. (d) Aeronautical Industry
39. (b) Off-the Job Training
40. (a) Degree Orientation
41. (d) All the above
42. (c) Promotion
43. (a) Transfer
44. (c) Retrenchment
45. (d) Upward Advancement of an employee
46. (a) Labour Turnover
47. (a) Performance Appraisal
48. (d) Organisational Climate Indicies
49. (d) All the above
50. (d) Both 'a' and 'b'
51. (a) Government Departments
52. (d) Peter F. Drucker
53. (c) Lay - Off
54. (a) Golden Hand Shake Plan
55. (c) Dismissal
56. (b) Payment for labour's services
57. (a) Peruisites
58. (a) Accident - relief
59. (c) Canteen and Uniform
60. (c) Minimum Wage Method
61. (a) Fair Wage Method
62. (a) Total earnings = Total Output x Rate per unit
63. (d) All the above
64. (b) 83% to 90%: 100% of Ordinary Piece rate [Guranteed rate]
65. (d) All the above
66. (d) Both 'a' and 'b'
67. (b) 30% of time saved
68. (d) Earnings = Rate Per hour x $\sqrt{\text{Standard hours x Actual hours worked}}$
69. (c) Long term benefit
70. (d) All the above
71. (b) Expectancy Model
72. (a) Adams
73. (c) Performance Satisfaction Model
74. (d) All the above
75. (b) Herzberg

76. (c) Herzberg Two Factor Theory
77. (d) All the above
78. (d) All the above
79. (a) Motivation x Instrumentability x Valence
80. (c) Both 'a' and 'b'
81. (c) Need for Achievement
82. (b) Motivation
83. (d) All the above
84. (d) Adam's Equity Theory
85. (d) Alderfer's ERG Theory
86. (d) All the above
87. (a) Social Needs
88. (d) All the above
89. (b) 5
90. (d) Physiological Needs
91. (a) Physiological Needs
92. (c) Child hood
93. (d) Safety Needs
94. (b) Physiological, Safety
95. (a) Recognition
96. (d) All the above
97. (a) Personnel Management
98. (d) All the above
99. (d) None of these
100. (b) Interview
101. (d) Panel (or) Board Interview
102. (c) Physical Test
103. (a) Existence, Relatedness and Growth
104. (a) David C. MC Clelland
105. (d) All the above
106. (d) Sex
107. (d) Both 'a' and 'b'
108. (d) All the above
109. (a) Communication
110. (a) Operational Information
111. (c) Both 'a' and 'b'
112. (a) Top Secrete
113. (d) All the above
114. (b) Downward Communication
115. (a) Upward Communication
116. (c) Boss
117. (a) He has prestige but no power
118. (b) Administrative Leader
119. (d) Incremental Influential Power
120. (a) Powers based on Primarily on Organisational factors.
121. (b) Legitimate Power
122. (a) Group Task Roles
123. (b) Individual Role
124. (b) Autocrat
125. (c) Expert
126. (b) Who is opportunistic and exploits people
127. (b) Leadership Style
128. (c) Supervisory Style
129. (a) Autocratic
130. (d) Both 'a' and 'b'
131. (b) Participative Leadership
132. (d) Both 'a' and 'b'
133. (c) Bureaucratic Leadership
134. (a) Autocratic
135. (b) Democratic
136. (a) Blakes and Mouton
137. (c) Reddin
138. (a) The Trait-Oriented Approach
139. (b) The Functional Approach
140. (a) Concern for production and concern for people
141. (c) Two-Dimensional Theory of Leadership
142. (a) Fielder's Theory of Leadership
143. (d) All the above
144. (a) Performance Appraisal
145. (a) Adjudication
146. (b) 1947
147. (c) V. V. Giri
148. (c) 1926
149. (a) Trade Unionism
150. (d) All the above
151. (a) N.K. Lohanda
152. (b) Bombay Mill Hands Association
153. (c) 1910
154. (b) 1947
155. (a) All-India Trade Union Federation
156. (d) National Apex Body

157. (a) Communist Party of India
158. (b) AITUC
159. (d) All the above
160. (b) Learning
161. (d) All the above
162. (b) Skinnerian Psychology
163. (a) Punishment
164. (b) Cognitive Learning
165. (d) Motive
166. (a) Emotions associated with an attitude object
167. (b) Hedonistic principles of pleasure
168. (a) Ago-idel
169. (b) the compromising element
170. (c) Both a and b
171. (d) Carl Jung
172. (c) Learning
173. (a) Trait Theories
174. (b) Accident
175. (d) All the above
176. (a) Accident Frequency Rate = Number of diabling work injuries x 1000000 x Total
177. (a) Severity Rate = Number of mandays lost x 1000000 x Total number of Man hours worked
178. (c) 2000
179. (a) 1000
180. (a) Engineering, Education and Enforcement
181. (a) Safety Regulation
182. (d) All the above
183. (d) All the above
184. (d) All the above
185. (d) All the above
186. (d) Employer deal with the workers directly
187. (b) Friendship Groups
188. (a) Apathetic Groups
189. (b) Strategic Groups
190. (c) A retirement punishment
191. (a) Personality
192. (b) Biological Factors
193. (a) Socialization
194. (c) Sigmund Frend
195. (d) All the above
196. (c) 1962
197. (c) Praja Socialist Party
198. (d) All the above
199. (c) Workers Participation
200. (a) Formal Groups
201. (d) All the above
202. (b) Exchange Theory
203. (a) Personal differences
204. (a) Military Personal
205. (a) Organisational Behaviour Modification
206. (d) Both a and b
207. (d) All the above
208. (d) All the above
209. (a) Summed-Rating Measure
210. (a) More number of employees move out of the organization
211. (b) Promotion
212. (d) Wage Policy
213. (b) M B O
214. (b) Immediate Supervisor
215. (c) Interviewing
216. (b) Merit
217. (c) Early retirement

*****

VII

FINANCIAL MANAGEMENT AND PROJECT MANAGEMENT

1. The basic objective of Financial Management is ____________

(a) Maximisation of wealth of the shareholders
(b) Maximisation of profit of a concern
(c) Strengthen sound financial position of a concern
(d) All the above

2. The Earnings Theory of Capitalization is suitable for _________

(a) Unorganised Concern (b) Newly proposed Concern
(c) Well established Companies (d) Sole Trader Concern

3. ____________ is more dangerous than Under Capitalisation

(a) Optimum Capital Structure (b) Over Capitalization
(c) Actual Capitalization (d) Proper Capitalization

4. ____________ is obtained when the market value per equity share is the maximum

(a) Optimum Capital Structure (b) Optimum Financial Structure
(c) Under Capitalization (d) Over Caitalisation

5. Trading on Equity is resorted to magnify____________

(a) Market value of per equity share (b) Earning per equity share
(c) Earning after tax (d) Operating profit

6. When liquidity increases ___________ decreases

(a) Prices (b) Interest (c) Profitability (d) Production

7. A statement estimating amount of capital and determining its composition is termed as ____________

(a) Production Plan (b) Financial Plan (c) Capital Plan (d) Organizational Plan

8. __________ is the funds required for the acquisition of assets that are to be used for a long period

(a) Fixed Capital (b) Working Capital
(c) Both 'a' and 'b' (d) Current Assets

9. The total amount of capital employed in a business is termed as _______

(a) Capital Structure (b) Capitalisation
(c) Treasurer (d) Pattern of Financing

10. __________ refers to make up a firm's capitalisation

(a) Financial Plan (b) Capital Structure
(c) Financial Structure (d) Organisation Structure

11. EBIT level at which EPS remains the same irrespective of the debt equity mix is termed as __________

(a) Point of Indifference (b) Break Even Level of EBIT
(c) Both 'a' and 'b' (d) None of these

12. Trading on equity is a situation where the ROI is more than ________ rate

(a) Interest (b) Profitability (c) Liquidity (d) Turnover

13. Net working capital is the part of current assets which is financed by _______

(a) Short term funds (b) Long term funds (c) Total fund (d) Working Capital

14. The term Permanent Working Capital also referred as ______

(a) Fixed Working Capital (b) Variable Working Capital
(c) Core Current Assets (d) Sources of Funds

15. ________ is the trade off between cost of carrying cash and required for maintaining liquidity.

(a) Production Management (b) Cash Management
(c) Financial Management (d) Working Capital Management

16. Management of receivables involves balancing the cost carrying receivables and the loss of sales due to ________

(a)Tight Cash Policy (b) Tight Credit Policy
(c) Liberal Credit Policy (d) Lenient Credit Policy

17. On effect of the implementions of the recommendation of the ______ the current ratio of the borrowers will improve further

(a) Chore Committee (b) Dehejia Committee
(c) Tamdon Committee (d) Malhothra Committee

18. Excess of current assets over current liabilities refers to _______

(a) Gross Working Capital (b) Gross Floating Capital
(c) Net Working Capital (d) Fixed Capital

19. In the case of lock – box system, the cheques are received by the _______

(a) Collections Centre (b) Post Office Box
(c) Separate Box at Local Bank (d) None of these

20. _____ is an attempt to maintain or expand scale of operations of the business with insufficient cash resources

(a) Over Trading (b) Under Trading

(c) Cash Management (d) Working Capital Management

21. Decrease in the credit period allowed to customers from 40 days to 20days results in _____ of working capital total requirements

(a) Increase (b) No change (c) Decrease (d) Not much change

22. Purchase of additional fixed assets to increase productions results in _____ total working capital requirements

(a) Decrease (b) No change (c) Not much change (d) Increase

23. Change in the method of depreciations results in _____ working capital total requirements

(a) No change (b) Increase (c) Decrease (d) Not much change

24. A decisions to increase the wage rate results in _____ working capital total requirements

(a) Decrease (b) Increase (c) No change (d) Not much change

25. Cash flows from a project can be worked out only on the basis of _____

(a) Certain probabilities (b) Certain assumptions

(c) Certain conditions (d) None of these

26. It is imperative to make an estimate regarding likely increase in costs on account of possibility of delay in _____

(a) Commencement of business (b) Expand the project

(c) Implementing the project (d) All the above

27. _____ determines the maximum rate of interest that a firm can afford to pay on the borrowings for a particular project

(a) Net Present Value (b) Accounting Rate of Return

(c) Internal Rate of Return (d) Pay-Back Method

28. _____ is considered while calculating the return on a project under Accounting Rate of Return Method

(a) Depreciations (b) Good Will (c) Discount (d) Time Value Money

29. Discounted Cash Flow technique takes into account the _____

(a) Market Value of Money (b) Time Value of Money

(c) Estimated Value of Money (d) Calculated Value of Money

30. The technique of long term planning for proposed capital outlays and their financing is known as _____

(a) Capital Budgeting (b) Operating Budget

(c) Financial Budgeting (d) Capital Expenditure Budget

31. The minimum rate of return expected of a capital investment project is called as _____

(a) Calculated Rate (b) Fixed Rate (c) Cut – off Rate (d) Estimate Rate

32. Which of the following related to the Annual Average Yield on a project?

(a) Internal Rate of Return
(b) Accounting Rare of Return
(c) Both a and b
(d) None of these

33. While calculating capital investment proposals, the time value of money is considered in the case of____

(a) Accounting Rate of Return Method
(b) Present Value Index Method
(c) Pay – Back Method
(d) Discounted Cash Flow Method

34. Which of the following method is not considered as the return after the pay-off period?

(a) Pay Back Method
(b) Accounting Rate of Return Method
(c) Discounted Cash Flow Method
(d) Present Value

35. Which of the following techniques is used for determining return/cash flows from a project for capital budgeting decisions?

(a) Sensitivity Analysis
(b) Probability Assignment
(c) Co-efficient Variation
(d) All the above

36. The Cost of Capital is the minimum return that will maintain the value of a firm's _______

(a) Equity Shares
(b) Preference Shares
(c) Subscribed Capital
(d) Debentures

37. Which of the following cost inclusive of all cost of capital from all sources?

(a) Composite Cost (b) Cost of Debt (c) Fixed Cost (d) Specific Cost

38. Which of the following cost is the weighted average cost of the new funds raised by the firm?

(a) Composite Cost (b) Cost of Equity (c) Marginal Cost (d)Historical Cost

39. Cost of capital consist of both business and _____ risks

(a) Capital (b) Financial (c) Personal (d) Property

40. Cost of each component of capital is known as _____

(a) Marginal Cost (b) Cost of Equity (c) Cost of Debt (d) Specific Cost

41. In case of traditional approach cost of capital is affected by _____

(a) Debt Equity Mix
(b) Dividend Price
(c) Rate of Return
(d) Return on Investment

42. According to _____ weights are assigned to each source of funds in proportions of financing inputs the firms intends to employ

(a) Modigliani – Miller Approach
(b) Marginal Weight Method
(c) Traditional Approach
(d) Co-efficient variation

43. In case of ______ approach the investor arrives at the market price of an equity share by capitalising the set of expected dividends payments

(a) Dividend Price Approach
(b) M M Approach
(c) Marginal Approach
(d) Traditional Approach

44. Cost of Capital serves as ______ for capital investment decisions

(a) Calculated Rate (b) Interest (c) Cut – off Rate (d) Estimated Rate

45. According to Modigliani Miller Approach assumes that ______ market are perfect

(a) Investment (b) Capital (c) Share (d) Stock

46. Which of the following is Badla?

(a) To buy Equity Shares (b) To buy Debentures
(c) To carry forward the transactions (d) All the above

47. The stock exchange deals with

(a) Issue of Equity Shares (b) Issue of Debentures
(c) Issue of Preference Shares (d) Secondhand Securities

48. An option to buy the Share/Debentures refers to

(a) Call (b) Put (c) Pull (d) Spread

49. Which of the following is an element of Investment?

(a) Risk only (b) Return only
(c) Return, risk & time (d) Capital

50. Which of the following relates to Capital Market?

(a) Market for short term funds (b) Market for long term funds
(c) Market for short and long term funds (d) Market for Medium term funds

51. Capital Market Theory is built on ________

(a) Maslows Work (b) Markowitz Work
(c) M.C. Millan Work (d) Traditional Approach

52. One of the following is not a mutual fund generator

(a) ONGC (b) L.I.C (c) UTI (d) SBI

53. Portfolios are nothing but ______

(a) Combinations of Liabilities (b) Combinations of Capital
(c) Combinations of Assets (d) Combination of Assets and Liabilities

54. All companies with initial issued capital of ______ are allowed to listed on OTC exchange

(a) 40 lakhs (b) 30 lakhs (c) 20 lakhs (d) 50 lakhs.

55. Where is the head office of National Stock Exchange?

(a) Bombay (b) Calcutta (c) Delhi (d) Bangelore

56. ______ refers to an increased means of accomplshing some purpose

(a) Leverage (b) Badla (c) Capital market (d) None of these

57. According to _______ leverage as "the employment of an asset or funds for which the firm pays a fixed cost or fixed return

(a) Waterman, Merwin (b) James Horne
(c) Hamptions Jhon (d) Brigham, Engene

58. Which of the following relates to high Break Even Point?

(a) Low Operating Leverage (b) Medium Operating Leverage
(c) High Operating Leverage (d) None of these

59. It is risky to have a high operating leverage, since even a slight fall in sales would result in a disproportionately ______

(a) Larger fall in profits (b) Larger increase in profits
(c) No effect in profits (d) Constant increase in profits

60. _____ describes that the change in taxable income on account of change in sales

(a) Financial Leverage (b) Operating Leverage
(c) Composite Leverage (d) Low financial Leverage

61. The ideal situations is to have a high financial leverage and ______

(a) High Operating Leverage (b) Low Operating Leverage
(c) Low Financial Leverage (d) Composite Leverage

62. It is risky to have both operating leverage and ______ at a high level

(a) Composite Leverage (b) Financial Leverage
(c) Both A and B (d) None of these

63. Financial leverage indicated disproportionate change in taxable income as a result of change in ______

(a) Operating Income (b) Non Operating Income
(c) Market Value (d) Contribution Margin

64. An ideal situations should be to maintain ______ low and _____ high

(a) Financial leverage, Operating leverage (b) Operating leverage, Financial leverage
(c) Composite leverage, Financial leverage (d) Composite leverage, Operating leverage

65. A management would be too cautious if both operating leverage and financial leverage are maintained ______

(a) High (b) Low (c) Ideal (d) None of these

66. The combined impact of operating leverage and financial leverage indicated by _____ of the two

(a) Multiplications (b) Subtractions (c) Divisions (d) Additions

67. Trading on Equity implies having a high ______

(a) Debt-Equity Ratio (b) Operating Ratio
(c) Protifitability Ratio (d) Turnover Ratio

68. The share holders of a company which has a high financial leverage stand to gain when the company's Return On Investment (ROI) is ______ as compared to ______ of debt

(a) Cost, higher (b) Cost, lower (c) higher, cost (d) lower, cost

69. Trading on Equity is suitable for ______ Financial Leverage

(a) Unfavourable (b) Favourable (c) Adverse (d) None of these

70. Raising funds through debentures is cheaper as compared to raising funds through _____

(a) Banks (b) Bonds (c) Shares (d) Private finance

71. As compared to Pledge, Borrowers prefers ______

(a) Hypothecations (b) Security (c) Lean (d) Hire purchase

72. ______ have a preferential right as to the repayment of capital in the event company's winding up

(a) Equity Shares (b) Debentures (c) Preference Shares (d) Bonds

73. Which of the following is the source of Trade Credit?

(a) Long Term Finance (b) Medium Term Finance

(c) Short Term Finance (d) External Finance

74. In the case of interest payable on debenture is ______

(a) A charge against profits (b) An appropriations of profits

(c) Revaluation of profits (d) General Reserve

75. Which of the following relates to Good Will?

(a) An Intangible Asset (b) A Tangible Asset

(c) Current Asset (d) Non-Current Liability

76. In the case of MM Approach, dividend policy has no effect on the ______

(a) Market value of a company (b) Share prices of a company

(c) Dividend rate of a company (d) Cost prices of a company

77. ______ is based on the relationship between 'r' and 'k'

(a) MM Approach (b) Prof. Walter's Model

(c) Millers Approach (d) None of these

78. 'Cum right' price is ______ 'ex – right' price of a share

(a) Higher than (b) Lower than (c) Equal to (d) None of these

79. Issue of right shares impact of dilutions of the market price of the company's

(a) Preference Shares (b) Equity Shares (c) Debentures (d) Bonus Shares

80. The policy concerning quantum of profits to be distributed as dividend is called as ______

(a) Tax Policy (b) Investment Policy

(c) Dividend Policy (d) Price Policy

81. In the case of MM hypothesis, the price of a company's share is measured by its investment policy and not by pattern of its ______

(a) Income distributions (b) Dividend

(c) Profit (d) Liquidity position

82. In case of companies having 'r' > 'k', the optimum dividend policy requires ______ dividend pay out ratio

(a) 100% (b) Zero (c) Higher (d) Constant

83. A company having 'r' < 'k' is also called as ______

(a) Declining Firm (b) Higher Firm (c) Constant Firm (d) None of these

84. The most appropriate dividend policy is payment of ______

(a) Market value of share (b) Constant dividend per share

(c) Earning per shares (d) Higher dividend per share

85. Issue of Bonus Shares are indicated as ______ of profit of a company

(a) Capitalisation (b) Dividend Policy (c) Leverage (d) None of these

86. The right shares are issued at a lower price as compared to ______

(a) Ex – right price (b) Cum–right price (c) Market price (d) Subscription price

87. Project Report is prepared by ______

(a) The Entreprenuer (b) The Financial Institutions

(c) Organizations (d) Auditors

88. Repayment capability is measured by ______

(a) Interest Coverage Ratio (b) Debt Service Coverage Ratio

(c) Both a and b (d) Pay Out Ratio

89. Application of Critical Path Method(CPM) is suitable for ______

(a) Projects of recurring nature (b) Projects of non – recurring nature

(c) Completed projects (d) Project which occurs only once

90. A project is said to be financially viable if

(a) It has adequate profit (b) There is a good scope for marketing

(c) It is technically sound (d) It is useful to the society

91. Which of the following relates to Project?

(a) Can be set up only by the govt. (b) Is a plan with some objectives

(c) Does not consume resources (d) Is always service oriented

92. ______ is the difference between the time available for completing an activity and the time necessary to complete the same

(a) Node (b) Burst (c) Float (d) Critical path

93. PERT is a technique involves ______ time estimates

(a) Single (b) Double (c) Three (d) Several

94. A dummy activity is a network which is otherwise called as ______ activity

(a) Concurrent (b) Zero time (c) Succeeding (d) Preceding

95. Which of the following refers to PERT?

(a) Is activity oriented (b) Is a deterministic model

(c) Involves three time estimates (d) Applies crashing

96. Term Loans are used for ______

(a) The purchase of stock (b) Settlement of books debts

(c) The purchase of current assets (d) The acquisitions of fixed assets

97. In BEP, Sales minus Variable Cost =

(a) Fixed Cost (b) Profit (c) Loss (d) Contributions

98. Which of the following refers to IDBI?

(a) Industrial Development Financial Institutions

(b) A Commercial Bank

(c) An Insurance Company

(d) Scheduled Bank

99. In the case of _______ considers time value of money

(a) ARR (b) IRR (c) Pay Back Period (d) Ratio Analysis

100. Industries which are concerned with reproducing and multiplying plants, animals etc are known as______

(a) Extractive Industries (b) Genetic Industries

(c) Botanical Industries (d) White Industries

101. Speciality in knowledge is required for a ______

(a) Business Man (b) Professional (c) Trader (d) Leader

102. Karta is head of a

(a) Family (b) Hindu Undivided Family

(c) Company (d) Firm

103. Minor partner is admitted only to the share of ______

(a) Profit and loss (b) Loss only (c) Profit only (d) Liability

104. Principles of 'one member one vote'is followed in the general body of______

(a) Public Ltd Company (b) Government Company

(c) Co-operative Society (d) Private Company

105. A broker who expects a rise in price of shares in the stock exchanges is termed as

(a) Bear (b) Bull (c) Lame Duck (d) Dealer

106. Mr. Weber has given a mathematical formula for plant locations it is known as

(a) Product Index (b) Material Index (c) Law of Intertia (d) Weber's Index

107. When a concern attains maximum benefits at minimum cost the concern is described as

(a) Higher Firm (b) Profitable Firm

(c) Optimum Firm (d) Firm at Break Even Point

108. Acquiring membership in the Chamber of Commerce is

(a) Voluntary (b) Compulsory (c) Recommendations (d) Optional

109. Depreciation is included in costs in case of ______

(a) Pay – Back Method (b) Internal Return Method

(c) Present Value Index Method (d) Return On Investment

110. Which of the following refers to Capitalisation?

(a) Balance Sheet value of stocks and bond outstanding

(b) Par value of share capital + Reserves and surplus + Long term loans

(c) Comprises of ownership capital

(d) All the above

111. Which of the following refers to Capital?

(a) The net worth of a business undertaking

(b) Assets minus liabilities of a business

(c) Net worth minus liabilities of a business

(d) All the above

112. Which of the following is not referring to Capital Structure?

(a) The make up of a firms capitalisations

(b) It represents the mix of different long term funds

(c) It include both long term and short term funds

(d) Capital structure is only a part of financial structure

113. The best time for floating of company's securities is the ______

(a) Boom Period (b) Recovery Period

(c) Recession Period (d) Depression Period

114. In case of Lock – Box System, the cheques are receive by _______

(a) Collections Centre (b) Post – Office Box (c) Local Bank (d) City Bank

115. The safety level for cash can be determined by ______

(a) Safety level of cash = Desired days of cash x Average daily cash outflows

(b) Safety level of cash = Desired days of cash x Average daily cash inflows

(c) Safety level of cash = Desired days of cash x Average of highest daily cash outflows

(d) None of these

116. In the case of Under trading, these is a fall in ______

(a) Working Capital to Sales Ratio (b) Return on Capital Employed

(c) Turnover Ratio (d) Debt Equity Ratio

117. Which of the following refers to Over Trading?

(a) Under utilisations of its resources by a firm

(b) Faulty financial policy

(c) Attempt to maintain or expand scale of operations of the business with insufficient cash resources

(d) Both 'b' and 'c'

118. A firm cannot have a strict credit policy in case of its ______

(a) Products are in demand

(b) Sales and receivables are likely to be high

(c) Recession period

(d) Inflation period

119. What will be the effect of working capital total requirements when decrease in the credit period allowed to customers from 20days to 10 days?

(a) Decrease of working capital (b) Increase of working capital

(c) No change of working capital (d) Not much change of working capital

120. Acquisitions of additional fixed assets to increase productions results in ______ of working capital total requirements

(a) Decrease (b) Increase (c) No change (d) Not much change

121. The decisions to store, in a larger quantity, the raw material whose price is expected to go up is future would results in _______ of working capital total requirement

(a) Decrease (b) Increase (c) No change (d) Not much change

122. Change in the method of depreciations would results in _______ working capital total requirements

(a) Decrease (b) Increase

(c) No change (d) Not much change

123. A decision to pay immediate cash to suppliers of raw materials for enjoying cash discounts would results in _______ of work capital total requirements

(a) Decrease (b) Increase

(c) No change (d) Not much change

124. A decisions to implement a scheme which reduces the productions period to half would results in _______ of working capital total requirements.

(a) Decrease (b) Increase

(c) Not much change (d) No change

125. A decisions to increase the wages rate would results _______ of working capital total requirements

(a) Decrease (b) Increase

(c) Not much change (d) No change

126. In the case of Pay – Back Period Method for evaluating capital investment proposals can be determined by _________

(a) $\text{Pay - Back Period} = \frac{\text{Original Investment}}{\text{Annual Average Cash Inflow}}$

(b) $\text{Pay - Back Period} = \frac{\text{Initial Investment}}{\text{Annual Average Cash Outflow}}$

(c) $\text{Pay - Back Period} = \frac{\text{Annual Investment}}{\text{Annual Cash Outflow}}$

(d) None of the above

127. For Financial Decisions Making, relevant cost are

(a) The Historical Cost (b) Future Costs

(c) Pre Determined Cost (d) Marginal Cost

128. According to MM Approach, cost of capital is _______

(a) Affected by firm's debt – equity mix

(b) Constant and it is independent of the method and level of financing

(c) Does not affect by the firms debt equity mix

(d) Both 'b' and 'c'

129. Retained Earnings have _______ to the firm

(a) No cost (b) Opportunity cost

(c) Absolutely cost free (d) Fixed operating cost

130. The Operating Leverage can be calculated by ______

(a) $\text{Operating Leverage} = \dfrac{\text{Profit}}{\text{Operating Profit}}$

(b) $\text{Operating Leverage} = \dfrac{\text{Contributions}}{\text{Operating Profit}}$

(c) $\text{Operating Leverage} = \dfrac{\text{Operating profit}}{\text{Profit before tax}}$

(d) None of the above

131. Composite leverage can be calculate by ______

(a) Composite Leverage = Operative Leverage x Financial Leverage

(b) $\text{Composite leverage} = \dfrac{\text{Contribution}}{\text{Operating profit}} \times \dfrac{\text{Operating profit}}{\text{Profit before tax}}$

(c) $\text{Composite leverage} = \text{Operating leverage} \times \dfrac{\text{Operating profit}}{\text{Profit before tax}}$

(d) All the above

132. Equity Shares entitled to dividend on the basis of ______

(a) Fixed Rate (b) Availability of divisible profit

(c) Intentions of the Directors (d) Both 'b' and 'c'

133. Public Deposits are used as a source of ______

(a) Long – Term Finance (b) Short Term Finance

(c) Medium Term Finance (d) Term Loans

134. Preference Shares are entitled to dividend on the basis of ______

(a) Fixed Rate (b) Availability of divisible profits

(c) Intention of the Directors (d) Fluctuated Rate

135. Issue of Bonus Shares is an indications of ______

(a) Higher future profits (b) Higher future dividends

(c) High psychological value (d) All the above

136. Share holders usually prefer ______

(a) Capital gains to current dividend

(b) Capital gains to sale of capital investments

(c) Capital gains to transfer of capital investments

(d) None of these

137. Investment in a project consists of the sum total of ________ required for the project

(a) Fixed capital and Working capital (b) Fixed capital and Current-assets

(c) Working capital and Provisions (d) Fixed asset and Capital employed

138. Which of the following 3A's are functions of Financial Management

(a) Anticipating financial needs, Acquiring financial resources, Allocating funds in business

(b) Anticipating financial needs, Allocation of financial resources, Apportionment of investments in business

(c) Allocating business needs, Acquiring financial resources, Ascertainment of cash

(d) None of these

139. The Traditional Approach of Financial Management is mainly focussed on ______

(a) Business Finance (b) Corporate Finance

(c) Industrial Finance (d) General Finance

140. Which of the following two theories are used to determine the amount capitalisations?

(a) Historical Theory, Cost Theory (b) Historical Theory, Earning Theory

(c) Both 'a' and 'b' (d) Maslows Theory, Markowitz Theory

141. The Leverage of a firm is required to ________ measure

(a) Cost (b) Profit

(c) Both Cost and Revenue (d) Investments

142. The term ______ explains the ratio between the stock and the fixed interest bearing securities of a company

(a) Marginal Leverage (b) Capital Gearing (c) Operating Leverage (d)Composite Leverage

143. The product of asset turnover and profit margin is termed as ________

(a) Profit (b) Contributions

(c) Return On Investment (d) None of these

144. A firm has a cash surplus when its ______ capital exceeds its ______ the surplus is normally invested ______

(a) Long term financing, cumulative capital requirements, marketable securities

(b) Short term financing, cumulative capital requirements, marketable securities

(c) Long term financing, marketable securities, debentures

(d) None of these

145. Short Term Financing Plans are developed by ____________ and ______ often aided by computerized ______

(a) Error, Trail, Business Models (b) Trail, Error, Financial Model

(c) Trail, Error, Mathematical Models (d) None of these

146. A Company can purchase its own

(a) Equity shares (b) Preference shares

(c) Debentures (d) All the above

147. Financial Management is refers to ______

(a) Branch of Finance (b) Applied Economics
(c) Branch of Investments (d) Branch of Business

148. The function of finance is to make ______ utilizations of funds

(a) Effective (b) Proper (c) both a and b (d) None of these

149. Financial Management is the applications of ______ principles to a particular financial operations

(a) General Management (b) Productions Management
(c) Marketing Management (d) Export Management

150. Financial Management is suitable for ______

(a) Big Companies (b) Small Organizations
(c) Medium Level Organizations (d) All the above

151. Certainty is always expressed as ____ an impossibility as ______

(a) One, Zero (b) Zero, One (c) One, One (d) Zero, Zero

152. The point at which shareholders feel that there is a trade off between risk and return is known as the ______

(a) Standard Point (b) Optimum Point (c) Zero Point (d) None of these

153. Which of the following methods can be measured for risks of investment proposals

(a) Standard Deviations
(b) Co-efficient of Variations
(c) Combining decisions tree with Standard Deviations
(d) All the above

154. ______ describes how the basic forecast of results in a decision will be affected by changes in the critical data inputs that influence those results

(a) Decision Tree Approach (b) Sensitivity Analysis
(c) Standard Deviation (d) Correlations Analysis

155. Capital Structure is the mix of ______ which would maximize the value of the equity stock

(a) Debt and Equity Securities (b) Asset and Liabilities
(c) Fixed and Current Liabilities (d) Income and Expenses

156. Which of the following is common approach to the theory of capital structure?

(a) Ezra Soloman's Approach (b) Modigliani – Miller Approach
(c) Both 'a' and 'b' (d) Jhon F. Childs Approach

157. According to ______ the optimal capital structure for a firm occurs at the point at which it can no longer take advantage of a favorable financial leverage

(a) Ezra Soloman's Approach (b) Varying Cost of Equity Capital Theory
(c) Fixed Ke Theory (d) None of these

158. Which of the following term is the same as Asset Turnover?

(a) Asset (b) Operating (c) Financial (d) Marginal Change

159. ______ Leverage indicates the impact of changes in sales on operating income

(a) Marginal (b) Asset (c) Financial (d) Operating

160. Financial Leverage is also termed as ______

(a) Return on Investment Leverage (b) Trading on Equity

(c) Operating Leverage (d) Asset Leverage

161. The term Capital Rationing indicates ______ in favour of more acceptable proposals

(a) Allocations of capital (b) Distributions of capital

(c) Both 'a' and 'b' (d) Acquiring capital

162. Which of the following is simplest technique of Capital Budgeting?

(a) Pay Back Method (b) Average Rate of Return

(c) Internal Rate of Return (d) Net Present Worth

163. ______ is the rate which equates the present value of expected future cash flows with the cost of the investment

(a) Pack Back Method (b) Internal Rate of Return

(c) Average Rate of Return (d) Net Present Worth

164. ______ is the relationship that exists between the present values of net cash inflows and the present values of cash outflows

(a) Profitability Index (b) Net Present Worth

(c) Average Rate of Return (d) None of these

165. Which of the following inventory models relates to Cash Management?

(a) Miller – Orr Model (b) EOQ Model

(c) Both a and b (d) Cash Tank Method

166. ______ indicates when an order should be placed

(a) Re Order Point (b) Economic Order Point

(c) Minimum Level Point (d) Normal Stock Level Point

167. Reductions of the number of items carries in an inventory is known by the term ______

(a) Fixed Reductions (b) Variety Reductions

(c) Average Reduction (d) Estimated Reductions

168. ______ is classifications of inventory control is attempted on the basis of value of items in storage

(a) VED (b) ABC (c) XYZ (d) HML

169. Which of the following basis relates to ABC Analysis?

(a) Value of items consumed (b) Unit price of the materials

(c) The importance or criticality of materials (d) Procurement difficulties

170. Cash Working Capital is measured on the basis of ______

(a) profit and Loss Account (b) Costing Profit and Loss

(c) Revaluations Account (d) Retained Earning Account

171. Conventional Method and Operating Cycle Method are used to estimate

(a) Working Capital Requirement (b) Permanent Capital Requirement

(c) Cash Requirement (d) All the above

172. The excesses of current assets over current liabilities can be expressed as ______

(a) Net Current Assets (b) Net Working Capital

(c) Both a and b (d) Liquid Capital

173. Which of the following Committees was appointed for examining credit limits for Commercial Banks in respect of the working capital requirements?

(a) V.T. Dehejia Committee (b) Prakash Tandon Committee

(c) K.B. Chore Committee (d) All the above

174. Which of the following term is related to most Liquid Assets in a business?

(a) Cheque (b) Cash (c) Inventory (d) Fund

175. The forecast to achieve the objective of the economic use of available cash is known as______

(a) Cash Forecast (b) Sales Forecast

(c) Demand Forecast (d) Productions Forecast

176. Which of the following method is used for preparing short range cash forecast?

(a) Receipts and Disbursements Method (b) Adjusted Income Method

(c) Capital Differential Method (d) All the above

177. Which of the following method is used for preparing long range cash forecast?

(a) Cash Book Method of Analysis (b) Cash Tank Method of Analysis

(c) Adjusted Income Method (d) Both a and b

178. ______ is the most inexpensive method of acquiring funds?

(a) Shares (b) Debenture (c) Retained Earning (d) Bonds

179. ______ is the part of the surplus which is not related directly to the operating results of each year

(a) Surplus (b) Capital surplus (c) Reserve (d) Revenue

180. ______ is the net income that remains after distributions of dividends to shareholders

(a) Surplus (b) Reserve (c) Revenue (d) Contribution

181. _______ is an accounting device for reducing the carrying value of an asset

(a) Revenue (b) Surplus (c) Reserve (d) Bonus

182. _______ is a distributions of the book surplus of a company among shareholders

(a) Profit (b) Dividend (c) Interest (d) Surplus

183. The term ______ refers to dividend promises to pay the stockholders at a future specific date

(a) Property (b) Special (c) Scrip (d) Bond

184. Extra dividends of the speculative type, which are large in amount, are called as ______

(a) Melons (b) Bonus (c) Surplus (d) Profit

185 Which of the following is a usual form of paying dividend?

(a) Bond (b) Cash (c) Stock (d) Optional

ANSWERS

1. (d) All the above
2. (c) Well Established Companies
3. (b) Over Capitalisation
4. (a) Optimum Capital Structure
5. (b) Earning per equity share
6. (c) Profitability
7. (b) Financial Plan
8. (a) Fixed Capital
9. (b) Capitalization
10. (b) Capital Structure
11. (c) Both a and b
12. (a) Interest
13. (b) Long Term Funds
14. (c) Core Current Assets
15. (b) Cash Management
16. (b) Tight Credit Policy
17. (a) Chore Committee
18. (c) Networking Capital
19. (b) Post Office Box
20. (a) Over Trading
21. (c) Decrease
22. (d) Increase
23. (a) No change
24. (b) Increase
25. (a) Certain probabilities
26. (d) All the above
27. (c) Internal Rate of Return
28. (a) Depreciation
29. (b) Time value of money
30. (a) Capital Budgeting
31. (c) Cut off Rate
32. (b) Accounting Rate of Return
33. (b) Present Value Index Method
34. (b) Accounting Rate of Return Method
35. (d) All the above
36. (a) Equity shares
37. (a) Composite Cost
38. (c) Marginal Cost
39. (b) Financial
40. (d) Specific Cost
41. (a) Debt Equity Mix
42. (b) Marginal Weight Method
43. (a) Dividend price
44. (c) Cut off Rate
45. (b) Capital
46. (c) To carry forward the transactions
47. (d) Secondhand Securities
48. (a) Call
49. (c) Return, Risk, and Time
50. (b) Market of long term fund
51. (b) Markowitz Work
52. (a) ONGC
53. (c) Combinations of Assets
54. (b) 30lakhs
55. (a) Bombay
56. (a) Leverage
57. (b) James Horne
58. (c) High Operating Leverage
59. (a) Larger fall in profits
60. (c) Composite Leverage
61. (b) Low operating leverage
62. (b) Financial Leverage
63. (a) Operating Income
64. (b) Operating and Financial
65. (b) Low
66. (a) Multiplication
67. (a) Debt Equity Ratio
68. (c) Higher, Cost
69. (b) Favorable
70. (c) Shares
71. (a) Hypothecation
72. (b) Debentures
73. (c) Short – Term Finance
74. (b) An appropriation of profits
75. (a) An Intangible Asset
76. (b) Share prices of company
77. (b) Prof. Walter's Model
78. (a) Higher than
79. (b) Equity share
80. (c) Dividend Policy

81. (a) Income Distribution
82. (b) Zero
83. (a) Declining firm
84. (b) Constant dividend per share
85. (a) Capitalization
86. (c) Market Price
87. (a) The Entrepreneur
88. (c) Both a and b
89. (a) Projects of recurring nature
90. (a) It has adequate profit
91. (b) Is a plan with some objectives
92. (c) Float
93. (c) Three
94. (b) Zero Time
95. (c) Involves three time estimates
96. (d) The acquisitions of fixed assets
97. (d) Contributions
98. (a) Industrial Development Financial Institution
99. (b) IRR
100. (b) Genetic Industries
101. (b) Professional
102. (b) Hindu Undivided Family
103. (c) Profit only
104. (c) Co-operative Society
105. (b) Bull
106. (b) Material Index
107. (c) Optimum Firm
108. (c) Recommendations
109. (a) Pay – Back Method
110. (d) All the above
111. (d) All the above
112. (c) It include both long term and short term funds
113. (b) Recovery Period
114. (b) Post – Office Box
115. (a) Safety level of cash = Desired day of cash x Average daily cash outflows
116. (b) Return on Capital Employed
117. (d) Both 'b' and 'c'
118. (b) Sales and receivables are likely to be high
119. (a) Decrease of Working Capital
120. (b) Increase
121. (b) Increase
122. (c) No change
123. (d) Not much change
124. (c) Not much change
125. (a) Increase
126. (a) Pay – Back Period = $\frac{\text{Original investment}}{\text{Annual Average cash inf low}}$
127. (b) Future Costs
128. (d) Both 'b' and 'c'
129. (b) Opportunity Cost
130. (b) Operating Leverage = $\frac{\text{Contributions}}{\text{Operating profit}}$
131. (d) All the above
132. (d) Both 'b' and 'c'
133. (b) Short Term Finance
134. (a) Fixed Rate.
135. (d) All the above
136. (b) Capital gains to sale of capital investments
137. (a) Fixed Capital and Working Capital
138. (a) Anticipating financial needs, Acquiring financial resources, Allocating funds in business
139. (b) Corporation finance
140. (a) Historical Theory, Cost Theory
141. (b) Profit
142. (b) Capital Gearing
143. (c) Return on Investment
144. (a) Long term financing, Cumulative capital requirements, marketable security
145. (b) Trail, Error, Financial Model
146. (c) Debenture
147. (b) Applied Economics
148. (c) Both 'a' and 'b'
149. (a) General Management
150. (d) All the above
151. (a) One, Zero

152. (b) Optimum Point
153. (d) All the above
154. (b) Sensitivity Analysis
155. (a) Debt and Equity Securities
156. (c) Both 'a' and 'b'
157. (c) Fixed Ke Theory
158. (a) Asset
159. (d) Operating
160. (b) Trading on Equity
161. (c) Both 'a' and 'b'
162. (a) Pay Back Method
163. (b) Internal Rate of Return
164. (a) Profitability Index
165. (c) Both 'a' and 'b'
166. (a) Re Order Point
167. (b) Variety reductions
168. (c) XYZ
169. (a) Value of items consumed
170. (a) Profit and Loss Account
171. (a) Working capital requirement
172. (c) Both 'a' and 'b'
173. (d) All the above
174. (b) Cash
175. (a) Cash Forecast
176. (d) All the above
177. (d) Both 'a' and 'b'
178. (c) Retained Earnings
179. (b) Capital Surplus
180. (a) Surplus
181. (c) Reserve
182. (b) Dividend
183. (c) Scrip
184. (a) Melons
185. (b) Cash

***

VIII

FINANCIAL ACCOUNTING

1. The Accounting Equation of Dual Aspect Concept is

(a) Capital + Liabilities = Assets
(b) Capital + Assets = Liabilities
(c) Liabilities + Assets = Capital
(d) None of these

2. The Balance Sheet based on ______ is not favaour to a potential investor

(a) Cost Concept
(b) Going Concern Concept
(c) Period Concept
(d) Money Measurement Concept

3. The principles of Accountancy which recognizes the double aspect of a business transactions is known as ________ Concept

(a) Entity Concept
(b) Dual Aspect
(c) Accrual Concept
(d) Objectivity Concept

4. According to Convention of Conservatism profits are not predetermined and all _____ are provided for

(a) Possible losses
(b) Possible revenues
(c) Estimate losses
(d) Estimated profits

5. 'Policy of planning safe' refers to

(a) Convention of Disclosure
(b) Convention of Materiality
(c) Convention of Consistency
(d) Conventions of Conservatism

6. The policy consideration of all possible losses and leave all possible profits due to

(a) Conventions of Consistency
(b) Conventions of Conservatism
(c) Convention of Disclosure
(d) None of these

7. All expenses and losses are

(a) Credited (b) Debited (c) Ignored (d) Understated

8. Any adverse effect on owner's equity is the result of _____ made by the business

(a) Profit (b) Loss

(c) Cost of productions (d) Both a and c

9. A debit to Equity Account ____ the balance

(a) Decrease (b) Increases (c) No changes (d) None of these

10. The Cash Book is an example of

(a) General Journal (b) Special Journal

(c) Ledger (d) Both Journal and Ledger

11. Decrease in one equity with no change in the asset will effect in ______ of another equity

(a) Increase (b) Decrease (c) No change (d) None of these

12. To match cost with revenue is the ______

(a) Income (b) Cost (c) Capital (d) All the above

13. Un expired cost is used to measure the value of ______

(a) Assets (b)Capital (c) Liabilities (d) Owner's Equity

14. Which of the following cost will be more under Straight Line Method?

(a) Un expired cost (b) Replacement cost

(c) Revalued cost (d) Standard Cost

15. Under _______ Depreciation charge will be more in the previous year

(a) Straight Line Method (b) Diminishing Balance Method

(c) Replacement Method (d) Sinking Fund Method

16. While valuing stock, during a period of rising prices _______

(a) LIFO (b) FIFO

(c) Simple Average Method (d) Base Stock Method

17. The conventional income statement is in the form of a T account indicating the _____ on the right side and _____ on the left side.

(a) Revenue, Expenditure (b) Expenditure, Revenue

(c) Assets, Liabilities (d) Liabilities, Assets

18. The _______ describes that profit can be shown after keeping the physical capital of the business

(a) Sum of Digits Methods (b) Historic Cost Method

(c) Current Value Method (d) CCA Method

19. Financial accounts of a company are prepared according to schedule IV of the ______

(a) Factories Act (b) Special Act (c) Societies Act (d) Companies Act

20. Company's Net worth refers to

(a) Equal to Shareholders Fund (b) Equal to Tangible Net Asset

(c) Equal to Authorized Capital (d) Equal to Subscribed Capital

21. Favorable company's Tangible Net Worth refers to

(a) The solvency of the company (b) The Profitability of the company

(c) Credit worthness of the company (d) Sound financial position of a company

22. Assets can be arranged in the Balance Sheet in the form of

(a) Permanence (b) Convention (c) Current (d) Liquidity

23. The Balance Sheet is prepared for a

(a) Particular period (b) Stipulated date (c) Financial period (d) All the above

24. Balance Sheet is a statement of ______

(a) Asset and liabilities (b) Income and Expenditure

(c) Receipts and Payments (d) Revenues and Capital

25. Journal is a book of ______

(a) Prime Entry (b) Secondary Entry (c) Closing Entry (d) Correcting Entry

26. The rule for personal account is _____ the receiver and ______ the giver

(a) Credit, Debit (b) Debit, Credit (c) Both a and b (d) None of these

27. Purchase Return Book is prepared on the basis of ________

(a) Debit Note (b) Credit Notes (c) Invoice Notes (d) Requisition Notes

28. The rule for Real Account is _______

(a) Debit what comes in and credit what goes out

(b) Debit the receiver and credit the giver

(c) Debit all expenses and losses and credit all gains and incomes

(d) None of the above

29. The rule of Debit all expenses and losses and Credit all gains and incomes relates to

(a) Personal Account (b) Real Account (c) Nominal Account (d) None of these

30. _______ is a subsidiary journal and ledger account

(a) Bills Receivable Book (b) Sales Book

(c) Sales Day Book (d) Cash Book

31. Credit note is the basis for ________

(a) Purchase Return Book (b) Sales Return Book

(c) Purchase Book (d) Cash Book

32. Sale of old machinery on account is recorded in

(a) Sales Book (b) Cash Book (c) Journal (d) Ledger

33. Outstanding income refers to

(a) Asset (b) Liability (c) Revenue (d) Capital

34. Prepaid expenses an example of

(a) Asset (b) Liability (c) Losses (d) Income

35. A schedule of balances drawn from the ledgers is called ____

(a) Trail Balance (b) Balance Sheet

(c) Income Statement (d) Trading Accounts

36. Any assets easily converted in to cash refers to

(a) Current Assets (b) Liquid Assets (c) Fixed Assets (d) Non-Current Assets

37. Appearing in the Trail Balance are shown in the balance sheet

(a) Prepaid expenses (b) Outstanding expenses

(c) Outstanding income (d) All the above

38. Provision for discount on creditors show ________

(a) Debit balance (b) Credit balance

(c) Debit or Credit balance (d) None of these

39. Which of the following refers to interest on capital?

(a) An appropriations of profits (b) Reserves

(c) Loss (d) Liability

40. Capital stock appearing in trail balance will be taken to

(a) Trading Account (b) Balance Sheet

(c) Profit and Loss A/c (d) Revaluation Account

41. Sales can be calculated by _____

(a) Net Profit + Expense + Cost of good sold

(b) Net Profit + Cost of goods sold– Non Trading expenses

(c) Gross profit + Cost of goods sold + Operating expenses

(d) None of these

42. The formula for calculations of Purchase is

(a) Cost of goods sold + Opening stock – Closing stock

(b) Cost of goods sold + Closing stock – Opening stock

(c) Cost of goods sold + Average stock

(d) Cost of goods sold + Net profit – Non operating expenses

43. The arithmetical accuracy of postings is the main principles of _______

(a) Trail Balance (b) Journal Book (c) Transactions (d) Ledger Book

44. Any discount made on debtor is a charge on ________

(a) An Appropriation of Profits (b) Revenue

(c) Capital (d) Non Trading Income

45. Excess sales over cost of goods sold is ________

(a) Gross profit (b) Net profit (c) Operating profit (d) Net operating profit

46. Provision for bad debts appearing is trail balance will figure in

(a) The Balance Sheet (b) The Profit and Loss Account

(c) Both a and b (d) Trading Account

47. Which of the following refers to outstanding expenses?

(a) Nominal Account (b) Representative Personal Account

(c) Real Account (d) Personal Account

48. The total equity of a business is Rs.2,40,000 of which creditors equity is Rs.80,000 the net worth of the business is

(a) 2,40,000 (b) 1,60,000 (c) Rs.80,000 (d) 60,000

49. Owner's Equity refers to

(a) Total equity – Creditors equity

(b) Total equity + Creditors equity

(c) Total equity + Creditors equity – Owner's equity

(d) Total equity

50. Non-Trading expenses are debited to _______ account

(a) Capital (b) Drawing (c) Assets (d) Liabilities

51. Good Will is an example of _______ assets

(a) Tangible (b) Intangible (c) Fictitious (d) Both b and c

52. The excess of Cost of goods sold over the sales proceeds is _______

(a) Net Profit (b) Operating Profit (c) Gross Profit (d) Gross Loss

53. Which of the following is to Errors of Principle?

(a) Wrong casting of subsidiary books

(b) Capital expenditure wrongly treated as revenue

(c) Posting the same amount twice to an account

(d) None of the above

54. Entering wrong amount in subsidiary books is an example of

(a) Errors of Principles (b) Errors of Omission

(c) Errors of Commission (d) Errors of Transfer

55. Any errors in the trail balance is recorded in

(a) Drawing Account (b) Personal Account

(c) A Suspense Account(d) Adjustment Account

56. Goods returned to Y the supplier are wrongly entered in the sales book this will affect

(a) Purchase Returns and Sales Account (b) Sales Account and Y's Account

(c) Purchase Returns and Y's Account (d) Purchase Account and Sales Account

57. Purchase of machinery entered in Purchase Day Book is an example of _______

(a) Errors of Principle (b) Errors of Omission

(c) Errors of Commission (d) Errors of Transfer

58. Short debit to an account increases the ______ side of the trail balance

(a) Debit (b) Credit (c) Debit or Credit (d) None of these

59. Bank Reconciliations Statement is stands for

(a) A Memorandum Statement (b) A Journal Account

(c) A Cash Book (d) A Pass Book

60. Which of the following is not relates to adjusting the cash errors?

(a) Errors in the Cash Book (b) Errors in the Pass Book

(c) Income debited in Cash Book (d) Rent credited in Pass Book

61. Bank Reconciliations Statement is prepared by

(a) Bankers (b) Accountant

(c) Internal Auditors (d) Creditors According to Bank Reconciliation Statement

62. Favorable bank balance indicates

(a) Credit balance in the Cash Book (b) Credit balance in the Pass Book

(c) Debit balance in the Cash Book (d) Debit balance in the Pass Book

63. Pass Book is the evidence of

(a) Customer Account (b) Bank Account (c) Both a and b (d) None of these

64. Cheque issued but not presented for payment, favorable balance as per cash book will be ______than that of the pass book

(a) Less (b) Larger (c) Smaller (d) Both a and c

65. Which of the following method used for valuing inventories?

(a) Cost Price Based (b) Sales Price Based

(c) Lower Cost or Sale Price (d) All the above

66. The ascertainment of value of stocks from account records is known as

(a) Continuous Stock Taking (b) Periodic Inventory

(c) Perpetual Inventory (d) Physically Counting the Stock

67. The value of stock is ascertained by physically counting the stock at the end of the year is known as ______

(a) Periodic Inventory (b) Perpetual Inventory

(c) Both a and b (d) None of these

68. In Job Order industries ________ are included in stock valuation

(a) Selling expenses (b) Office expenses

(c) Distribution expenses (d) Factory expenses

69. A Chronological record of transactions may be found in

(a) Journal (b) Ledger (c) Trail Balance (d) Balance Sheet

70. Bills Receivable Account is a nature of

(a) Real Account (b) Personal Account (c) Nominal Account (d) None of the above

71. On the acceptance of a bill the acceptor debits____ account

(a) Payee's Account (b) Creditors Account

(c) Bills Payable Account (d) Bills Receivable Account

72. Which of the following Act relates to Bill of Exchange?

(a) Negotiable Instrument Act (b) Companies Act

(c) Factories Act (d) Special Act passed by the Parliament

73. _______ is a bill of exchange drawn on a specified banker and not expressed to be payable otherwise than on demand.

(a) Promissory notes (b) Cheque (c) Bill of Exchange (d) Bonds

74. According to Bill of Exchange, bills are drawn by ____ and accepted by ______

(a) Creditor, Debtor (b) Debtor, Creditor (c) Drawee, Drawer (d) Payee, Payer

75. In Bill of Exchange, noting charges account is debited by

(a) Payee (b) Acceptor (c) Endorser (d) Bank

76. When a bill is endorsed credit is given to

(a) Bills Payable Account (b) Endorser's Account

(c) Bills Receivable Account (d) Bank Account

77. Payment before the date of maturity is termed as _____

(a) Accommodation Bills (b) Retiring a Bills

(c) Renewal of Bill (d) Dishonour of Bills

78. Revenue expenditure is useful for

(a) Current period (b) Future period (c) Short term period (d) Long term period

79. According to Kohler capital expenditure is any expenditure benefiting a _______

(a) Current period (b) Future period (c) Definite period (d) None of these

80. Heavy expenditure of revenue nature incurred for getting benefit over a number of years is classified as _______

(a) Deferred Revenue Expenditure (b) Capital Expenditure

(c) Revenue Expenditure (d) Non-Operating Expenditure

81. Salaries paid for furniture are debited to

(a) Salaries (b) Furniture

(c) Profit and Loss Account (d) Both a and b

82. Preliminary expenses is an example of

(a) Capital Receipt (b) Revenue Expenditure

(c) Deferred Revenue Expenditure (d) Capital Expenditure

83. Expenditure resulting in the acquisitions of building to

(a) Revenue Expenditure (b) Deferred Revenue Expenditure

(c) Capital Expenditure (d) Capital Receipt

84. Receipts and Payment Account is a nature of

(a) Real Account (b) Nominal Account

(c) Personal Account (d) Representative Personal Account

85. Sale of old scraps recorded on the credit side of

(a) Cash Book (b) Income and Expenditure Account

(c) Profit and Loss Account (d) Sales Book

86. Receipts and Payments Account is prepared on the basis of

(a) Cash Book (b) Income and Expenditure Account

(c) Balance Sheet (d) Trial Balance

87. Donations received for a specific purpose is

(a) Capital Receipt (b) Revenue Receipt

(c) Liability (d) Asset

88. Any gains arising from special fund will be credited to

(a) Special Fund in the Balance Sheet (b) Income and Expenditure Account

(c) Receipts and Payment Account (d) Revaluation Account

89. When goods are sent on Consignment it is debited to

(a) Consignee's Account (b) Consignment Account

(c) Bank Account (d) Consignor's Account

90. In Consignment Account the Conginor and the Consignee is like a

(a) Principal and Agent (b) Buyer and Seller

(c) Debtor and Creditor (d) Payer and Payee

91. According to Consignment, goods sent at cost price or at higher price is known as ____

(a) Invoice Price (b) Market Price (c) Actual Price (d) None of these

92. Losses arising in Consignment due to theft, fire etc is

(a) Normal (b) Abnormal (c) Total (d) Contingent

93. Overriding Commission is usually paid for ________

(a) In order to avoid bad debts (b) Pushing a new product in the market

(c) To avoid normal loss (d) To avoid abnormal loss

94. Consignee's Account is a nature of

(a) Normal Account (b) Personal Account

(c) Real Account (d) Representative Personal Account

95. Delcredere Commission is calculated on

(a) Cash sales (b) Credit sales (c) Trial sales (d) Estimated sales

96. Goods Send by a Manufacturer to an agent for the purpose of sale on commission basis is called ______

(a) Consignment (b) Account Sale (c) Sales (d) Abnormal Loss

97. In Consignment any abnormal loss is credited to ______ Account

(a) Consignee's (b) Consignment (c) Sales (d) Abnormal Loss

98. The document showing the description of goods sent to the consignee by the consigner is known as _______

(a) Account Sale (b) Pro-Forma Invoice

(c) Consignment (d) Consignment Inward

99. Any loss of goods arising due to natural causes is called as ________

(a) Normal Loss (b) Total Loss (c) Abnormal Loss (d) Contingent Loss

100. The periodical statement rendered by the consignee to the consignor showing the sale proceeds less expenses, commission, remittances and the resultant balance due by him is called an________.

(a) Pro-Forma Invoice (b) Settlement A/c

(c) Consignment A/c (d) Account Sale

101. Joint Venture Account is a nature of

(a) Personal Account (b) Real Account

(c) Nominal Account (d) Representative Personal Account

102. Income and Expenditure Account is a nature of ______

(a) Real Account (b) Personal Account

(c) Nominal Account (d) Representative Personal Account

103. Any amount given to a non-trading concern as per the will of a deceased person is termed as ______

(a) Legacy (b) Donation (c) Specified Fund (d) Annuity Funds

104. In the book of X, joint venture account with Y is an example of ______

(a) Personal Account (b) Real Account

(c) Nominal Account (d) None of these

105. The account current method in which the days are calculated from the date of transaction to the commencement date is known as______

(a) Daily balance Method (b) Epoch Method

(c) Backward Method (d) Both b and c

106. The method of account current usually employed by the banker is known as______

(a) Daily Balance Method (b) Red Ink Interest

(c) Epoch Method (d) Forward Method

107. Any payment is made on the Average Due Date it results in

(a) Loss of interest to the creditor (b) Loss of interest to the debtors

(c) No loss of creditor and debtor (d) None of these

108. Which of the following is not Self Balancing?

(a) For bad debts written off recovered (b) For commission allowed

(c) For bills receivable dishonoured (d) For discount allowed

109. A person from whom such goods in which the firm deals are purchase on credit basis is called as ______

(a) Trade Debtors (b)Trade Creditors (c) Supplier (d) Accounts Payable

110. In Self Balancing System, any ledger is meant for keeping personal accounts of trade debtors is also called as ______

(a) Sold Ledger (b) Sales Ledger (c) Both a and b (d) Bought Ledger

111. ______ is allocated so as to charge a fair proportion of the depreciable amount in each accounting period during the expected useful life of the asset.

(a) Depletion (b)Amortization (c) Dilapidation (d) Depreciation

112. External causes of depreciation are

(a) Wear and Tear (b) Obsolencence (c) Time Factor (d) Depletion

113. Depreciation is the process of

(a) Allocation of cost (b) Valuation of assets

(c) Both 'a' and 'b' (d) Allocation of revenue

114. Any reduction in the service capacity of an asset refers to

(a) Depreciation (b) Depletion (c) Obsolencence (d) Amortization

115. Profit prior to incorporation is an example of

(a) Capital Reserve (b) Revenue Reserve (c) Secret Reserve (d) General Reserve

116. Which of the following method of depreciation is suitable to lives stock

(a) Retirement Method (b) Appraisal Method

(c) Depletion Method (d) Straight line Method

117. According to ______ of depreciations are used because assets are more productive in the early years of economic life

(a) Straight Line Method (b) Written Down Value Method

(c) Accelerated Method (d) Annuity Method

118. Under ________ depreciation is charged at fixed rate on the reducing balance every year.

(a) Written Down – Value Method (b) Fixed Percentage on Declining Base Method

(c) Both a and b (d) Sum – of – Years – Digits Method

119. The total amount of depreciation to be written off life of an asset is equal to the cost of the asset less its__________

(a) Scrap value (b) Profit (c) Loss (d) Contribution

120. Wear and Tear is the _______ causes of depreciation

(a) Internal (b) Economic (c) Inadequacy (d) Effluxion of time

121. In the case of wasting assets the amount of charge is determined on the basis of exhanstion of the asset known as________

(a) Depreciation (b) Depletion (c) Obsolescence (d) Wear and Tear

122. Any Secret Reserve is not shown is _______

(a) Profit and Loss Account (b) Balance Sheet

(c) Trading Account (d) General Reserve Account

123. General reserves can be utilized for declaring dividend subject to the restrictions imposed by the ______

(a) Companies Act 1956 (b) Companies Act 1972

(c) Companies Act 1962 (d) Companies Act 1976

124. When a reserve is invested in outside securities it is termed as ________

(a) Secret Reserve (b) General Fund

(c) Capital Reserve (d) Reserve Fund

125. Construction of building is an example of ________

(a) Job (b) Contract (c) Investment (d) Batch

126. Purchase made and expenses paid from out of Joint Bank Account are debited to _____ account

(a) Real (b) Contract (c) Joint venture (d) Personal

127. Any profit or loses in Manufacturing Account is taken to ______

(a) Manufacturing A/c (b) General Profit and Loss A/c
(c) Costing Profit and Loss A/c (d) Trading A/c

128. Cost sheets are prepared on the basis of _______

(a) Schedule (b) Statement (c) Report (d) Budget

129. Sum total of Direct Material Direct Labour and Direct Expenses is

(a) Prime cost (b) Factory cost (c) Work cost (d) Total cost

130. Which of the following is the aim of Manufacturing Account?

(a) To ascertain factory cost of production (b) To disclose operating profit
(c) Cost control and ascertainment of cost (d) To find out total cost

131. Gross work cost + opening WIP – closing WIP =

(a) Net Work Cost (b) Factory Cost of Production
(c) Prime Cost (d) Total Cost

132. Any profit revealed by Cost Sheet is ______

(a) Gross Profit (b) Net Profit (c) Operating Profit (d) Net Operating Profit

133. In the receipts and payments account the payments are recorded on the ______ side.

(a) Credit (b) Debit
(c) Either Credit or Debit (d) None of these

134. The Income and Expenditure Account is prepared on the basis of ________ system of accounting.

(a) Cash (b) Mercantile (c) Profit (d) Non-profit

135. Any amount received towards Endowment fund is a _________ receipt

(a) Capital (b) Revenue (c) Special (d) None of these

136. Subscriptions received in advance are shown in __________

(a) Trading A/c (b) Income and Expenditure A/c
(c) Receipts and Payment A/c (d) Balance Sheet

137. Any revenue expenditure relating to special fund must be deducted from______

(a) Revenue Receipts (b) Capital Fund (c) Special Fund (d) General Fund

138. In Bills of Exchange, Bills are drawn by ______ and accepted by ______

(a) Creditors, Debtors (b) Debtors, Creditors
(c) Drawer, Drawee (d) Payee, Payer

139. Purchase of an asset is called ______

(a) Expenditure (b) Investment (c) Income (d) Sources of fund

140. The first part of the income statement is called ______

(a) Profit and Loss Account (b) Balance Sheet

(c) Trading Account (d) Trading, Profit and Loss Account

141. Journal entry require for – transferring them to Trading Profit and Loss Account is called ______

(a) Ledger (b) Posting

(c) Closing Entry (d) Post Closing Trail Balance

142. "Old customers will resort to the old place" means

(a) Leaseholds (b) Goodwill (c) Copyrights (d) Patents

143. Patents and Copyrights are the example of ______

(a) Current Assets (b) Liquid Assets

(c) Tangible Assets (d) Contingent Assets

144. Presentation of fixed assets as per ______ of the Companies Act 1956

(a) Schedule I (b) Schedule II (c) Schedule VI (d) Schedule IV

145. Journal is also called as ______

(a) Books of Original Entry (b) Books of Subsidiary Record

(c) Books of Prime Entry (d) All the above

146. Which of the following is Special Journal

(a) Sales Book (b) Purchase Book (c) Sales returns Book (d) All the above

147. Recording the transactions in the main book is called ______

(a) Journal Entry (b) Journalising (c) General Journal (d) Special Journal

148. Insurance Company's Account is an example of ______

(a) Natural Person's Account

(b) Artificial Persons and Body of Persons Account

(c) Representative Personal Account

(d) None of the above

149. Trade Mark is the nature of ______

(a) Real Account (b) Tangible Real Account

(c) Intangible Real Account (d) Nominal Account

150. Good Will arises when

(a) A new partner is admitted

(b) An existing partner retires

(c) A business concern is acquired by another

(d) All the above

ANSWERS

1. (a) Capital + Liabilities = Assets
2. (a) Cost Concept
3. (b) Dual Aspect
4. (a) Possible Losses
5. (a) Convention of Disclosure
6. (b) Convention of Conservatism
7. (b) Debited
8. (d) Both a and c
9. (a) Decrease
10. (d) Both Journal and Ledger
11. (a) Increase
12. (d) All the above
13. (a) Assets
14. (a) Unexpired Cost
15. (b) Diminishing Balance Method
16. (b) FIFO (First In First Out)
17. (a) Revenue, Expenditure
18. (c) Current Value Method
19. (d) Companies Act
20. (a) Equal to shareholders fund
21. (a) The solvency of the company
22. (a) Permanence
23. (a) Particular period
24. (a) Asset and Liabilities
25. (a) Prime Entry
26. (b) Debit, Credit
27. (a) Debit Notes
28. (a) Debit what comes in and credit what goes out
29. (c) Nominal Account
30. (d) Cash Book
31. (b) Sales Return Book
32. (c) Journal
33. (a) Asset
34. (a) An Asset
35. (a) A Trail Balance
36. (b) Liquid Assets
37. (d) All of the above
38. (a) Debit Balance
39. (a) An appropriation of profits
40. (a) Trading Account
41. (a) Net income + Expenses + Cost of goods sold
42. (b) Cost of goods sold + Closing stock – Opening stock
43. (a) Trail Balance
44. (b) Revenue
45. (a) Gross Profit
46. (c) Both a and b
47. (b) Representative Personal Accounts
48. (b) Rs.1,60,000
49. (a) Total Equity – Creditors Equity
50. (b) Drawings
51. (c) Both b and c
52. (d) Gross Loss
53. (b) Capital expenditure wrongly treated as revenue
54. (c) Errors of Commission
55. (c) A Suspense Account
56. (a) Purchase Returns and Sales Account
57. (a) Errors of Principle
58. (a) Debit
59. (a) A Memorandum Statement
60. (b) Errors in the Pass Book
61. (b) Accountant
62. (a) Credit Balance in the Cash Book
63. (a) Customers Account
64. (d) both a and c
65. (d) All the above
66. (c) Perpetual Inventory
67. (a) Periodic Inventory
68. (a) Selling expenses
69. (a) Journal
70. (a) Real Account
71. (b) Creditor's Account
72. (a) Negotiable Instrument Act
73. (b) Cheque
74. (a) Creditor, Debtor
75. (b) Acceptor

76. (c) Bills receivable Account
77. (b) Retiring a Bills
78. (a) Current period
79. (c) Future period
80. (a) Deferred Revenue Expenditure
81. (b) Furniture Account
82. (c) Deferred Revenue Expenditure
83. (c) Capital Expenditure
84. (a) Real Account
85. (b) Income and Expenditure Account
86. (a) Cash Book
87. (a) Capital Receipt
88. (a) Special Fund in the Balance Sheet
89. (b) Consignment Account
90. (a) Principal and Agent
91. (a) Invoice Price
92. (b) Abnormal
93. (b) Pushing a new product in the market
94. (b) Personal Account
95. (c) Total sales
96. (a) Consignment
97. (b) Consignment
98. (b) Pro – Forma Invoice
99. (a) Normal Loss
100. (d) Account Sale
101. (c) Nominal Account
102. (c) Nominal Account
103. (a) Legacy
104. (a) Personal Account
105. (d) Both b and c
106. (a) Daily Balance Method
107. (c) No loss of interest to either of them
108. (a) For bad debts written off recovered
109. (b) Trade Creditors
110. (c) Both a and b
111. (d) Depreciation
112. (b) Obsolescence
113. (a) Allocation of cost
114. (b) Depletion
115. (a) Capital Reserve
116. (b) Appraisal Method
117. (c) Accelerated Method
118. (c) Both a and b
119. (a) Scrap Value.
120. (b) Economic
121. (b) Depletion
122. (b) Balance Sheet
123. (a) Companies act 1956
124. (d) Reserve Fund
125. (b) Contract
126. (c) Joint Venture
127. (b) General Profit and Loss A/c
128. (b) Statement
129. (a) Prime Cost
130. (a) To ascertain the factory cost of production
131. (a) Net Work Cost
132. (c) Operating Profit
133. (a) Credit
134. (b) Mercantile
135. (a) Capital
136. (d) Balance Sheet
137. (c) Special Fund
138. (a) Creditors, Debtors
139. (a) Expenditure
140. (c) Trading Account
141. (c) Closing Entry
142. (b) Good Will
143. (d) Contingent Asset
144. (c) Schedule VI
145. (d) All the above
146. (d) All the above
147. (b) Journalising
148. (b) Artificial Persons and Body of Persons Accounts
149. (c) Intangible Real Account
150. (d) All the above

****

IX

MANAGEMENT ACCOUNTING

1. **Determinations of profit is the main purpose of preparing**
   (a) Financial Accounting (b) Cost Accounting
   (c) Management Accounting (d) Auditing
2. **Financial Accounting is prepared on the basis of**
   (a) Actual figures (b) Budgeted figures (c) Standard figures (d) Estimated figures
3. **The term Management Accountancy was first used in**
   (a) 1930 (b) 1970 (c)1950 (d) 1990
4. **Presentations of accounting data is the objective of**
   (a) Financial Accounting (b) Cost Accounting
   (c) Management Accounting (d) Company Accounting
5. **According to law Management Accounting is**
   (a) Obligatory (b) Compulsory (c) Optional (d) Essential
6. **Accounting designed for use in the operational needs of the business is termed as ________**
   (a) Cost Accounting (b) Management Accounting
   (c) Financial Accounting (d) Auditing
7. **The one which distinguishes between individual and business**
   (a) Business Entity Concept (b) Management Accounting Concepts
   (c) Dual Concern Concept (d) Product Concept
8. **Which of the following is Cost Concept?**
   (a) Market values (b) Cost and Market value
   (c) Estimated value (d) Actual amount paid

9. Which of the following is refers to Accounting Concept?

(a) Facts and figures (b) Assumptions

(c) Opinion and thoughts (d) Accounting records

10. Financial Statements is prepared under

(a) Income Tax Act (b) Company Act

(c) Business Law (d) Consumer Protection Act

11. Management Accounting provides necessary information to

(a) Shareholders (b) Top Management

(c) Shareholders and outside agencies (d) All the above

12. Retained Earnings Statement refers to

(a) Appropriations of profits (b) Non-operating profits

(c) Estimated cost (d) Operating profits

13. A Summary of accounts is

(a) Cost Accounting (b) Financial Accounting

(c) Management Accounting (d) Auditing

14. The term Financial Analysis refers to

(a) Analysis of financial statement (b) Interpretations of financial statements

(c) Both a and b (d) Preparations of financial statements

15. Form of Horizontal Analysis of income statements refers to

(a) Comparative Statements Analysis (b) External Analysis

(c) Internal Analysis (d) Trend Analysis

16. Common–size statements and financial ratios of income statements are use in

(a) Horizontal Analysis (b) Vertical Analysis

(c) Trend Analysis (d) Financial Analysis

17. ______ is an arithmetical relationship of one number to another number

(a) Ratio (b) Unit (c) Cost (d) Percentage

18. Current asset and current liabilities are the elements of

(a) Current Ratio (b) Liquid Ratio (c) Gross Profit Ratio (d) Turnover Ratio

19. Liquid Ratio is also termed as

(a) Turnover Ratio (b) Acid Test Ratio (c) Proprietary Ratio (d) Current Ratio

20. Current Liabilities are payable in

(a) More than 5 years (b) Between 2 to 5 years

(c) A year (d) More than two years

21. The ideal thump of Current Ratio is

(a) 1:1 (b) 3:1 (c) 2:1 (d) 2:2

22. The relationship between outsiders funds and shareholders fund is measured by______

(a) Debt Equity Ratio (b) Gross Profit Ratio (c) Turnover Ratio (d) Fixed Assets Ratio

23. The formula of $\frac{\text{Operating cost}}{\text{Net sales}} \times 100$ refers to

(a) Operating Profit Ratio (b) Net Profit Ratio
(c) Operating Ratio (d) Gross Profit Ratio

24. Inventory is a part of _______

(a) Current Assets (b) Fixed Assets
(c) Non-Current Assets (d) Liquid Assets

25. The ideal standard for Liquid Ratio is

(a) 2:1 (b) 1:1 (c) 2:2 (d) 2:3

26. _______ is to measures overall profitability of a concern

(a) Gross Profit Ratio (b) Overall Profitability Ratio
(c) Net Profit Ratio (d) Return on Investment Ratio

27. Long term solvency is a part of _______

(a) Price Earnings Ratio (b) Operating Ratio
(c) Solvency Ratio (d) Liquid Ratio

28. _______ is to measures the profitability of a business

(a) Return on Investment Ratio (b) Current Ratio
(c) Gross Profit Ratio (d) Net Profit Ratio

29. The difference between current assets and current liabilities refers to

(a) Capital (b) Expenditure (c) Revenue (d) Fund

30. _______indicate increase or decrease of working capital

(a) Cash Flow Statement (b) Cash From Operation
(c) Fund Flow Statement (d) Schedule Change in Working Capital

31. Increase in current assets means _______

(a) Increase in working capital (b) Decrease in working capital
(c) Fund lost in operations (d) Fund from operations

32. Any transactions results in increase of working capital is a _______

(a) Application of Funds (b) Source of Cash
(c) Uses of Funds (d) Source of Funds

33. Purchase of plant will mean _______ in working capital

(a) Decrease (b) Increase (c) No flow of funds (d) None of these

34. Issue of share capital will mean _______ in working capital

(a) Decrease (b) Increase (c) No flow of funds (d) None of these

35. Good Will is a _______

(a) Non Current Liabilities (b) Non Current Assets
(c) Tangible Assets (d) Current Assets

36. When one account is _______ and another a ______ it result in flow of funds

(a) Current, Current (b) Non – Current, Non – Current

(c) Current, Non – Current

37. Which of the following is included is current assets?

(a) Bills Receivable (b) Bills Payable (c) Machinery (d) Trade Investment

38. Which of the following is a Non – Current Assets?

(a) Bank Balance (b) Sundry Debtors (c) Good Will (d) Cash Balance

39. State which of the following is a Non-current liability?

(a) Long term loan (b) Bank loan (Short term)

(c) Sundry creditors (d) Outstanding expenses

40. Depreciations on plant and machinery results in

(a) Applications funds (b) Cash from operations

(c) No flow of funds (d) Source of funds

41. Which of the following is Non – current liabilities?

(a) Payment of salaries (b) Sundry debtors

(c) Cash balance (d) Profit and loss account

42. Fund Flow Statement is also termed as _________

(a) Summary of Financial Operations

(b) Fund Generated and Expended

(c) Statement of Sources and Application of Fund

(d) All the above

43. Which of the following will result into outflow of funds?

(a) Purchase of building(b) Issue of share capital

(c) Sale of plant (d) Decrease of debtors

44. Cash Flow Statement is based upon ______ of accounting

(a) Cash Basis (b) Accrual Basis

(c) Both Cash and Accrual Basis (d) None of these

45. Cash Flow Statement is important for _________

(a) Long Term Financial Analysis (b) Medium Term Financial Analysis

(c) Short Term Financial Analysis (d) Working Capital Analysis

46. Reductions in stocks is a ________

(a) Source of cash (b) No effect on cash flow

(c) Both a and b (d) Applications of cash

47. Increase in creditors is a ______

(a) Cash from operations (b) Outflow of cash

(c) No flow of cash (d) Inflow of cash

48. Raising of short term loan results in _______

(a) Inflow of cash (b) Outflow cash

(c) No flow of cash (d) Fund from operation

49. Income tax refund is a ______ of cash

(a) Outflow (b) Source (c) Applications (d) Uses

50. In a narrow sense fund mean ______

(a) Working capital (b) Fund (c) Cash (d) Bank

51. ________ is prepared by taking the opening balance of cash

(a) Cash Flow Statement (b) Fund Flow Statement

(c) Income Statement (d) Financial Statement

52. Budgetary control is a system of controlling __________

(a) Profit (b) Price (c) Units (d) Cost

53. _______ indicates duties and responsibilities of various executives concerned with budgets

(a) Budget Manual (b) Planning (c) Budget Strategy (d) Key Factor

54. A factor which influences all other budgets in called ______ factor

(a) External (b) Internal (c) Key (d) Both a and b

55. _______ incorporates all functional budgets

(a) Sales Budget (b) Master Budget

(c) Productions Budget (d) Material Budget

56. Zero – Base Budgeting was introduced by ______

(a) Jimmy cater (b) Herzberg (c) Keynes (d) Drucker

57. ________ is to measure the ratio between actual and budgeted days

(a) Efficiency Ratio (b) Calendar Ratio (c) Turnover Ratio (d) Activity Ratio

58. ________ will be appropriate in areas where output is not related to productions

(a) Performance Budgeting (b) Zero Base Budgeting

(c) Flexible Budgeting (d) Master Budget

59. Change with different level of activity is to be measured by

(a) Master Budget (b) Fixed Budget

(c) Flexible Budget (d) Productions Budget

60. Budgeting may be ______

(a) An act of determining costing standards (b) Act of building budgets

(c) System of controlling cost (d) None of these

61. For preparations of flexible budget, expenses are divided into

(a) Past and Current expenses

(b) Fixed, Semi – variable and Variable expenses

(c) Operating and Non–operating expenses

(d) Direct and Indirect expenses

62. Capital Budgeting is also termed as ______

(a) Investment Decision Making (b) Profitability Index

(c) Internal Rate of Return (d) None of these

63. Planning of capital expenditure is referred to

(a) Budget Manual (b) Budget Period (c) Capital Budgeting (d) Budget Center

64. Capital investment decisions are generally of ______ nature

(a) Irreversible (b) Reversible (c) Accrual (d) Recurring

65. ______ is also termed as benefit/cost ratio

(a) Activity Index (b) Efficiency Index (c) Turnover Index (d) Profitability Index

66. Which is the simplest capital budgeting technique?

(a) Draw – Back Period Method (b) Pay – Back Period Method

(c) Return on Investment (d) None of these

67. ______ is calculated by deducting cost of investments and present value of cash inflows

(a) Capital Return (b) Net Present Value of Inflows

(c) Internal Rate of Return (d) Time, Adjusted Rate of Return

68. Net present value of inflows is calculated by deducting ______

(a) Cost of productions (b) Cost of sales

(c) Cost of investment (d) Cost of Administration

69. ________ is to measures the true profitability of projects

(a) Pay Back Period Method (b) Rate of Return Method

(c) Net Present Value Method (d) Profitability Index Method

70. Internal rate of return is also known as ______

(a) Pay back period method (b) Time Adjusted rate of Return

(c) Profitability index (d) Turnover Index

71. ______ refers to a situations where a firm is not in a position to invest in all profitable projects due to the constraints on availability of funds

(a) Capital Budgeting (b) Capital Expenditure Budget

(c) Capital Rationing (d) Budgetary Control

72. Internal Rate of Return Method takes into

(a) Account the time value of money

(b) Account the earnings over the entire life of the project

(c) Objective of maximum profitability

(d) None of these

73. _______ takes into account the earnings over the entire life of the project

(a) Internal Rate of Return (b) Time Adjusted Rate of Return

(c) Net Present Value Method (d) Pay Back Period Method

74. Pay – Back Period Method is also called as _______

(a) Payout Period Method (b) Pay off Period Method

(c) Both a and b (d) None of these

75. Where budget for single measure of activity refers to

(a) Flexible Budget (b) Fixed Budget (c) Master Budget (d) Zero–Base Budget

76. Which of the following refers to Liquid Assets?

(a) Cash and Bills Receivable
(b) Cash and Debtors
(c) Cash and Debtors (Except provision for bad debtors)
(d) Cash and Debtors (Except bad debts) and marketable securities

77. Which of the following include in Liquid Liabilities?

(a) Bills Payable (b) Bank Loan and Bills Payable
(c) Creditors (d) None of these

78. Current Ratio is a ____ ratio

(a) Profit and Loss (b) Balance Sheet (c) Trading (d) Manufacturing

79. Which of the following item is not included in Current Ratio?

(a) Good Will (b) Sundry Debtor (c) Sundry Creditor (d) Bills Receivable

80. Which of the following item is not included in quick ratio?

(a) Bank Balance (b) Cash Balance (c) Bank Over Draft (d) Sundry Debtors

81. Loss on sale of old machinery is an expenses referred to

(a) Operating expenses (b) Non operating expenses
(c) Trading expenses (d) Manufacturing expenses

82. The Debtors Turnover Ratio may be calculated by

(a) $\frac{\text{Total sales}}{\text{Average creditors}}$ (b) $\frac{\text{Credit sales}}{\text{Average debtors}}$

(c) $\frac{\text{Cash sales}}{\text{Average debtors}}$ (d) $\frac{\text{Credit sales}}{\text{Debtors}} \times \text{Days in a year}$

83. Stock Turnover Ratio is a ____

(a) Solvency Ratio (b) Current Ratio (c) Liquidity Ratio (d) Profitability Ratio

84. The Stock Turnover Ratio can be calculated by

(a) $\frac{\text{Turnover at selling prices}}{\text{Stock at cost}}$ (b) $\frac{\text{Turnover at cost prices}}{\text{Stock at cost}}$

(c) $\frac{\text{Turnover at selling prices}}{\text{Stock at selling prices}}$ (d) All the above

85. Which of the following is the test of the long term liquidity of a business?

(a) Current Ratio (b) Liquid Ratio
(c) Stock Turnover Ratio (d) Interest Coverage Ratio

86. The Stock Turnover Ratio is referred to

(a) Buying in small lots (b) Buying in big lots and selling slowly
(c) Buying in small lots and selling quickly (d) None of these

87. The Gross Profit Ratio is the ratio that indicates Gross profit to

(a) Total Capital Employed (b) Net credit sales

(c) Net cash sales (d) Net total sales

88. Which of the following formula is used to calculate the Net Profit Ratio?

(a) $\frac{\text{Net profit}}{\text{Net sales}} \times 100$ (b) $\frac{\text{Gross profit}}{\text{Net sales}} \times 100$

(c) $\frac{\text{Operating profit}}{\text{Net sales}} \times 100$ (d) $\frac{\text{Net profit}}{\text{Total sales - sales return}} \times 100$

89. Fixed Assets Turnover Ratio is useful to measure the _______

(a) Liquidity position of the company (b) Capacity utilizations

(c) Return on overall investment (d) Utilization of Resources

90. Which of the following is not an operating expenses?

(a) Administrative expenses (b) Stationary expenses

(c) Interest received (d) Advertising expenses

91. _______ is to measure the relationships expressed in mathematical terms between two figures

(a) Turnover Ratio (b) Overall Profitability Ratio

(c) Accounting Ratio (d) Current Ratio

92. 'Net Worth' of business refers to

(a) Preference share capital (b) Total capital

(c) Total assets (d) Total assets minus Total liabilities

93. Return on Investment Ratio is to measure the relationship between

(a) Investment and Profit (b) Turnover and Capital employees

(c) Net profit and Capital employed (d) Profit and Sale

94. Window Dressing is prohibited by the ______

(a) Accrual Concept (b) Conventions of Materiality

(c) Convention of Disclosure (d) Convention of Conservatism

95. Which of the following is not a Capital Reserve?

(a) Premium on issue of shares (b) Profits prior to incorporations

(c) profit on sale of fixed assets (d) Dividend equalizations reserve

96. Which of the following is the Non-current liability?

(a) Share capital (b) Equity share capital

(c) Debentures (d) outstanding wages

97. Redemptions of preference share capital results into ______ of funds

(a) Inflow (b) Outflow (c) No flow (d) None of these

98. Conversion of debenture into equity share capital results into ______ of fund

(a) Inflow (b) Outflow

(c) No flow (d) Fund from operations

99. Sales of building results in ______ of fund

(a) Inflow (b) Applications

(c) No flow (d)Funds from operations

100. When rate is paid, it results into ______

(a) Source of Fund (b) Applications of Fund

(c) No flow of Fund (d) None of these

101. Cash Accounting mainly helps the management in ________

(a) Earning more profits

(b) Providing necessary information's to the management for decisions making

(c) fixing selling price

(d) Cost control

102. Variable cost per unit ________

(a) Remain constant

(b) Variable with the volume of production

(c) No change with the volume of productions

(d) None of the above

103. Fixed cost per unit increases when

(a) Production volume decreases (b) Productions volume increases

(c) Variable cost per unit increases (d) Variable cost per unit decreases

104. Which of the following financial statement are most useful for management ?

(a) Income Statement, Statement of Retained Earnings and Balance Sheet

(b) Income Statement, Balance Sheet and Statement of Changes in Financial Position

(c) Income Statement of Retained Earnings, Fund Flow Statement and Cash Flow Statement

(d) Balance Sheet, Cash Flow Statement and Retained Earnings

105. In the case of Limited Company, the term Financial Statements includes

(a) Profit and Loss A/c and Balance Sheet

(b) P & L A/c, Profit and Loss Appropriations A/c and Balance Sheet

(c) Trading A/c and Balance Sheet

(d) None of these

106. The term Current Assets does not include

(a) Payments in advance (b) Bills Receivable

(c) Long term differed charges (d) Stock

107. Which of the following is a recorded fact?

(a) Market value of investment (b) Debtors

(c) Replacement cost of machinery (d) None of these

108. The term Fixed Assets includes ____

(a) Stock in trade (b) Furniture

(c) Payment in advance (d) Bank

109. Which of the following relates to Ratio of Net Sales to Net Working Capital?

(a) Working Capital Turnover Ratio (b) Current Ratio

(c) Over all profitability Ratio (d) Solvency Ratio

110. Which of the following advantages result to Ratio Analysis?

(a) Simplifies financial statements (b) Facilities inter–firm comparison

(c) Helps is planning (d) All the above

111. Which of the following Ratio relates to net profit before interest and tax to sales?

(a) Operating Profit Ratio (b) Turn Over Ratio

(c) Current Ratio (d) Acid – Test Ratio

112. Which of the following is not relating to profitability ratio?

(a) Operating Ratio (b) Net Profit Ratio

(c) Gross Profit Ratio (d) Current Ratio

113. Balance Sheet is a statement of ______ of a business at a specific moment of time

(a) Matches (b) Financial position

(c) Liquidity (d) None of these

114. Profit and Loss Account is also called as the ______ Statement of

(a) Income (b) Finance (c) Revaluation (d) Both a and b

115. Financial Statement disclose only ______ facts

(a) Historical (b) Actual (c) Quantitative (d) Estimated

116. Increase in an asset due to purchase is ______

(a) Source of Funds (b) Fund From Operation

(c) Application of Funds (d) Cash From Operation

117. Net profit earned plus non – working capital expenses is equal to

(a) Funds provided by operations (b) Use of Funds

(c) Sinking Fund (d) Outflow of Funds

118. Dividend paid indicates ______

(a) Applications of Funds (b) Source of Funds

(c) No Flow of Fund (d) Cash From Operation

119. Opening stock results in ______

(a) Outflow of Funds (b) Inflow of Funds

(c) No Flow of Funds (d) Cash From Operations

120. Closing stock results in ______

(a) Outflow of Funds (b) Inflow of Funds

(c) No Flow of Funds (d) Cash From Operations

121. An increase in the share premium account result in ______

(a) Outflow of Funds (b) Inflow of Funds

(c) No Flow of Funds (d) Cash From Operations

122. **Sale of investments results in**
(a) Source of Funds (b) Applications Funds
(c) Fund From Operation (d) No Flow of Funds

123. **Flow of funds refer to change in ______ capital**
(a) Working capital (b) Long term (c) Authorized (d) Share

124. **_______ is to measures the inflows and outflows of net working capital that result from any type of business activity**
(a) Income Statement (b)Fund Flow Statement
(c) Cash Flow Statement (d) Statement of Changes in Financial Positions

125. **Any dividend received result in ______**
(a) Outflow of Funds (b) Inflow of Funds
(c) No Flow of Funds (d) Cash From Operations

126. **Any gain on sale of Non – current assets should be _______ from the net profit for the determining funds from operations**
(a) Added (b) Deducted (c) Divided (d) None of these

127. **Cash From Operations is equal to**
(a) Net profit plus increase in outstanding expenses
(b) Net profit plus increase in debtors
(c) Net profit plus increase in stock
(d) None of the above

128. **Which of the following relates to Cash Flow Statement?**
(a) Movement of cash (b) Movement of working capital
(c) Movement of fund (d) Both a and b

129. **Increase in provision for doubtful debts should be added back in order to find out ______**
(a) Fund for Operations (b) Cash From Operations
(c) Fund Flow Statement (d) Income Statement

130. **Production Budget is prepared on the basis of _______**
(a) Sales Budget (b) Flexible Budget
(c) Expenditure Budget (d) Cash Budget

131. **In the case of plant the limiting factor may be**
(a) Insufficient capacity (b) Shortage of experienced salesmen
(c) General shortage of power (d) None of these

132. **______is a summary of the budget schedules in capsule from made for the purpose of presenting is on report the highlights of the budget forecast**
(a) Mater Budget (b) Sales Budget (c) Flexible Budget (d) Production Budget

133. **The priorities of functional budget determines**
(a) Principal Budget Factor (b) Budget Period
(c) Budget Manual (d) Plan and Control

134. Zero – Base Budgeting is a technique first used in _______

(a) USA (b) Germany (c) India (d) England

135. Which of the following functions of Management Accounting?

(a) Provides data (b) Modifies data
(c) Serves as a means of communication (d) All the above

136. The budget which commonly takes the form of budgeted profit and loss account and balance sheet is _______

(a) Cash Budget (b) Master Budget (c) Flexible Budget (d) Productions Budget

137. A system by which budgets are used as a means of planning and controlling all aspect of a business is called _______

(a) Budget (b) Budgetary Control
(c) Budget Planning (d) Budget Program

138. Which of the following main objectives of budgetary control?

(a) Planning (b) control (c) Decision making (d) All the above

139. _____ indicates the expected sources and utilizations of cash

(a) Master Budget (b) Income and Expenditure Budget
(c) Cash Budget (d) Sales Budget

140. Financial Statements is also called as __________

(a) Income statements (b) Financial Reports
(c) Both a and b (d) Financial Documents

141. _______is concerned with determining the quantity of raw materials required for production

(a) Material Budget (b) Productions Budget
(c) Master Budget (d) Flexible Budget

142. Cash Budget is a _______ term budget

(a)Short (b) Long (c) Medium (d) All the above

143. A budget which consolidates the organizations overall plan is called _______

(a) Budget Center (b) Budget Manual (c) Master Budget (d) Cash Budget

144. A _______ is a document which set out the utilizations of the persons engaged in budgetary control

(a) Budget Program (b) Budget Manual (c) Budget Planning (d) Master Budget

145. Operating budget consists of two parts called as ______ budget and ______ budget

(a) Program, Responsibility (b) Income, Expenditure
(c) Program, Accountability (d) Receipts, Payment

ANSWERS

1. (a) Financial Accounting
2. (a) Actual figures
3. (c) 1950
4. (c) Management Accounting
5. (c) Optional
6. (b) Management Accounting
7. (a) Business Entity Concept
8. (d) Actual Amount paid
9. (a) Facts and figures
10. (b) Company's Act
11. (d) All the above
12. (a) Appropriation of profit
13. (b) Financial Accounting
14. (c) Both Analysis and Interpretation
15. (a) Comparative Statements
16. (b) Vertical Analysis
17. (a) Ratio
18. (a) Current Ratio
19. (b) Acid test Ratio
20. (c) A year
21. (c) 2:1
22. (a) Debt Equity Ratio
23. (c) Operating Ratio
24. (a) Current Assets
25. (b) 1:1
26. (b) Overall Profitability Ratio
27. (c) Solvency Ratio
28. (a) Return on Investment Ratio
29. (d) Fund
30. (c) Fund Flow Statement
31. (a) Increase in working capital
32. (d) Sources of Funds
33. (a) Decrease
34. (b) Increase
35. (b) Non current assets
36. (c) Current and Non-current
37. (a) Bills Receivable
38. (c) Good Will
39. (a) Long term loan
40. (d) Source of Funds
41. (d) Profit and Loss Account
42. (d) All the above
43. (a) Purchase of building
44. (a) Cash basis
45. (c) Short term financial analysis
46. (a) Source of Cash
47. (d) Inflow of Cash
48. (a) Inflow of Cash
49. (b) Source
50. (c) Cash
51. (a) Cash Flow Statement
52. (d) Cost
53. (a) Budget Manual
54. (c) Key
55. (b) Master Budget
56. (a) Jimmy Cater
57. (b) Calendar Ratio
58. (b) Zero Base Budgeting
59. (c) Flexible Budget
60. (b) Act of Building
61. (b) Fixed, Semi – Variable and Variable expenses
62. (a) Investment decision making
63. (c) Capital Budgeting
64. (a) Irreversible
65. (d) Profitability Index
66. (b) Pay - Back Period Method
67. (b) Net present value of inflows
68. (c) Cost of investment
69. (b) Rate of Return Method
70. (b) Time Adjusted Rate of Return
71. (c) Capital Rationing
72. (a) Account the time value of money
73. (c) Net Present Value Method
74. (c) Both a and b
75. (b) Fixed Budget
76. (d) Cash and Debtors [except bad debts] and marketable securities
77. (c) Creditors
78. (b) Balance Sheet

79. (a) Good Will
80. (c) Bank Over Draft
81. (a) Operating expenses
82. (b) $\frac{\text{Credit sales}}{\text{Average debtors}}$
83. (c) Liquidity Ratio
84. (d) All the above
85. (d) Interest Coverage Ratio
86. (b) Buying the big lots and selling slowly
87. (d) Net Total Sales
88. (d) $\frac{\text{Net profit}}{\text{Total sales - sales return}} \times 100$
89. (b) Capacity utilization
90. (c) Interest received
91. (c) Accounting Ratio
92. (d) Total assets minus Total liabilities
93. (c) Net profit and Capital Employed
94. (d) Convention of Conservatism
95. (d) Dividend equalization reserve
96. (d) Outstanding wages
97. (b) Outflow
98. (c) No flow
99. (a) Inflow
100. (b) Application of Fund
101. (b) Providing necessary information to the management for decision making
102. (b) Variable with the value of production
103. (d) Variable cost per unit decreases
104. (b) Income Statement, Balance Sheet and Statement of Changes in Financial Position
105. (b) P&L A/c, Profit and Loss Appropriation A/c and Balance Sheet
106. (c) Long term differed charges
107. (b) Debtors
108. (b) Furniture
109. (a) Working Capital Turnover Ratio
110. (d) All the above
111. (a) Operating Profit Ratio
112. (d) Current Ratio
113. (b) Financial Position
114. (a) Income
115. (b) Actual
116. (c) Application of Funds
117. (a) Funds provided by operations
118. (a) Application of Funds
119. (b) Inflow of Funds
120. (a) Outflow of Funds
121. (b) Inflow of Funds
122. (a) Source of Funds
123. (a) Working Capital
124. (b) Fund Flow Statement
125. (a) Inflow of Fund
126. (b) Deducted
127. (a) Net profit plus increase in outstanding expenses
128. (a) Movement of cash
129. (b) Cash From Operation
130. (a) Sales Budget
131. (a) Insufficient Capacity
132. (a) Flexible Budget
133. (a) Principal Budget Factor
134. (a) USA
135. (a) Multi – Activity Method
136. (b) Master Budget
137. (b) Budgetary Control
138. (d) All the above
139. (c) Cash Budget
139. (d) Principal Budget Factor
140. (c) Both a and b
141. (a) Materials Budget
142. (c) Master Budget
143. (a) Budget - Centre
144. (b) Budget Manual
145 (a) Program, Responsibility

*****

X

COST ACCOUNTING

1. **Costing is a technique of ________**
   (a) Income determination (b) External reporting
   (c) Ascertaining cost (d) Internal reporting
2. **Which of the following function relates to Cost Accounting?**
   (a) Internal Reporting (b) External Reporting
   (c) Interim Reporting (d) Routine Reporting
3. **________ is useful not only to ascertain the cost but also to control the cost**
   (a) Management Accounting (b) Cost Accounting
   (c) Auditing (d) Income Tax
4. **One of the functions of cost accounting is proper matching of _____ with revenue**
   (a) Cost (b) Production (c) Sales (d) Stock
5. **Cost Accounting Assists Financial Accounting with regard to the ______**
   (a) Valuation of inventory (b) Determinations of income
   (c) Ascertaining the financial positions (d) Determination of cost
6. **Cost Accounting is a tool of ______**
   (a) Financial Accounting (b) Management Accounting
   (c) Auditing (d) Company Accounts
7. **Cost Accounting is based on ______ figures**
   (a) Actual (b) Estimated (c) Accrual (d) Historical
8. **Incremental Cost is a type of _________**
   (a) Differential Cost (b) Conversions Cost (c) Job Cost (d) Historical Cost

9. _______ is the cost which fluctuates with volume of production

(a) Fixed cost (b) Variable cost (c) Semi variable cost (d) Controllable cost

10. ________ per unit increases when production volume decreases

(a) Variable cost (b) Semi variable cost
(c) Controllable cost (d) Fixed cost

11. ______ is useful for making managerial decisions

(a) Conversion cost (b) Opportunity cost (c) Fixed cost (d) Incremental cost

12. ________ is the sum total of Direct Wages, Direct Expenses and Factory Overheads

(a) Opportunity Cost (b) Differential Cost
(c) Variable Cost (d) Conversion Cost

13. Cost of goods produced include ________

(a) Work in progress and total cost (b) Cost of production and prime cost
(c) Cost of productions and work in progress (d) None of the above

14. Multiple Costing Method is used in ________

(a) knitwear textile industry (b) Cement industry
(c) Chemical industry (d) Car manufacturing industry

15. Factory overheads = ________

(a) Work cost (b) prime cost (c) Total cost (d) Cost of goods sold

16. Direct material + Direct labour + Direct expenses = ______

(a) Factory on cost (b) Prime cost (c) Cost of goods sold (d) Total cost

17. ______ costing used in chemical works

(a) Operating (b) Single (c) Contract (d) Process

18. The method of costing used in constructional works is ________

(a) Job costing (b) Batch costing
(c) Process costing (d) Operating costing

19. In a educational institutions, cost unit is ________

(a) Office staff (b) Students (c) Children's (d) Teachers

20. In hospitals, cost unit is________

(a) Per tone Km (b) Number (c) Per Doctor (d) Per bed per day

21. Which of following costing methods represent for group of identical products?

(a) Batch (b) Uniform (c) Contract (d) Standard

22. Rent, interest and wages of self owned resources are the examples of

(a) Direct cost (b) Notional cost
(c) Selling over heads (d) Distribution over heads

23. A statement that sets out the divisional classification of costs is known as ________

(a) Income Statement (b) Statement of Cost and Profit
(c) Cost Sheet (d) Financial Statement

24. Which of the following is the main aims of Cost Accounting ?

(a) Cost Control (b) Cost Ascertainment
(c) Price Fixation (d) All the above

25. Whereas direct cost is allocable to cost unit or cost centers indirect cost can be ______

(a) Allocated (b) Collected (c) Apportioned (d) None of these

26. Direct material is an example of ______

(a) Fixed cost (b) Variable cost
(c) Semi – variable cost (d) Office on cost

27. Which of the following documents is used for issuing materials to the production department

(a) Materials Inspection Note (b) Stores Ledger Note
(c) Stores Material Control Record (d) Materials Requisition

28. ______ is a schedule of materials needed for a job.

(a) Bill of Materials (b) Purchase Requisition
(c) Stock Verification Inventory Sheet (d) Materials Transfer Note

29. Proportional Parts Value Analysis is called as ______

(a) Demand and Supply Method (b) Perpetual Inventory System
(c) ABC Analysis (d) Break Even Analysis

30. ______ is a tool for controlling inventory

(a) Economic Order Quantity (b) Budgeting
(c) Fore Casting (d) Standard Costing

31. The rate of change in the material usage is called ______

(a) Efficiency Ratio (b) Turnover Ratio (c) Activity Ratio (d) Capital Ratio

32. Bin card and the stores ledger are important for ______ records

(a) Economic Order Quantity (b) Perpetual Inventory
(c) ABC Analysis (d) Trend Analysis

33. Average Consumption X Maximum Re-order Period for emergency purchases=

(a) Maximum level (b) Minimum level (c) Re order level (d) Danger level

34. Which of the following example is Multiple Costing?

(a) Spare parts manufacturing (b)Constructional works
(c) Bicycle manufacturing (d) Brick works

35. ______ = Maximum Consumptions x Maximum Re – order period

(a) Danger level (b) Minimum level (c) Re order level (d) Maximum level

36. The quantity of material to be ordered one time is called as ______

(a) ABC Analysis (b) Economic Order Quantity
(c) Perpetual Inventory System (d) Ordering Level

37. ______ helps management to ascertain stock without physical verifications

(a) Material Turnover Ratio (b) Perpetual Inventory System
(c) Re Order Level (d) Economic Order Quantity

38. ______ used for calculating the values of materials on the basis of order of purchase

(a) FIFO (b) LIFO
(c) Specific Price Method (d) Weighted Average Price Method

39. _______ is useful for bulky and non-perishable type of materials

(a) LIFO (b) FIFO

(c) Simple Average Method (d) Weighted Average Method

40. Base Stock Method of pricing materials issue may adopt _______

(a) FIFO (b) LIFO

(c) Both a and b (d) Specific Price Method

41. _______ is credited with saleable value of normal spoilage

(a) Process A/c (b) Normal Loss A/c

(c) Abnormal Loss A/c (d) Costing Profit and Loss A/c

42. Material losses due to abnormal reasons should be transferred to_______

(a) Profit and Loss A/c (b) Costing Profit and Loss A/c

(c) Material Loss A/c (d) Abnormal Loss A/c

43. _______ forms part of cost of productions

(a) Abnormal waste (b) Scrap

(c) Normal waste (d) None of these

44. Goods damaged beyond rectifications refers to

(a) Spoilage (b) Scrap (c) Depreciations (d) Defects

45. The cost of abnormal spoilage is transferred to _______

(a) Good units of Output (b) Costing Profit and Loss Account

(c) Manufacturing Account (d) Trading Profit and Loss Account

46. Wage Sheet is prepared by _______

(a) Production Department (b) Human Resource Department

(c) Finance Department (d) Payroll Department

47. Time and Motion study is conducted by _______

(a) Research Department (b) Engineering Department

(c) Stores Department (d) Purchase Department

48. The basic elements of cost are labour cost, Over head cost and_______

(a) Material cost (b) Distributions cost

(c) Selling cost (d) Controllable cost

49. Under Replacement Method, labour turnover is calculate by _______

(a) $\frac{\text{Number of workers left during the period}}{\text{Average No. of workers during the period}} \times 100$

(b) $\frac{\text{Number of workers addition during the period}}{\text{Average No. of workers during the period}} \times 100$

(c) $\frac{\text{Number of workers replaced during the period}}{\text{Average No. of workers during the period}} \times 100$

(d) None of the above

50. Time Booking is essential for

(a) Idle time workers (b) Piece workers

(c) Time workers (d) Efficient workers

51. _______ suitable to measure individual efficiency

(a) Time Wage System (b) Piece Wage System

(c) Flat time Rate System (d) Differential Time Rate

52. When time saved is 50% of the standard time, the total earnings of a worker are same under _____

(a) Halsey Plans (b) Rowan Plan

(c) Halsey and Rowan Plans (d) Emerson's Plan

53. Taylor's Differential Piece Rate System describes _______

(a) Two Wage Rates System (b) Three Wage Rates System

(c) Four Wage Rate System (d) More than Four Wage Rates System

54. _______ Provides for higher rate to efficient workers

(a) Halsey Plan (b) Taylor's Differential Piece Rate

(c) Merrick's Multiple Piece Rate System (d) Rowan Plan

55. If any scrap arises due to change in the method of production refers to _____

(a) Legitimate Scrap (b) Administrative Scrap

(c) Defective Scrap (d) Saleable Scrap

56. _______ is the aggregate of indirect material cost indirect wages and indirect expenses

(a) Prime Cost (b) Cost of Production

(c) Overhead Cost (d) Total Cost

57. _______ remain constant by changes in the level of production

(a) Fixed Overheads (b) Variable Overheads

(c) Semi-Variable Overheads (d) All the above

58. ______ means charging of overheads to cost units

(a) Apportionment (b) Absorption

(b) Cost Ascertainment (d) Allocation

59. Charging of overheads to cost center refers to

(a) Apportionment (b) absorptions (c) Allocations (d) Distribution

60. The closing balance in cost of sales account transferred to

(a) Costing Profit and Loss Account (b) Profit and Loss Account

(c) Trading Account (d) Manufacturing Account

61. The closing balance in costing profit and loss account indicates ______

(a) Trading Profit and Loss (b) Non-Trading Profit and Loss

(c) Costing Profit and Loss A/c (d) None of these

62. The work in progress control account is credited with

(a) Cost of finished goods (b) Cost of raw materials

(c) Cost of productions (d) Cost of work in progress

63. In costing books ______ is valued at cost of production

(a) Opening stock (b) Closing stock
(c) Both a and b (d) None of these

64. Job Costing is most appropriate for ________

(a) Specific order concerns (b) Large production concerns
(c) Continuous productions concerns (d) Small production concerns

65. _______is suitable for readymade garment industry

(a) Process Costing (b) Batch Costing
(c) Job Costing (d) Contract Costing

66. In contract costing payment cash is made on the basis of ________

(a)Work certified (b) Estimated profit
(c) Contract price (d) Work in progress

67. ________ in a contract, describes that the contract price cover up the excess cost on the happing of specified contingency

(a) Escalation Clause (b) Work Certified
(c) Cost Plus Contract (d) Estimated Profit

68. When the contract is complete, profit is transferred to Profit and Loss A/c is equal to _____

(a) $\frac{2}{3}$ x Notional profit x $\frac{\text{Cash received}}{\text{Work certified}}$ (b) Estimated profit x $\frac{\text{Work certified}}{\text{Contract price}}$

(c) Work completions certificate (d) None of the above

69. The stage where joint products are separated from each other is known as ______

(a) Angle of Incidence (b) Economic Order Quantity
(c) Split of Point (d) Break Even Point

70. Contribution is the difference between ______ and variable cost

(a) Total cost (b) Fixed cost (c) Sales (d) Break Even Sales

71. Breaks, Even Point is indicate

(a) No profit No loss (b) Total cost equal to Total revenues
(c) Both a and b (d) None of these

72. Contributions is also termed as ______

(a) Net Margin (b) Gross Margin (c) Margin of Safety (d) P/v Ratio

73. Marginal Costing Equation is ______

(a) Marginal costing = Prime cost + Variable overheads
(b) Sales = Variable cost + Fixed cost ± Profit or loss
(c) Contributions = Fixed cost + Profit
(d) All the above

74. _______ is used to measure the relationship of contribution to sales

(a) P/v Ratio (b) Break Even Point (c) Key Factors (d) Margin of Safety

75. _______ is the excess of actual sales over sales at Break Even Point

(a) Break Even Point (b) Margin of Safety

(c) Profit Volume Ratio (d) Key Factors

76. Margin of safety can be improved by _______

(a) Increasing selling price (b) Reducing selling price

(c) Reducing the fixed cost (d) Increasing variable cost

77. P/v Ratio can be improved by _________

(a) Increasing selling price (b) Decreasing selling price

(c) Increasing variable cost (d) Reducing fixed cost

78. Marginal Costing and Differential Cost Analysis both are used for

(a) Decision Making (b) Cost Control

(c) Cost Ascertainment (d) All the above

79. $\_\_\_\_\_ = \dfrac{\textbf{Number of actual working day in a period}}{\textbf{Number of working days in the budget period}} \textbf{ x 100}$

(a) Calender Ratio (b) Capacity Ratio (c) Activity Ratio (d) Efficiency Ratio

80. $\_\_\_\_\_ = \dfrac{\textbf{Actual hours worked}}{\textbf{Budgeted hours}} \textbf{ x 100}$

(a) Efficiency Ratio (b) Capacity Ratio (c) Activity Ratio (d) Calendar Ratio

81. $\_\_\_\_\_ = \dfrac{\textbf{Standard hours for actual production}}{\textbf{Actual hours worked}} \textbf{ x 100}$

(a) Efficiency Ratio (b) Turnover Ratio (c) Capacity Ratio (d) Profitability Ratio

82. $\_\_\_\_\_ = \dfrac{\textbf{Standard hours for actual production}}{\textbf{Budgeted standard hours}} \textbf{ x 100}$

(a) Current Ratio (b) Activity Ratio (c) Calendar Ratio (d) Capacity Ratio

83. _____ is a predetermined cost

(a) Standard cost (b) Marginal cost (c) Historical cost (d) Batch Cost

84. Management by Exception is applied in control over _______

(a) Favorable items (b) Unfavorable items

(c) Both a and b (d) None of these

85. Fixed cost + Profit =

(a) Contribution (b) Margin of Safety

(c) Marginal Cost (d) Profit Volume Ratio

86. Material Price Variance = _______ (standard price – Actual price)

(a) Standard quantity (b) Actual quantity

(c) Estimated quantity (d) None of these

87. _______ = Idle hours x Actual rate

(a) Idle time variance
(b) Sales price variance
(c) Material price variance
(d) Material usage variance

88. Material Mix Variance = Standard cost of Standard Mix --

(a) Actual cost of Actual Mix
(b) Standard cost of Actual Mix
(c) Actual cost of materials
(d) Standard rate

89. _______ = [Budgeted Fixed Overheads – Actual Fixed Overhead]

(a) Calendar Variance
(b) Sales Mix Variance
(c) Material Yield Variance
(d) Expenditure Variance

90. Sales price variance = (Actual price – Standard price) x ______

(a) Standard Quantity
(b) Actual Quantity
(c) Actual Rate
(d) Idel Hours

91. _______ = Material Mix Variance + Yield Variance

(a) Total Labour Cost Variance
(b) Sales Price Variance
(c) Material Usage Variance
(d) Idle Time Variance

92. Three types of standards are Current standard, Basic standard and ______

(a) Normal standard
(b) Abnormal standard
(c) Future standard
(d) Actual standard

93. Cost Audit is concerned with the ________

(a) Financial Accounts
(b) Verifications of Cost Accounts
(c) Verifications of Company Account
(d) None of these

94. Material Usage Variance = (Standard usage – Actual usage) x _______

(a) Standard price
(b) Actual price
(c) Standard quantity
(d) Actual quantity

95. _________ through graphs, charges and diagrams can be preferred to descriptive reports

(a) Oral Reports
(b) Special Reports
(c) Visual Reporting
(d) Operating Reports

96. The report should draw managements attention immediately to exceptional matters so that ________ may be carried out effectively

(a) Management Information System
(b) Management by Exceptions
(c) Management by Objectives
(d) None of these

97. Cost Audit helps the ________

(a) Financial Auditor
(b) Company Auditor
(c) Both a and b
(d) None of these

98. Which of the following functions relates to cost control?

(a) Corrective function
(b) Preventive functions
(c) Eliminated functions
(d) None of these

99. Cost Reduction is a ________

(a) Corrective functions
(b) Estimating standards
(c) Preventive functions
(d) Decision making function

100. The Value Analysis is a systematic ______

(a) Effective tool for cost reduction (b) confined to already known facts
(c) Identifications of unnecessary costs (d) Approach for find out necessary costs

101. Cost Accounting has been developed because of ______ of financial Accounting

(a) Limitations (b) Scientific Methods
(c) Modern Concept (d) Scope

102. Cost Accountancy is the Science, Art and ______ of a cost accountant

(a) Professions (b) Practice (c) Key (d) Both 'a' and 'c'

103. Cost Accounts deal partly with facts and partly with ______

(a) Figures (b) Estimates (c) Both 'a' and 'b' (d) Accrual

104. Cost Accounting provide data for managerial ______

(a) Decision making (b) Control (c) Planning (d) All the above

105. Cost Accounting provides the detailed information about ______ of various products, processes, services and operations

(a) Merits (b) Costs (c) Actual (d) Facts and figures

106. Which of the following type of costing refers to Railways ?

(a) Process costing (b)Operating costing
(c) Contract costing (d) Batch costing

107. Indicate which of the following fall under the category "Method of costing"?

(a) Contract costing (b) Differential costing
(c) Standard costing (d) Process costing

108. Which of the following is the Technique of Costing?

(a) Contract costing (b) Differential costing
(c) Uniform costing (d) Job costing

109. Which of the following is the System of Costing?

(a) Process costing (b) Service costing (c) Standard costing (d) Batch costing

110. Job Costing refers to

(a) Methods of costing (b) Techniques of costing
(c) Systems of costing (d) None of these

111. Historical costing refers to

(a) Methods of costing (b) Systems of costing
(c) Continuous costing (d) Technique of costing

112. Marginal Costing refers to

(a) Standard costing (b) Marginal costing
(c) Techniques of costing (d) None of these

113. The total of all direct elements of cost refers to ______

(a) Prime cost (b) Factory cost
(c) Office on cost (d) Cost of productions

114. ________ costs are partly fixed and partly variable in relations to out put

(a) Semi – variable cost (b) Sunk cost

(c) Research cost (d) Policy cost

115. Which of the following refers to opportunity cost?

(a) The benefit foregone (b) The disadvantage foregone

(c) Multiple costing (d) Cash outlays

116. Work Cost is a total of ________

(a) Prime cost + Office on cost

(b) Direct material + Direct labour + Direct expenses + Work expenses

(c) Prime cost + Selling overheads

(d) Prime cost + Distribution overheads

117. The sacrifices that are made when returns are rejected are known as ______

(a) Production cost (b) Opportunity cost (c) Replacement cost (d) Conversion cost

118. Depreciation is the nature of ______

(a) Variable cost (b) Semi variable cost

(c) Fixed cost (d) Controllable cost

119. Added Value is the change in ______

(a) Notional value (b) Municipal value (c) Market value (d) Actual value

120. Rent of factory premises is an example of

(a) Variable cost (b) Semi variable cost

(c) Fixed cost (d) None of these

121. ______ refers to depreciated value of plant at the time of considering the replacement of that plant

(a) Imputed cost (b) Standard cost (c) Sunk cost (d) Marginal cost

122. Rent on own building is one of the example of the following cost

(a) Sunk cost (b) Imputed cost

(c) Out of pocket cost (d) opportunity cost

123. Which of the following costs are not assigned to products?

(a) Period costs (b)Marginal cost (c) Standard costs (d) Sunk costs

124. Which of the following refers to Material Control?

(a) Purchase of materials, storing of materials and issue of material

(b) Production, financing and marketing

(c) Allocation, ascertainment and estimations

(d) None of these

125. Which of the following aspect relates to Material Control?

(a) Financial aspect and production aspect (b) Accounting aspect and operational aspect

(c) Material handling and financial aspect (d) None of these

126. ________ is adopted to ascertain the cost of operating a department .

(a) Operation costing (b) Operating costing
(c) Departmental costing (d) Multiple costing

127. Stock Verification Sheets are maintained to record on the basis

(a) Day to day verifications (b) Auditing
(c) Physical verifications (d) Continuous verifications

128. A cost which can be influenced by the action of a specified number of an undertaking is known as ________

(a) Controllable cost (b) Variable cost
(c) Uncontrollable cost (d) Normal cost

129. The quantity of material to be ordered at one time is known as ________

(a) Re – Order Quantity (b) Economic Order Quantity
(c) Minimum Reorder Level (d) Maximum Reorder Level

130. A Cost which cannot be influenced by the action of a specified number of an undertaking is known as ________

(a) Controllable cost (b) Fixed cost
(c) Uncontrollable cost (d) Conversion cost

131. Re – Ordering Level = Maximum Re – Order Period X ________

(a) Minimum Re – order period (b) Average Inventory
(c) Maximum Consumption (d) Normal Re – order period

132. Inventory Turnover Ratio = Cost of Inventory during the period

(a) Cost of inventory consumed during the period
(b) Cost of average inventory held during the period
(c) Economic Order Quantity
(d) Total inventory

133. ________ is a quantitative record of receipts, issues and balances of items.

(a) Bin Card (b) Store Ledger
(c) Inspection Report (d) Goods Received Note

134. Bin Card is maintained by ________

(a) Material Manager (b) Store keeper (c) Supervisor (d) Accountant

135. Materials are issued by the store keeper against ________

(a) Material Issue Analysis Sheet (b) Store Debit note
(c) Material Requisitions Note (d) Material Return Note

136. ________ is an analytical statement of materials issued to different jobs.

(a) Bin Card System (b) Stores Ledger
(c) Material Abstract (d) Goods Received Note

137. Which of the following method of valuing material issues is suitable in times of raising prices?

(a) First In First Out Method (FIFO) (b) Last In First Out Method (LIFO)
(c) Simple Average Method (d) Specific Price Method

138. Which of the following method of valuing material issues is suitable in time of falling prices?

(a) First In First Out Method (FIFO) (b) Last In First Out Method (LIFO)
(c) Market Price Method (d) Inflated Price Method

139. _______ is suitable for materials which shrink in size or lose in weight with the passage of time.

(a) Average Cost Method (b) Base Stock Method
(c) Specific Price Method (d) Inflated Price Method

140. ________ is suitable for valuing material issued for a particular job or work or contract

(a) Specific Price Method (b) Inflated Price Method
(c) Standard Price Method (d) Market Price Method

141. ______ is suitable, when materials issued are valued at a price at which they can be replaced

(a) Market Price Method (b) FIFO
(c) LIFO (d) Base Stock Method

142. Bill of Material is suitable for ______

(a) Material inspections (b) Material receipts
(c) Material requisitions(d) Stock of materials

143. _______ does not forms part of cost of productions

(a) Material losses (b) Normal waste
(c) Abnormal waste (d) None of these

144. Any loss caused by abnormal conditions should be transferred to ______

(a) Costing Profit and Loss A/c (b) Production A/c
(c) Trading P & L A/c (d) Manufacturing Process A/c

145. _______ is a second major elements of cost

(a) Material cost (b) Labour cost (c) Other expenses (d) Overhead cost

146. _______ is a method of evaluating the job in terms of its money value

(a) Job Prescription (b) Job Analysis (c) Job Evaluations (d) Merit Rating

147. Which of the following methods is used to measure time keeping?

(a) Manual method and mechanical methods
(b) Costing methods and financial methods
(c) Qualitative methods and quantitative methods
(d) None of these

148. _______ is suitable for evaluation of the workers for wages increase, promotion and training.

(a) Merit Rating (b) Job Evaluations (c) Job Card (d) Job Analysis

149. Which of the following documents are used for Time Booking?

(a) Daily Time Sheets (b) Job Cards (c) Job Tickers (d) All the above

150. Cost of abnormal idle time is should be charged to ______

(a) Costing Profit and Loss A/c (b) Manufacturing Process A/c

(c) Trading P & L A/c (d) Work in Progress A/c

151. Which of the following costs relate to labour turnover?

(a) Contract costs and Process costs (b) Job costs and Batch costs

(c) Preventive cost and Replacement costs (d) Uniform costing and Job costing

151. The cost of overtime premium arises due to any abnormal reason is debited to ______

(a) Profit and Loss Account (b) Costing Profit and Loss Account

(c) Production Account (d) Manufacturing Process Account

152. When the idle capacity is beyond control, the cost of the same is debited to______

(a) Cost Profit and Loss Account (b) Profit and Loss Account

(c) Plant and Machinery Account (d) Manufacturing Process Account

153. Inventory Control Technique may be employed in

(a) Manufacturing business (b) Merchandising business

(c) Both a and b (d) None of these

154. Which of the following methods of wage payment does not guarantee wages on time basis

(a) Halsey Premium System (b) Rowan Premium System

(c) Piece Rate System (d) Time Rate System

155. Time keeping facilitate ______

(a) Preparation of Payroll (b) Job Evaluation

(c) Labour Turnover (d) Merit Rating

156. Taylor's differential piece rate system provides for higher rate to ______ workers

(a) Efficient (b) Inefficient (c) Skilled (d) Casual

157. ______ is most suitable when quality of work is of prime importance

(a) Piece Wage System (b) Time Wage System

(c) Premium Bonus Plan (d) None of these

159. Under Merrick's Multiple Piece Rate System, 110% of the ordinary piece rate is given to workers whose level of performance between ______ of the standard output

(a) 84% to 100% (b) 83% to 120% (c) 83% to 100% (d) 80% to 100%

160. Overhead cost is the aggregate of Indirect Material Cost, Indirect Wages an ______

(a) Direct material (b) Direct labour. (c) Direct expenses (d) Indirect expenses

161. ______ refers to those fixed overhead costs which continue to be incurred even when there is no productions

(a) Fixed cost (b) Overhead cost (c) Committed cost (d) Variable cost

162. he apportionment of stores service expenses is on the basis of ______

(a) Value of materials consumed (b) Number of employees

(c) Quantity of materials (d) Stock of materials

163. Supervisor's salary is an example of _____

(a) Indirect materials cost (b) Indirect labour cost

(c) Direct labour cost (d) Indirect other expenses

164. Basis of Apportionment of advertising expenses is _____

(a) Actual expenses (b) Percentage of sales

(c) Total cost (d) Both a and b

165. Basis of Apportionment of electric power expenses is _____

(a) Horse – Power of Machines (b) KWH

(c) Both a and b (d) No. of light points

166. The expenses of ordinary packing is relates to _______

(a) Cost of materials (b) Prime cost (c) Office on cost (d) Both a and b

167. In case the amount of over or under absorbed overheads is charged is _______

(a) Profit and Loss Account (b) Costing Profit and Loss Account

(c) Factory Overheads Account (d) Production Overhead Account

168. Discount and allowances cost is an item of _______

(a) Selling overhead (b) Office on cost (c) Factory cost (d) Works cost

169. Which of the following relates to storage cost ?

(a) Office overhead (b) Distributions overhead

(c) Selling cost (d) Factory on cost

170. Which of the following expenses are incurred for taking managerial decisions?

(a) Credit and collection costs (b) Notional expenses

(c) Normal expenses (d) Administration cost

171. A Cost Sheet is prepared on the basis of actual cost data is termed as _______

(a) Historical Cost Sheet (b) Estimated Cost Sheet

(c) Cost Statement (d) Income Statement

172. Which of the following is considered to determine the rate of depreciation of plant and machinery?

(a) Time and usage factor (b) Element of maintenance

(c) Element of interest (d) All the above

173. When speed of production is beyond control, the suitable method of wage payment is

(a) Time Rate System (b) Piece Rate System

(c) Halsey Premium System (d) Rowan Bonus Plan

174. Rent of owned building is ______ back to costing profit to reconcile it with profit as per financial books

(a) Added (b) Deducted (c) Both a and b (d) None of these

175. Dividend received but not included in cost accounts is to be ______ back to costing profit in reconciling profit with financial profit

(a) Deducted (b) Added (c) Both a and b (d) None of these

176. Donation paid is a nature of ________

(a) Financial Accounts (b) Cost Accounts
(c) Both a and b (d) Real Account

177. Interest on capital is a nature of ________

(a) Financial Account (b) Cost Accounts (c) Both a and b (d) Nominal Account

178. Under Integral Accounting System, cost and financial accounts are ____ in one ledger

(a) Separated (b) Merged (c) Both 'a' and 'b' (d) Different

179. _____ of accounts is possible under integrated accounting system

(a) Duplications (b) Commission (c) Omission (d) Malpractice

180. There is _____ of reconciling cost and financial accounts under integrated accounts

(a) Need (b) No need (c) Both 'a' and 'b' (d) None of these

181. The need for reconciliation of cost and financial results arise in cases where cost accounts are maintained _____of financial accounts.

(a) Dependent (b) Independent (c) Separated (d) Both b ad c

182. Dividend paid is the nature of ______

(a) Marginal profit (b) Net profit
(c) Appropriation of profit (d) Revenue expenses

183. Closing stock in cost accounts is valued at ______

(a) Factory cost (b) Prime cost
(c) Both a and b (d) Cost price or Market price

184. In Job Costing each _____ is a cost unit to which all costs are assigned

(a) Batch (b) Process (c) Job (d) Contract

185. Opening or closing stock in financial accounts is valued at _______

(a) Factory cost (b) Cost price or market price whichever is less
(c) Prime cost (d) Cost of production

186. Any loss raised on an in complete contract is transferred to ________

(a) Costing Profit and Loss A/c (b) Contract A/c
(c) Profit and Loss A/c (d) Normal Loss A/c

187. Contract which have completed more than half, the profit to be credited to Profit and Loss A/c will be equal to ________

(a) $\frac{2}{3}$ x Notional profit x $\frac{\text{Cash received}}{\text{Work certified}}$ (b) $\frac{2}{4}$ x Notional profit x $\frac{\text{Work certified}}{\text{Cash received}}$

(c) $\frac{2}{3}$ x Notional profit x $\frac{\text{Work certified}}{\text{Contract price}}$ (d) None of the above

188. Which of the following concerns prefer cost–plus contract?

(a) Small Concerns (b) Large Concerns
(c) Government Company (d) Building Contractors

189. Operating Costing is also known as _______

(a) Service Costing (b) Incremental Costing
(c) Marginal Costing (d) Process Costing

190. In contract costing payment of cash to the contractor is made on the basis of _________ work

(a) Estimate (b) Completed (c) Certified (d) Contract price

191. Contract is a nature of _____

(a) Big job (b) Small work (c) Medium job (d) All the above

192. When actual loss is more than the estimated loss the difference between two is considered to be _______

(a) Normal loss (b) Estimated loss (c) Actual loss (d) Abnormal loss

193. When actual loss is less than the estimated loss the difference between loss is considered as

(a) Normal gain (b) Abnormal gain (c) Abnormal loss (d) Normal loss

194. Which of the following is included in work in progress under contract costing?

(a) Work Certified (b) Work Uncertified (c) Both a and b (d) Contract Price

195. When 2000 units are 60% complete in a process, it is equivalent to ________ completed units

(a) 1000 (b) 600 (c) 1200 (d) 1500

196. Work uncertified is valued at _______

(a) Cost price (b) Contract price (c) Cost plus profit (d) All the above

197. Abnormal process loss should be transferred to ______

(a) Profit and Loss A/c (b) Abnormal Loss A/c
(c) Costing and Loss A/c (d) Process A/c

198. The cost of ______ process loss is absorbed in the cost of production of good units

(a) Normal (b) Abnormal (c) Material (d) Productions

199. Repairs are done within a factory or at customers premises refers to ______

(a) Job costing (b) Batch costing (c) Contract costing (d) Process costing

200. Equivalent Units represent the production process in terms of ______

(a) Completed Units (b) Incompleted Units
(c) Estimated Units (d) Both a and b

201. The method of costing used in electricity company is termed as ______

(a) Process costing (b) Batch costing (c) Job costing (d) Operating costing

202. Profit = Contribution _______

(a) Variable cost (b) Fixed cost (c) Marginal cost (d) Prime cost

203. ______ means that the profit are made at higher rate and vice verse

(a) Limiting Factor (b) Angle of Incidence
(c) Margin of Safety (d) Break Even Point

204. _________ is useful to the management for profit planning

(a) Marginal costing (b) Historical costing
(c) Uniform costing (d) Process Costing

205. Marginal Costing is suitable for price fixation during the period of ____

(a) Regression (b) Boom (c) Depression (d) Introductions

206. Selling goods below marginal cost can be adopted for _______

(a) Long period (b) Medium period
(c) Shorter period (d) Day to day affairs

207. ______ is taken in to considerations to decide the probability of different products due to shortage of materials

(a) Marginal Costing (b) Make or Buy Decision
(c) Key Factors (d) Productions Planning

208. _______ is made by comparing variable cost with outside's purchase price

(a) Uniform Costing (b) Key Factors
(c) Productions Planning (d) Make or Buy Decisions

209. Marginal cost = _________ + Variable Overheads

(a) Prime cost (b) Works cost (c) Factory cost (d) Fixed cost

210. Master Budget is _________ incorporating its component functional budgets

(a) Productions Budget (b) Sales Budget
(c) Cash Budget (d) Summary Budget

211. Zero – Base Budgeting is useful in budgeting process because of it tries to overcomes the weakness of ______

(a) Master Budget (b) Conventional Budgeting
(c) Functional Budgeting (d) Flexible Budgeting

212. Contribution can be calculated by _______

(a) Sales x P/V Ratio (b) Sales x (1 – P/V Ratio)
(c) B.E.P. x P/V Ratio (d) None of these

213. Standard Costing is more suitable in _______ industries

(a) Service (b) Contract
(c) Process and Engineering (d) Agriculture

214. _______ is defined as a budget which is prepared for use unrelated over a long period of time

(a) Flexible Budget (b) Basic Budget
(c) Zero – Base Budget (d) Master Budget

215. Volume Variance = Standard Rate (Actual output - ______)

(a) Budgeted Output (b) Actual Rate
(c) Actual Usage (d) None of these

216. Profit Volume Ratio can be calculated by ______

(a) $\frac{\text{Contribution}}{\text{Sales}} \times 100$ (b) Sales x Contribution per unit

(c) $\frac{\text{Fixed cost}}{\text{Contribution per unit}} \times 100$ (d) None of the above

217. A group of columns in a purchase card is known as a ______

(a) Data processing (b) Hard ward (c) Field (d) Verifier

218. Financial Audit aims at verification of ______

(a) Financial Accounts (b) Cost Accounts

(c) Both a and b (d) Company Accounts

219. The technique of Marginal Costing can be used in conjunction with ______

(a) Standard costing (b) Budgetary control

(c) Both a and b (d) Absorption costing

220. Which of the following cost is suitable for decision making ?

(a) Absorption costing (b)Marginal costing

(c) Direct costing (d) Both b and c

221. Payment of ideal time is adopted when the workers are paid on ______

(a) Time basis (b) Output basis

(c) Time and Output (d) Time, Out put and Time saving

222. Standard costing works on the principles of ______

(a) Management by Objectives (b) Management by Exceptions

(c) Budgotary Control (d) Marginal Costing

223. Equivalent units indicate the production process of ______

(a) Completed units (b) Uncompleted units

(c) Estimated units (d) Anticipated units

224. Overhead Cost Variance is the difference between

(a) Recovered overheads and Budgeted overheads

(b) Budgeted overheads and Actual overheads

(c) Budgeted overheads and Standard overheads

(d) None of these

225. Overhead Expenditure Variance is the difference between

(a) Recovered overheads and Budgeted overheads

(b) Budgeted overheads and Actual overheads

(c) Standard overheads and Actual overheads

(d) None of these

226. Andard hour is refers to ______

(a) Estimated hour (b) Ideal hour (c) Hypothetical hour (d) None of these

227. ______ is used for pricing issues of costly materials

(a) Specific Price Method (b) Periodic Weighted Average Price Method

(c) First In First Out Method (d) Market Price Method

228. Period cost means ______

(a) Variable cost (b) Fixed cost

(c) Prime cost (d) Semi – variable cost

229. Which of the following cost relates to fixed cost?

(a) Setting–up costs (b) Material cost

(c) Labour cost (d) Other overheads

230. Which of the following is most suitable for cost control?

(a) Standard costing (b) Post costing

(c) Continuous costing (d) Job costing

231. Budgetary Control and Standard Costing are

(a) Independent on each other (b) Same

(c) Interrelated with each other (d) Unrelated with each other

232. One of the objectives of standard costing is to

(a) Promote and measure performance (b) Control and reduce costs

(c) Simplify productions operation (d) Set cost of manufacture

233. Which of the following relates to appropriations of profits?

(a) Dividend paid (b) Commission paid (c) Interest paid (d) Income tax paid

234. Sales value variance is the difference between ______

(a) Actual sales and Budgeted overheads

(b) Budgeted sales and Actual sales

(c) Budgeted sales and Actual over heads

(d) None of these

235. ______ refers to works cost before adjusting stock of work in progress

(a) Gross works cost (b) Net works cost

(c) Cost of production (d) Cost of goods sold

236. The system which determines what should be the cost in advance of productions is called ______ system

(a) Process costing (b) Standard costing

(c) Historical costing (d) Batch costing

237. Which of the following formula is used for the calculation of Break Even Point in units?

(a) $\frac{\text{Contribution}}{\text{Sales}} \times 100$ (b) $\frac{\text{Fixed cost}}{\text{Contributions permit}} \times 100$

(c) $\frac{\text{Fixed cost}}{\text{P / V ratio}} \times 100$ (d) None of the above

238. Standard for overheads is based on budgeted _____

(a) Output (b) Input

(c) Semi finished products (d)Income and expenditure

239. Costing method in which fixed factory overheads are added to inventory is

(a) Direct costing (b) Marginal costing

(c) Absorptions costing (d) Standard costing

240. When P/V ratio is 50% and fixed cost is Rs.20,000 the Break Even Point will be

(a) 10,000 (b) 40,000 (c) 60,000 (d) 50,000

241. When Profit – Volume Ratio is 40% and sales value Rs.20,000 the variable costs will be

(a) Rs.3000 (b) Rs.8000 (c) Rs.5000 (d) Rs.12000

242. When Margin of Safety is 20% and p/v ratio is 60% the profit will be

(a) 15% (b) 30 (c) 12% (d) 24%

243. When sales are Rs.1,00,000 fixed cost Rs.10,000 p/v ratio 20% the amount of profit will be

(a) Rs.15,000 (b) Rs.4000 (c) Rs.6000 (d) Rs.10000

ANSWERS

1. (c) Ascertaining Cost
2. (a) Internal Reporting
3. (b) Cost Accounting
4. (a) Cost
5. (a) Valuation of inventory
6. (b) Management Accounting
7. (b) Estimated
8. (a) Differential cost
9. (b) Variable cost
10. (d) Fixed cost
11. (b) Opportunity cost
12. (d) Conversion cost
13. (c) Cost of production and work in progress
14. (d) Car manufacturing industry
15. (a) Works cost
16. (b) Prime cost
17. (d) Process
18. (a) Job costing
19. (b) Students
20. (d) Per bed per day
21. (a) Batch
22. (b) Notional Costs
23. (c) Cost Sheet
24. (d) All the above
25. (c) Apportioned
26. (b) Variable cost
27. (d) Materials Requisition
28. (a) Bill of Materials
29. (c) ABC Analysis
30. (a) Economic Order Quantity
31. (b) Turnover Ratio
32. (b) Perpetual Inventory
33. (d) Danger Level
34. (c) Bicycle Manufacturing
35. (c) Re – Order Level
36. (b) Economic Order Quantity
37. (b) Perpetual Inventory System
38. (d) Weighted Average Price Method
39. (a) LIFO
40. (c) Both a and b
41. (a) Process A/c
42. (b) Costing Profit and Loss A/c
43. (c) Normal waste

44. (a) Spoilage
45. (b) Costing Profit and Loss A/c
46. (d) Pay roll Department
47. (b) Engineering Dept
48. (a) Material cost
49. (c) $\frac{\text{No. of workers replaced during the period}}{\text{Average No. of workers during the period}} \times 100$
50. (c) Time works
51. (b) Piece Wage System
52. (c) Halsey and Rowan Plans
53. (a) Two Wage Rates
54. (b) Taylor's Differential Piece Rate
55. (b) Administrative scrap
56. (c) Over head cost
57. (a) Fixed overheads
58. (b) Absorption
59. (a) Apportionment
60. (a) Costing Profit and Loss Account
61. (c) Costing Profit and Loss Account
62. (a) Cost of finished goods
63. (b) Closing stock
64. (a) Specific order concern
65. (c) Job costing
66. (a) Work Certified
67. (a) Escalation Clause
68. (b) Estimated profit $\times \frac{\text{Work Certified}}{\text{Contract Price}}$
69. (c) Split off Point
70. (c) Sales
71. (c) Both 'a' and 'b'
72. (b) Gross Margin
73. (d) All the above
74. (a) P/v Ratio
75. (b) Margin of Safety
76. (c) Reducing the fixed cost
77. (a) Increasing selling price
78. (d) All the above
79. (a) Calendar Ratio
80. (b) Capacity Ratio
81. (a) Efficiency Ratio
82. (b) Activity Ratio
83. (a) Standard cost
84. (b) Unfavorable items
85. (a) Contribution
86. (b) Actual quantity
87. (a) Idle Time Variance
88. (b) Standard Cost of Actual Mix
89. (d) Expenditure Variance
90. (b) Actual Quantity
91. (c) Material Usage Variance
92. (a) Normal Standard
93. (b) Verification of Cost Accounts
94. (a) Standard Price
95. (c) Visual Reporting
96. (b) Management by Exception
97. (c) Both A and B
98. (b) Preventive function
99. (a). Corrective function
100. (c) Identification of unnecessary costs
101. (a) Limitations
102. (b) Practice
103. (c) Both a and b
104. (a) Decision Making
105. (b) Costs
106. (b) Operating costing
107. (a) Contract costing
108. (b) Differential costing
109. (c) Standard costing
110. (a) Methods of costing
111. (b) Systems of costing
112. (c) Techniques of costing
113. (a) Prime cost
114. (a) Semi – variable cost
115. (a) The benefit foregone
116. (b) Direct material + Direct labour + Direct expenses + Work expenses
117. (b) Opportunity cost
118. (b) Semi Variable cost
119. (c) Market Value
120. (c) Fixed cost
121. (c) Sunk cost
122. (b) Imputed cost
123. (a) Period cost

124. (a) Purchase of materials, Storing of materials and Issue of materials
125. (b) Accounting aspect and operational Aspect
126. (c) Departmental costing
127. (c) Physical verification
128. (a) Controllable cost
129. (b) Economic Order Quantity
130. (c) Uncontrollable cost
131. (c) Maximum consumption
132. (a) Cost of average inventory held during the period
133. (a) Bin Card
134. (b) Store keeper
135. (c) Material Requisition Note
136. (c) Materials Abstract
137. (b) Last In First Out Method (LIFO)
138. (a) First In First Out Method (FIFO)
139. (d) Inflated Price Method
140. (a) Specific Price Method
141. (a) Market Price Method
142. (c) Material Requisition
143. (c) Abnormal Waste
144. (a) Costing Profit and Loss A/c.
145. (b) Labour cost
146. (c) Job Evaluation
147. (a) Manual Methods and Mechanical Methods
148. (a) Merit Rating
149. (d) All the above
150. (a) Costing Profit and Loss A/c
151. (c) Preventive costs and Replacement cost
152. (b) Costing Profit and Loss Account
153. (a) Costing Profit and Loss Account
154. (c) Both a and b
155. (c) Piece Rate System
156. (a) Preparation of payroll
157. (a) Efficient
158. (b) Time Wage System
159. (c) 83% to 100%
160. (d) Indirect expenses
161. (c) Committed costs
162. (a) Value of materials consumed
163. (b) Indirect labour cost
164. (d) Both a and b
165. (a) Horse-power of machines
166. (d) Both a and b
167. (b) Costing Profit and Loss Account
168. (a) Selling Over head
169. (b) Distribution Over head
170. (b) Notional expenses
171. (a) Historical Cost Sheet
172. (d) All the above
173. (a) Time Rate System
174. (a) Added
175. (b) Added
176. (a) Financial Account
177. (b) Cost Accounts
178. (b) Merged
179. (a) Duplication
180. (b) No need
181. (d) Both b and c
182. (c) Appropriation of profits
183. (c) Both a and b
184. (c) Job
185. (b) Cost price or Market price whichever is less
186. (c) Profit and Loss A/c
187. (a) $\frac{2}{3}$ x Notional profit x $\frac{\text{Cash received}}{\text{Work certified}}$
188. (c) Government
189. (a) Service Costing
190. (c) Certified
191. (a) Big job
192. (a) Abnormal loss
193. (b) Abnormal gain
194. (c) Both a and b
195 (c) 1200
196. (a) Cost price
197. (c) Costing profit and Loss A/c
198. (a) Normal
199. (a) Job Costing
200. (b) Incompleted Units

201. (d) Operating costing
202. (b) Fixed cost
203. (b) Angle of Incidence
204. (a) Marginal Costing
205. (c) Depression
206. (c) Shorter Period
207. (c) Key factors
208. (d) Make (or) Buy Decisions
209. (a) Prime cost
210. (d) Summary Budget
211. (b) Conventional Budgeting
212. (a) Sales X P/V Ratio
213. (c) Process and Engineering
214. (b) Basic Budgets
215. (a) Budgeted Output
216. (a) $\frac{\text{Contribution}}{\text{Sales}} \times 100$
217. (c) Field
218. (a) Both a and b
219 (c) Both a and b
220. (d) Both b and c
221. (a) Time Basis
222. (b) Management by Exception
223. (a) Completed Units
224. (a) Recovered overheads and Actual overheads
225 (b) Budgeted overheads and Actual overheads
226. (b) Hypothetical hours
227. (a) Specific Price Method
228. (b) Fixed cost
229. (a) Setting–up costs
230. (a) Standard Costing
231. (c) Interrelated with each other
232. (b) Control and reduce costs
233. (a) Dividend paid
234. (b) Budgeted sales and Actual sales
235. (a) Gross works cost
236. (b) Standard costing
237. (b) $\frac{\text{Fixed cost}}{\text{Contributions per unit}}$
238. (a) Output
239. (c) Absorption Costing
240. (a) Rs.40,000
241. (b) Rs.12,000
242. (c) 12%
243. (a) 10,000

*****

XI

BUSINESS LAW

1. **Law of Contract is**
   (a) Contract as an agreement enforceable by law
   (b) Is intention to create legal relationship
   (c) Lawful consideration
   (d) Both b and c
2. **Which of the following Principles relate to law of contract?**
   (a) An agreement (b) Its enforceability by law
   (c) Rights of Parties (d) Both a and b
3. **Agreement is**
   (a) Agreement = Capacity + Acceptance
   (b) Agreement = Offer + Acceptance
   (c) Agreement = Considerations + Acceptance
   (d) Agreement = Offer
4. **An agreement is a voidable contract when it is _________**
   (a) Enforceable by law at the options of the aggrieved party
   (b) Enforceable by both parties
   (c) Not enforceable by both parties
   (d) None of these
5. **An agreement not enforceable by law is ______**
   (a) Valid (b) Voidable (c) Void (d) Legal Contract

6. **_______ means an agreement which is enforceable by law at the options of one party there to, but not at the option of other**

(a) Void Agreement (b) Void Contract (c) Illegal Agreement (d) Voidable Contract

7. **A contract in which the terms are stated in words by the parties is called as _______**

(a) Express Contract (b) Implied Contract (c) Implied Contract (d) Quasi Contract

8. **An obligation created by law, regardless of agreement is refers to**

(a) Express Contract (b) Quasi Contract (c) Implied Contract (d) Executory Contract

9. **A contract in which the promises of both the parties have yet to be performed is called as _____**

(a) Unilateral Contract (b) Executed Contract
(c) Executory Contract (d) Quasi Contract

10. **A contract in which both the parties have yet to perform their obligation is called as ______**

(a) Bilateral Contract (b) Unilateral Contract
(c) Executory Contract (d) Executed Contract

11. **An offer made to a particular person is called as _______**

(a) Specific Offer (b) General Offer
(c) Implied Offer (d) Gross Offer

12. **Which of the following not a legal rules in an offer?**

(a) It must be certain
(b) It must be intended to create legal relations
(c) It must be communicated to the offeree
(d) None of these

13. **Which of the following is relates to lapse of offer or comes to an end?**

(a) By lapse of the specified or reasonable time
(b) By death or insanity of the offeror
(c) By counter offer
(d) All the above

14. **There is a counter offer when**

(a) The offeree gives conditional acceptance
(b) The offeror makes a fresh offer
(c) The offeree makes some query
(d) None of the above

15. **When offer is made to the world at large is called as _______**

(a) Specific Offer (b) General Offer (c) Implied Offer (d) Both a and b

16. **Communication of offer by auctions is ______**

(a) An offer (b) An invitation to offer
(c) No offer (d) None of these

17. ________ is an expression by the offeree of his willingness to be bound by the terms of the offer

(a) Offer (b) Consideration (c) Agreement (d) Acceptance

18. Which of the following is considerations?

(a) Must move at the desire of the promissor

(b) May move from the promissor

(c) May move at the desire of any third party

(d) None of the above

19. _______ means something in return from the promise or any other person

(a) Offer (b) Acceptance (c) Considerations (d) Agreement

20. Consideration in a contract is refers to

(a) May be past, present or future (b) May be present or future only

(c) Must be present (d) Must be future

21 A stranger to a contract

(a) Can not sue (b) Can sue

(c) Can sue only in well recognized cases (d) None of these

22. Consideration must be something which the promissor

(a) is already bound to do (b) is not already bound to do

(c) may do voluntarily (d) may not do voluntarily

23. A promise to compensate wholly or in part, a person who has already voluntarily done something for the promissor

(a) Is enforceable

(b) Is not enforceable because it is without considerations

(c) Is not enforceable

(d) None of these

24. An agreement made without considerations is ________

(a) Valid (b) Voidable (c) Void (d) None of these

25. When an agreement with or by a minor is ________

(a) Void (b) Voidable at the option of the minor

(c) Voidable at the option of the other party (d) None of these

26. On the attaining the age of majority a minor's agreement is

(a) Can be ratified (b) Can not be ratified

(c) Void (d) Valid

27. State the following person can not be competent to enter into contract?

(a) Minors

(b) Persons of unsound mind

(c) Persons disqualified by any law to which they are subject

(d) All the above

28. A Minor _______ into a contract of partnership.

(a) Can not enter (b) Can enter (c) May enter (d) None of these

29. A lunatic can enter is to a contract when

(a) he is of sound mind (b) he is a minor

(c) he has not attained eighteen years of age (d) he is an insolvent

30. A minor enters into a contract for the purchase of certain necessaries in such case

(a) he is not personally liable to pay (b) he is liable to pay

(c) his estate is liable to pay (d) None of these

31. A person who is usually of unsound mind, but occasionally of sound mind

(a) may enter into a contract when he is of sound mind

(b) may not enter into a contract even when he is of sound mind

(c) Can not enter into a contract

(d) None of these

32. During the war an Indian citizen _______ into a contract with an alien enemy

(a) Can not enter (b) Can enter

(c) May enter (d) None of these

33. The contractual capacity of a statutory corporation is regulated by

(a) Its Memorandum of Association and the provisions of the Companies Act

(b) The terms of contract entered into with a third party

(c) The term of contract entered into with a company

(d) None of these

34. An agreement with minor is

(a) Void Contract (b) Voidable Contract

(c) Valid Contract (d) Quasi –Contract

35. S. Shanmugam Pillai Vs.K.S. Pillai (1973) 2,SCC 312 Case deals with

(a) Communications of offer (b) An agreement of idiot

(c) A minor's agreement (d) Fraud

36. Where consent is caused by fraud or misrepresentations the contract is

(a) Void

(b) Not affected

(c) Voidable at the options of the party whose consent is so caused

(d) Valid

37. Where both the parties to an agreement are under a mistake as to a matter of fact essential to the agreement. The agreement is

(a) Voidable (b) Absolutely void (c) Valid (d) Not affected

38. Where only one of the parties is under a mistake as to a matter fact, the contract is not

(a) Voidable (b) Void (c) Valid (d) Affected

39. Where a person is made to enter into a contract through the inducement of another but through no fault of his own, there is a mistake as to the nature of the contract, and the contract is ________

(a) Voidable (b) Void (c) Valid (d) Not affected

40. Which of the following refers to Coercion?

(a) Physical character (b) Treat of an offence
(c) Involves a criminal Act (d) Moral character

41. Which of the following is not refers to undue influence?

(a) Consent is given under moral influence (b) Mainly of physical character
(c) No criminal act is involved (d) Influence of moral character

42. Coercion does not include

(a) Fear (b) Physical compulsion
(c) Menace to goods (d) None of these

43. Fraud exists when it is shown that a false representation has been made

(a) Without belief in its truth
(b) Knowingly
(c) Recklessly, not carrying whether it is true of false
(d) All the above

44. Which one of the following there is cases no presumption of undue influence?

(a) Husband and wife (b) Landlord and tenant
(c) Creditor and debtor (d) All the above

45. Which of the following is not fraud?

(a) Intentions to deceive the other party
(b) The act is deliberate or willful
(c) Making suggestions in which the party does not believes it to be true
(d) None of these

46. The consent is given under the threat of an offence is ________

(a) Coercion (b) Undue influence (c) Misrepresentation (d) Fraud

47. Which one of the following relationship raises presumption of undue influence?

(a) Doctor and Patient (b) Parent and Child
(c) Teacher and Student (d) All the above

48. ________ is defined as an erroneous belief about something

(a) Mistake (b) Misrepresentations
(c) Fraud (d) Coercion

49. If there is error in cause, the contract is

(a) Void (b) Voidable (c) Valid (d) Not affected

50. If there is error in consensus, the agreement is

(a) Voidable (b) Valid (c) Not affected (d) Void

51. If there is a unilateral mistake as regards identity caused by fraud of the other party, the contract is

(a) Valid (b) Voidable (c) Void (d) Not affected

52. If there is a fraudulent misrepresentations as to the contents of the title to the subject matter the contract is

(a) Void (b) Voidable (c) Valid (d) Not affected

53. If there is a fraudulent misrepresentations to the quality of the subject matter the contract is

(a) Void (b) Voidable (c) Valid (d) Not affected at all

54. Solwer Vs Potter (1940) I K B 271 case deals with

(a) Coercion (b) Undue influence

(c) Misrepresentations (d) Mistake as regards identity

55. When consideration or object is unlawful, the contract is

(a) Void (b) illegal (c) Voidable (d) Not affected

56. An agreement made with an alien enemy is unlawful

(a) On the ground of public policy

(b) Because it becomes difficult to be performed

(c) Both 'a' and 'b'

(d) None of these

57. Where the consideration is an act of sexual immorality, the agreement is _______

(a) Void (b) Voidable (c) Valid (d) Not affected

58. An agreement between a husband and wife for future separation is _______

(a) Voidable (b) Valid (c) Void (d) Not affected

59. Regulations as to the opening and closing of business in a market are

(a) Unlawful because they are in restraint of trade

(b) Valid

(c) Not lawful

(d) None of the above

60. Which of the following agreement have been held to be opposed to public policy?

(a) Agreements of trading with enemy

(b) Agreement to commit a crime

(c) Agreements interfering with administrations of justice

(d) All the above

61. An employee, by the terms of his service agreement, is prevented from accepting a similar engagement after the terminations of his service. The restraint is

(a) Valid (b) Voidable (c) Void (d) Not affected at all

62. A Voidable Contract becomes ______

(a) Valid

(b) Voidable

(c) Not affected at all

(d) Void when the party whose consent is not free rescinds the contract

63. A contract of life insurance.

(a) is a contract of indemnity (b) is not a contract of indemnity
(c) may be a contract of indemnity (d) None of these

64. An agreement, the meaning of which is not certain or capable of being made certain is

(a) Void (b) Voidable (c) Valid (d) Not affected at all

65. _______ means to pay money or moneys worth on the happening or non happening of a specified uncertain event

(a) Uncertain Agreement (b) Valid Agreement
(c) Wagering Agreements (d) None of these

66. _______ means return of the benefit received from the plaintiff under a void contract

(a) Restitution (b) Void Contract
(c) Wagering Contract (d) None of these

67. An agreement to do an act impossible is _____

(a) Void (b) Voidable (c) Valid (d) Enforceable

68. Wagering Agreement is

(a) Forbidden by law (b) Immoral
(c) Against public system (d) None of these

69. Which one of the following is Wagering Agreements?

(a) Picture puzzles (b) An agreement to buy a ticket for a lottery
(c) Commercial transactions (d) Both 'b' and 'c'

70. Which one of the following is Contingent Contract?

(a) Contract of Insurance (b) Contract of Guarantee
(c) Wagering Contract (d) Both 'a' and 'b'

71. Contingent contract is

(a) Void (b) Valid (c) Voidable (d) Affected

72. If a contingent contract depends on its performance fro doing an act by the promissor, the contract becomes _______

(a) Void (b) Voidable (c) Valid (d) Not affected at all

73. Contingent Contract depend on the happening of an uncertain future event cannot be enforced until the event has happened because contract becomes _______

(a) Void (b) Valid (c) Voidable (d) Not affected at all

74. When two or more persons have made a joint promise then unless a contrary to intention appears from the contract, all such persons must fulfill the promise

(a) Individually (b) Severally (c) Jointly (d) None of these

75. X agrees to pay Y Rs.5,000, if Y will marry X's daughter, B.B. was dead at the time of agreement. The agreement is _______

(a) Valid (b) Voidable (c) Void (d) None of these

76. A release by the promisee of any one of the joint promissors _____

(a) Discharges from liability (b) Does not discharge liability
(c) The other joint promissors from liability (d) None of these

77. Each party is a promissor and promisee

(a) In every contract (b) In case of past consideration
(c) In case of present considerations (d) In case of reciprocal promises

78. Promises which form the consideration or part of the considerations for each other are called as________

(a) Promises (b) Reciprocal promises
(c) Demand performance (d) None of these

79. If a contract contains an undertaking to perform an impossibility, it is

(a) Void (b) Voidable (c) Void at initio (d) Not affected

80. An agreement to do an act impossible in itself is

(a) Void (b) Voidable (c) Not affected (d) Valid

81. In the performance of a contract both the parties are ignorant of the destruction of subject matter the contract is

(a) Voidable (b) Valid (c) Void (d) Not affected at all

82. A contract is entered into between two parties on the basis of a continued existence or occurrence of a particular state of things, the contract is

(a) Discharged (b) Not discharged (c) Void (d) Not affected

83. X contracts to take in cargo for Y at a foreign port. X's government afterwards declares war against the country in which the port is situated. The contract becomes________

(a) Valid (b) Not affected (c) Void (d) Voidable

84. X sold to Y certain goods supposed to be on a voyage. The goods had ceased to exist due to the perils of the sea. The contract was________

(a) Void (b) Valid (c) Voidable (d) Not affected

85. Which of the following relates to Quasi Contract?

(a) A contract to get employment (b) An agreement to many
(c) Agreement to attend tea party (d) Finding a watch on the street

86. L.J. Ralli Bros V. Compania Neviera (1920) 2 K.B. 287 case deals with

(a) Agency (b) Contract of Guarantee
(c) Impossibility of Performance (d) Agreement opposed to Public Policy

87 ________ refers to when new contract is substituted for an existing one either between the same parties or between the new parties

(a) Alteration (b) Recission (c) Remission (d) Novation

88. ______ means intentional relinquishment or giving up of a right by a party entitled there to under a contract

(a) Waiver (b) Merger (c) Remission (d) Novations

89. _________ refers to when all or some of the terms of the contract are cancelled

(a) Waiver (b) Merger (c) Remission (d) Alteration

90. Where a contract could not be performed because of the default by a third person on whose work the promiser relied, it is ________

(a) Discharged (b) Not Discharged (c) Void (d) Voidable

91. When a contract is entered into for several objects, the failure of one of them ____ the contract

(a) Discharges (b) Does not discharge

(c) Invalidates (d) None of these

92. A minor has been supplied necessaries on credit

(a) He is not liable (b) He is personally liable

(c) His estate is liable (d) None of the above

93. A person to whom money has been paid, or anything delivered, by mistake or under coercion

(a) Must return it to the person who paid it by mistake

(b) Need not repay or return it

(c) May be return it

(d) None of the above

94. A person who finds goods belonging to another and takes them into his custody, is subject to the same responsibility as ______

(a) Bailor (b) Bailee (c) Promissor (d) Promisee

95. Quantum Meruit is also known as ________

(a) As much as earned (b) As much as merited

(c) Both a and b (d) None of these

96. A, trade man, leaves goods at B's house by mistake B treats the goods as his own

(a) B is bound to pay for them to A (b) B is not bound to pay for them to A

(c) It becomes void (d) None of these

97. The court may grant recession where the contact is

(a) Voidable at the option of the plaintiff (b) Void

(c) Valid (d) Not affected at all

98. Seth Kanhaya Lal Vs. National Bank of India (1913) 40 I.A. 56 case deals with

(a) Coercion (b) Supply of necessaries

(c) Mistake (d) Both a and c

99. Damages for breach of contract are given by way of

(a) Punishment for wrong inflicted (b) Compensation for loss suffered

(c) None of these

100. Union of India V.B Prahald & co AIR (1976) Delhi 236, 237 case deals with

(a) Anticipatory breach of contract (b) Injunction

(c) Supervening impossibility (d) Mitigation of damages

101. ______is a contract to perform the promise or discharge the liability of a third person in case of this default

(a) Contract of Indemnity (b) Contract of guarantee

(c) Surety (d) None of these

102. Which of the following is the object of an indemnity?

(a) To save the indemnity holder from any likely loss

(b) It provides security against loss

(c) Provide security for the debt

(d) Both 'a' and 'b'

103. The person for whom the guarantee is given is called the _______

(a) Surety (b) Principal Debtor

(c) Creditor (d) None of these

104. The person who gives the guarantee is called as _____

(a) Surety (b) Principal Debtor (c) Creditor (d) Indemnifier

105. The person to whom the guarantee is given is called as _______

(a) Surety (b) Principal Debtor (c) Creditor (d) Indemnifier

106. A document issued by the Railway Acknowledging Receipt of Goods is called as__________

(a) Delivery Order (b) Railway Receipt

(c) Dock Warrant (d) Bill of Lading

107. The person who delivers the goods in a bailment contract is called as________

(a) Bailee (b) Bailor (c) Pledger (d) Pledgee

108. The person to whom goods are delivered is called the _______

(a) Bailor (b) Bailee (c) Pledger (d) Pledgee

109. If in a bailment no considerations passes between the bailor and the bailee it is called as________

(a) Bailment (b) Gratuitous Bailment

(c) Non – Gratuitous Bailment (d) Bailment for regard

110. Which of the following is an example of Non – Gratuitous Bailment?

(a) Cloth given to a tailor for stitching for a charge

(b) When a cycle is taken for hire

(c) Both 'a' and 'b'

(d) A lends his scooter to his friends for a journey

111. _______ refers to the right of a person who has lawful possession of goods belonging to another to retain such goods until the debt due to him is repaid

(a) Lien (b) Ownership (c) Right (d) Power

112. _______ refers to the right to retain only that particular property or goods in respect of which the debt of liability is outstanding

(a) Particular Lien (b) Special Lien (c) Both a and b (d) General Lien

113. Bailee is entitled to exercise only_______

(a) General Lien (b) Bankers Lien (c) Particular Lien (d) None of these

114. Banker is entitled to exercise only ______

(a) Particular Lien (b) Special Lien (c) General Lien (d) None of these

115. Under Which of the following circumstances a contract of bailment terminates?

(a) When the object is achieved (b) Death of either the bailor or the bailee

(c) Expiry of the period of bailment (d) All the above

116. The bailment of goods as security for payment of a debt or performance of a promise is called as ______

(a) Bailment (b) Finder of Goods (b) Pledge (d) Lien

117. Which of the following is not pledge?

(a) Bailment of goods for specific purpose (b) Entrustment of goods for any purpose

(c) On default has a right of sale (d) None of these

118. If one of the co – owners is in possession of goods with the consent of other co – owners, he can make a contract is ______

(a) Valid (b) Void (c) Voidable (d) None of these

119. A contract which creates the relationship of principal and agent is called ______

(a) Bailment (b) Pledge (c) Contract of Agency (d) None of these

120. When a person acts as an agent without the knowledge and authority of the principal and gets the act adopted later by the principal, it is called ______

(a) Agency by Ratifications (b) Export Facto Agency

(c) Agency by Holding Out (d) Both 'a' and 'b'

121. A factor is a ______ who is in actual possession of goods belonging to the principal

(a) Mercantile Agent (b) Special Agent

(c) Universal Agent (d) General Agent

122. ______ is practically a consignee who guarantees to his principal that all his debtors will pay off their debts

(a)Commission Agent (b) Broker (c) Special Agent (d) Delcreadere Agent

123. ______ is a person employed to do any act for another or to represent another in dealing with third persons

(a) Servant (b) Mediator (c) Agent (d) Dealer

124. The person for whom such act is done or who is represented is called as______

(a) Agent (b) Principal (c) Owner (d) None of these

125. An agent appointed to sell a house is an example of ______

(a) Universal Agent (b) Commercial Agent

(c) Special Agent (d) Commission Agent

126. Which of the following commission gets by Delcreadere Agent?

(a) Brokerage (b) Normal Commission

(c) Delcreadere Commission (d) Over Riding Commission

127. The authority that is usually given to an agent for carrying on the assigned work is called as ______

(a) Ostensible Authority (b) Apparent Authority

(c) Delegation of Authority (d) Both 'a' and 'b'

128. A person employed by, and acting under the control of the original agent in the business of agency is called

(a) Agent (b) Sub Agent (c) Substituted Agent (d) Servant

129. Which of the following does not relate to sub agent?

(a) Works under the control of the agent (b) Delegates a part of his duties

(c) Not responsible to the principal (d) Is directly responsible to the principal

130. Which of the following relates to the Substituted Agent?

(a) Is directly responsible to the principal (b) Delegating work does not arise

(c) Is responsible to the principle (d) All the above

131. _______ is appointed to work for his master and to carry out the work strictly according to the direction and control of the master

(a) Agent (b) Sub Agent (c) Servant (d) Substituted Agent

132. An Agency may be terminated by _______

(a) By the Act of the parties (b) By the operation of Law

(c) On the expiry of the fixed period (d) All the above

133. Which of the following cases an agency is irrevocable?

(a) When the agency is coupled with interest

(b) When the agent has incurred personal liability

(c) When the authority has been partly exercised by the agent

(d) All the above

134. _______ is the relation between persons who have agreed to share the profits of a business carried on by all or any of them acting for all

(a) Partnership (b) Company

(c) Hindu undivided family (d) Co – operatives

135. A person who undertakes to do a piece of work for another in return for a contract price is called _______

(a) Universal Agent (b) Independent Contractor

(c) Sub Agent (d) Auctioneer

136. Attorneys, solicitors and insurance agents are the example of _______

(a) Commercial Agent (b) Mercantile Agents

(c) Non-Mercantile Agent (d) Special Agents

137. _______ refers to the complete extinctions of contractual relationship among all the partners and to the stoppage of business

(a) Dissolutions of the firm (b) Dissolutions of partnership

(c) Winding up of the partnership (d) None of these

138. _______ means contract whereby the seller transfers or agrees to transfer the property in goods to the buyer for a price

(a) Agreement Sell (b) Contract of Sale of Goods

(c) Rights of Lien (d) Contract of Agency

139. Which of the following is not refers to contract of sales?

(a) Sale (b) Agreement to sell

(c) Transfer of ownership (d) Seller has to bear the loss

140. ________ is a contact whereby the seller agrees to transfer to the hire purchaser the property therein after the entire price is paid in installments

(a) Consignment on Sale (b) Agreement to Sell

(c) Hire Purchase Agreement (d) Contract of Agency

141. When an agency can not be put an end to, it is said to be _____

(a) Revocation by the Agent (b) Irrevocable Agency

(c) Agency is not Irrevocable (d) None of these

142. Goods which are owned and possessed by the seller at the time of entering into contract are called as ______

(a) Existing Goods (b) Specific Goods

(c) Ascertained Goods (d) Future Goods

143. Goods identified and agreed upon at the time of marking the contract of sale are called as______

(a) Generic Goods (b) Specific Goods

(c) Future Goods (d) Contingent Goods

144. Goods which the seller does not own or possess at the time of the contract but which he will manufacture or acquire after the making of the contract are called as________

(a) Unascertained Goods (b) Specific Goods

(c) Future Goods (d) Contingent Goods

145. Which of the following is the requisites of Bailment?

(a) Contract

(b) Delivery of possession of goods for some purpose

(c) Return of goods when the purpose is accomplished

(d) All the above

146. According to Sale of Goods Act _______ is a stipulation essential to the main purpose of the contract the breach of which gives rise to right to treat the contract as repudiated

(a) Warranty (b) Conditions (c) Guarantee (d) None of these

147. According to Sale of Goods Act, stipulations is only collateral to the main purpose of the contract and its breach gives rise to claim for damages only, it is called as _______

(a) Warranty (b) Conditions (c) Guarantee (d) None of these

148. Which of the following refers to Caveat Emptor?

(a) Let the buyer beware (b) Buyer's duty to choose the goods

(c) Buyer must examine them thoroughly (d) All the above

149. According to Carriage of Goods Act _______ refers to one who under takes to carry goods from place to place for all persons who employ him for sale

(a) Common Carrier (b) Private Carrier

(c) Both 'a' and 'b' (d) Carriage of Goods by Sea

150. According to Carriage of Goods Act ______ refers to who occasionally carriers goods for other under special agreement

(a) Private Carrier (b) Common Carrier
(c) Carriage of Goods by Air (d) None of these

151. The contract of carriage of goods by sea is called ______

(a) Contract of Charter Party (b) Contract of Sale of Goods
(c) Contract of Affraightment (d) None of these

152. Which of the following does not relates to Bill of leading?

(a) A document acknowledging the receipt of goods
(b) A contract for the carriage of goods
(c) A document of title to goods
(d) None of these

153. Which of the following refers to Charter Party?

(a) Contract of hire (b) Can be for a particular voyage
(c) Is a quasi negotiable instrument (d) Both 'a' and 'b'

154. If the master stakes in the bill of leading that the goods received on board the ship are in good order and conditions it is known as ______

(a) Clean Bill of Lading (b) Bill of Lading
(c) Both 'a' and 'b' (d) Charter Party

155. According to Carriage of Goods Act, if it is remarked in the bill that goods received are in bad conditions the bill of lading is known as ________

(a) Qualified Bill of Lading (b) Dirty Bill of Lading
(c) Foul Bill of Lading (d) All the above

156. If the cargo covered by bill of lading is to be carried partly by sea and party by land and a composite freight has been charged for sea and land transportation, the bill of lading is called as _____

(a) Clean Bill of Lading (b) Qualified Bill of Lading
(c) Through Bill of Lading (d) None of these

157. When a vessel is hired for a specified period of time it is called as ____

(a) Time Charter Party (b) Voyage Charter Party
(c) Charter Party (d) None of these

158. When a vessel is hired for a particular voyage it is called as______

(a) Time Charter Party (b) Voyage Charter Party
(c) Charter without dismiss (d) None of these

159. Which of the following refers to implied warranties in a contract of carriage by sea?

(a) Sea worthiness of the ship (b) Non – Deviation of the voyage
(c) Commencement of voyage (d) All the above

160. According to Contract of Agency, an agent ______ his authority to another.

(a) Can delegate (b) Can not delegate (c) May be delegate (d) May not delegate

ANSWERS

1. (a) Contract as an agreement enforceable by law
2. (d) Both a and b
3. (b) Agreement = Offer + Acceptance
4. (a) Enforceable by law of the option of the aggrieved party
5. (c) Void
6. (a) Void Agreement
7. (a) Express Contract.
8. (b) Quasi – Contract
9. (c) Executory Contract
10. (a) Bilateral Contract
11. (a) Specific Offer
12. (d) None of these
13. (d) All the above
14. (a) The offeree gives conditional acceptance
15. (b) General Offer
16. (b) An invitation to offer
17. (d) Acceptance
18. (a) Must move at the desire of the Promissor
19. (c) Consideration
20. (a) May be past, present, or future
21. (a) Can not sue
22. (b) Is not already bound to do
23. (a) Is enforceable
24. (c) Void
25. (a) Void
26. (b) Cannot be ratified
27. (d) All the above
28. (a) Can not enter
29. (b) He is of sound mind
30. (c) His estate is liable to pay
31. (a) May enter into a contract when he is of sound mind
32. (a) Can not enter
33. (a) Its Memorandum of Association and the provisions of the Companies Act
34. (a) Void Contract
35. (c) A minors agreement
36. (c) Voidable at the option of the party whose consent is so caused
37. (b) Absolutely void
38. (a) Voidable
39. (b) Void
40. (d) Moral character
41. (b) Mainly at physical character
42. (d) None of these
43. (d) All the above
44. (d) All the above
45. (d) None of these
46. (a) Coercion
47. (d) All the above
48. (a) Mistake
49. (a) Void
50. (d) Void
51. (c) Void
52. (b) Voidable
53. (a) Void
54. (d) Mistake as regards identity
55. (b) Illegal
56. (a) On the ground of public policy
57. (a) Void
58. (c) Void
59. (c) Not lawful
60. (d) All the above
61. (c) Void
62. (a) Void
63. (b) Is not a Contract of Indemnity
64. (a) Void
65. (c) Wagering Agreements
66. (a) Restitution
67. (a) Void
68. (a) Forbidden by law
69. (d) Both 'b' and 'c'
70. (d) Both 'a' and 'b'
71. (a) Void
72. (a) Void
73. (a) Void
74. (c) Jointly

75. (c) Void
76. (b) Does not discharge liability
77. (d) Incase of reciprocal promises
78. (b) Reciprocal promises
79. (d) Not affected
80. (a) Void
81. (c) Void
82. (a) Discharged
83. (c) Void
84. (a) Void
85. (a) A contract to get employment
86. (c) Impossibility of performance
87. (d) Novation
88. (a) Waiver
89. (c) Rescission
90. (b) Not Discharged
91. (b) Does not discharge
92. (c) His estate is liable
93. (a) Must repay (or) return it to the person who paid it by mistake
94. (b) Bailee
95. (c) Both a and b
96. (a) B is bound to pay for them to A
97. (a) Voidable at the option
98. (a) Coercion
99. (b) Compensation for loss suffered
100. (d) Mitigation of damages
101. (b) Contract of Guarantee
102. (d) Both 'a' and 'b'
103. (b) Principal Debtor
104. (a) Surety
105. (c) Creditor
106. (b) Railway Receipt
107. (b) Bailor
108. (b) Bailee
109. (b) Gratuitous Bailment
110. (c) Both 'a' and 'b'
111. (a) Lien
112. (c) Both 'a' and 'b'
113. (c) Particular Lien
114. (c) General Lien
115. (d) All the above
116. (c) Pledge
117. (b) Entrustment of goods for any purpose
118. (a) Valid
119. (c) Contract of Agency
120. (d) Both 'a' and 'b'
121. (a) Mercantile Agent
122. (d) Delcreadere Agent
123. (c) Agent
124. (b) Principal
125. (c) Special Agent
126. (c) Delcreadere commission
127. (d) Both 'a' and 'b'
128. (b) Sub Agent
129. (d) Is directly responsible to the principal
130. (d) All the above
131. (c) Servant
132. (d) All the above
133. (d) All the above
134. (a) Partnership
135. (b) Independent Contractor
136. (c) Non-Mercantile Agents
137. (a) Dissolution of the firm
138. (b) Contract of sale of goods
139. (d) Seller has to bear the loss
140. (c) Hire Purchase Agreement
141. (b) Irrevocable Agency
142. (a) Existing Goods
143. (b) Specific Goods
144. (c) Future Goods
145. (d) All the above
146. (b) Condition
147. (a) Warranty
148. (d) All the above
149. (a) Common Carrier
150. (a) Private – Carrier
151. (c) Contract of Affreightment
152. (d) None of these
153. (d) Both 'a' and 'b'
154. (a) Clean Bill of Lading
155. (d) All the above
156. (c) Through Bill of Lading
157. (a) Time Charter Party
158. (b) Voyage Charter Party
159. (d) All the above
160. (b) Can not delegate

*****

XII

COMPANY LAW

1. A company is one formed and registered under this Act or an existing company which is described by

(a) According to Sec. 3 (1) I of Indian Companies Act

(b) According to Sec. 4 (1) I of Indian Companies Act

(c) According to Sec 3 (2) I of Indian Companies Act

(d) None of these

2. According to Law, person can be defined as _______ and _____

(a) Natural persons, Political persons (b) Natural persons, Legal person

(c) Business persons, Professional persons (d) National, Internationals

3. Who observed "Members may come and go but the company can go on for ever"

(a) N.D. Kapoor (b) Mr. Palmer (c) Gower (d) Justice Cave

4. _______ refers to a voluntary associations of individuals formed for the purpose of attaining a common social or economical end

(a) Hind Undivided Family (b) Sole Trader

(c) Firm (d) Company

5. A company is ______ according to Law

(a) Juristic person (b) Legal person (c) Artificial person (d) All the above

6. Which of the following is the principal merit of companies?

(a) Limited liability (b) Possibilities for expansions

(c) Capital formations is easy (d) All the above

7. Which of the following is the limitation of Companies?

(a) Long life
(b) Long drawn process
(c) Capital formations
(d) Democratic Management

8. Common Seal is the

(a) Official Signature of the Company
(b) Privileges of the Company
(c) Corporate Form of Enterprise
(d) None of these

9. Piercing the Corporate, Veil is also termed as ________

(a) Doctrine of Corporate Entity
(b) The Veil of incorporation
(c) Lifting the Corporate Veil
(d) All the above

10. Which of the following circumstances the Veil can be lifted by the Court?

(a) When company tries to avoid legal obligations
(b) Where a fraud is suspected
(c) Where the company acts as an agent
(d) All the above

11. A company is regulated and controlled by ________

(a) Partnership Act
(b) Companies Act
(c) Factories Act
(d) Central Government

12. Registration of Partnership Firm is ______ under Partnership Act

(a) Compulsory
(b) Obligatory
(c) Not Compulsory
(d) Optional

13. Life Time of a Company is ______

(a) Mere aggregations of individuals
(b) Death of a Director
(c) Mere obstruction of law
(d) Insolvency of its member

14. Company shares can be ______

(a) Freely transferable
(b) Not freely transferable
(c) Transfer with consent of management
(d) None of these

15. A Private Company should have a minimum of ______ members

(a) 4 (b) 3 (c) 2 (d) 5

16. A Private Company should have a maximum of ______ members

(a) 45 (b) 50 (c) 55 (d) 60

17. Public Limited Company should have a minimum of ______ members

(a) 5 (b) 6 (c)7 (d) 8

18. A Partnership Firm should have minimum of ______ and maximum of ______ persons

(a) 2, 20 (b) 4, 20 (c) 6, 20 (d) 5, 20

19. If a Public Company does not have its own Memorandum of Associations it may adopt Table B given in ______

(a) Schedule II (b) Schedule I (c) Schedule III (d)Schedule IV

20. A document to be considered as Prospectus must invite ________ to subscribe for shares/ debentures

(a) Directors (b) Shareholders (c) Public (d) Employees

21. Till allotment takes place ________ do not exist

(a) Debentures (b) Capital (c) Bonds (d) Shares

22. A transfer of shares to be valid must be registered with the ________

(a) Registrar (b) Auditor
(c) Government (d) Company Law Board

23. Which of the following does not affect the membership of a party?

(a) Transfer (b) Forfeiture (c) Subscription (d) Redemptions

24. The directors are prohibited from borrowing beyond the aggregate of ________of the company

(a) Subscribed (b) Call up (c) Nominal (d) Paid up

25. An official liquidator in a compulsory winding up is appointed by the ________

(a) Registrar (b) Central Government
(c) Court (d) Directors

26. Company is refers to a ________

(a) Citizen (b) Person (c) Human being (d) All the above

27. Debentures can be issued by ________

(a) Partnership Firm (b) Private Limited Company
(c) Joint Stock Company (d) Sole Trader Concern

28. Management of the company is in the hands of

(a) Representative of share holders (b) Professionals
(c) Members themselves (d) Both a and b

29. Quick decision making is possible in the case of ________

(a) Partnership Firm (b) Sole Trader Concern
(c) Company (d) All the above

30. The main motto of the Co – Operative Society is ________

(a) Render service to the society (b) To earn maximum profit
(c) To render service to its members (d) To render service to the government

31. According to Co – Operative Societies Act the rate of dividend can not exceed ________

(a) 6 1/4% (b) 7 1/4% (c) 8 1/4% (d) 9 1/4%

32. The minimum number of members required to form a Co- Operative Society is ________

(a) 11 (b) 10 (c) 9 (d) 8

33. Which of the following is not Incorporated Companies?

(a) Chartered Companies (b) Statutory Companies
(c) Registered Companies (d) Public Companies

34. Popular method of sale of New Share in India

(a) Public Issue (b) Offer for Sale (c) Private Placement (d) Right Issue

35. Incorporated Companies which are established by ________

(a) Companies Act (b) Special Act (c) Charter (d) All the above

36. East India Company is ________

(a) Chartered Company (b) Statutory Company
(c) Holding Company (d) Registered Company

37. Charter can be granted by ________

(a) Government (b) Kings (c) Queens (d) Both b and c

38. ________are companies which are established by Special Act of Central Legislature

(a) Statutory Companies (b) Registered Companies
(c) Holding Companies (d) None of these

39. Which of the following is a Statutory Company?

(a) The Bank of England (b) Chartered Bank of China
(c) State Bank of India (d) East India Company

40. Companies established under the Companies Act 1956 are called as ________

(a) Statutory Companies (b) Registered Companies
(c) Chartered Companies (d) None of these

41. Companies in which liability of the member is unlimited is known as ________

(a) Company Limited by Shares (b) Company Limited by Guarantee
(c) Unlimited Company (d) Limited Company

42. A Private Company should have minimum of ______ and maximum of ________ members

(a) 2, 50 (b) 7, 50 (c) 2, 60 (d) 2, 70

43. Formations of Public Company should have a minimum of not less than ________ members

(a) 6 (b) 2 (c) 7 (d) 5

44. Which of the following company to issues of share warrant?

(a) Private Company (b) Public Companies
(c) Partnership Firm (d) Charter

45. Founder's shares can be issued by ______

(a) Private Company (b) Public Company
(c) Statutory Company (d) Incorporated Company

46. Over all managerial remunerations of a Public Company should not exceed ______ of the net profit

(a) 10% (b)11% (c) 12% (d) 13%

47. Managing Director of a Public Company can not be appointed for more than ________ years

(a) 5 (b) 7 (c) 3 (d) 6

48. Quorum for a meeting of Public Company is ______

(a) 7 (b) 6 (c) 5 (d) 4

49. When one company has control over another it is called as ________

(a) Subsidiary Company (b) Holding Company
(c) Government Company (d) Public Company

50. Holding Company holds more than _____ of the equity share capital of another company

(a) 40% (b) 60% (c) 50% (d)70%

51. A Government Company holds _____

(a) More than 50% of equity share capital

(b) More than 50% of nominal value of equity share capital

(c) Not less than 50% of paid up share capital

(d) None of these

52. Both Holding and Subsidiary Companies are _______

(a) Incorporated Companies (b) Separate Legal Entity

(c) Both a and b (d) None of these

53. Auditor of a Government Company is appointed by _______

(a) State Government (b) Central Government

(c) Reserve Bank of India (d) Registrar of Companies

54. Audit Report of a Govt. Company should be sent to ______

(a) Central Government (b) State Government

(c) Comptroller of Auditor General of India (d) Department of Income Tax

55. Which of following is not the process of formations of company?

(a) Promotion (b) Registrations

(c) Commencement of business (d) Winding up of Company

56. The person who undertakes all activities to create a company is known as ________

(a) Promoter (b) Auditor

(c)Managing Director (d) Secretary

57. Form No 1A along with a fees of Rs.100 relates to _______

(a) Registrations of Company (b) Incorporation of Company

(c) Both a and b (d) Winding up of Companies

58. Certificates of Incorporations is issued by _______

(a) Promoter (b) Registrar (c) Secretary (d)Central Government

59. When a certificate is issued the new company is born this means _______

(a) Certificate of Incorporations (b) Memorandum of Association

(c) Articles of Associations (d) Statutory Provisions

60. Certificate of Incorporation can be cancelled by ________

(a) Court (b) Registrar

(c) Both a and b (d)Central Government

61. Memorandum of Associations and Articles of Association are drafted by _____

(a) Auditor (b)Registrar (c) Secretary (d) Director

62. Letter of no objections from the registrar relates to _______

(a) Commencement of Business (b) Incorporation of Company

(c) Approval of the proposed name (d) All the above

63. **According to Sec 2(28) of the Companies Act______of a company is originally framed or altered from time in pursuance of any previous companies law or of this Act**
(a) Memorandum of Associations (b) Articles of Associations
(c) Prospectus (d) Certificate of Incorporations

64. **Memorandum of Associations is a ________**
(a) Prospectus (b) Certificates (c) Documents (d) Schedule

65. **Which of the following clause is not relates to Memorandum of Associations?**
(a) Liability Clause (b) Capital Clause
(c) Object Clause (d) Management Clause

66. **________ is refers to the doing of an act which is beyond the legal power and authority of the company**
(a) Doctrine of Ultra Virus (b) Certificate of Incorporations
(c) Statement in Lieu of Prospectus (d) Pre – Incorporations Contracts

67. **Articles of Association of a company is framed under**
(a) Sec 2 (28) of the Companies Act (b) Sec 2 (2) of the Companies Act
(c) Sec 12 (2) a of the Companies Act (d) Sec (11) of the Companies Act

68. **Articles of Associations is the ________**
(a) Principal Document (b) Secondary Document
(c) Subordinate to the Companies Act (d) None of these

69. **Memorandum of Associations explains**
(a) Defines the relationship between company and outsiders
(b) Defines the relationship between company and its members
(c) Specifies the scope of authority and the objectives
(d) Both a and c

70. **Which of the following is not relating to Articles of Associations?**
(a) Alternations is difficult (b) Alterations is comparatively easy
(c) Internal regulations of the company (d) Secondary Document

71. **Authorized Capital is also termed as ______**
(a) Nominal Capital (b) Registered Capital
(c) Both 'a' and 'b' (d) Borrowed Capital

72. **The share capital issued to public can not exceed the ______**
(a) Authorized Capital (b) Subscribed Capital
(c) Paid up Capital (d) Called up Capital

73. **Called up capital is the part of ______**
(a) Issued Capital (b) Subscribed Capital
(c) Reserve Capital (d) Paid up Capital

74. **The amount not paid by the shareholder on the calls made is known as ______**
(a) Called up capital (b) Uncalled capital (c) Calls in arrears (d) Paid up capital

75. Which one of the following method is not used to raising the capital from the public?

(a) By directly selling the shares to the public

(b) By entering into an underwriting contract with the underwriters

(c) By placing shares

(d) By making securities with third parties

76. SEBI is described as ______

(a) Securities and Stock Exchange Board of India

(b) Stock and Securities Exchange Board

(c) Stock Exchanges and the Securities and Exchange Board of India

(d) Securities and Exchange Board of India

77. Guideline issued by SEBI with regard to issue of shares is termed as ______

(a) Methods for Disclosure and Investor Protections

(b) Guidelines for Disclosure and Investor Protections

(c) Procedure for Disclosure and Investor Protections

(d) Advisable for Disclosure and Investor Protections

78. ______ refers to an interest having a money value and make up of diverse rights specified under the articles of associations

(a) Debenture (b) Share (c) Owned capital (d) Bonds

79. Which of the following rights relate to Preference Shares?

(a) To claim dividend during the life time of the company

(b) To claim repayment of capital on the winding up

(c) Conversion to satisfy legal requirements

(d) both a and b

80. Equity shares are also called as ______

(a) Deferred Shares (b) Ordinary Shares (c) Risk Capital (d) Both 'b' and 'c'

81. The shares which are issued to the founders or promoters are called as ______

(a) Ordinary Shares (b) Equity Shares

(c) Deferred Shares (d) Preference Shares

82. The holders of deferred shares can get dividend only after ______

(a) Preference share holders (b) Equity share holders

(c) Debenture holders (d) Preference and Equity share holders

83. ______ refers to share or stock which does not have any face value or par value

(a) Deferred Shares (b) No Par Share

(c) Cumulative Preference Share (d) Risk Capital

84. 'Call' on shares can be expressed as ______

(a) Demand for money (b) Obligatory (c) Debt due (d) All the above

85. Which of the following condition does not relate to for Forfeiture of Shares?

(a) Authority to forfeit (b) Board resolutions

(c) Notice to defaulting shareholders (d) All the above

86. _______ refers to the right to retain the shares of another for non fulfillment of an obligations

(a) Share Certificate (b) Lien on Shares

(c) Surrender of Shares (d) Share Warrant

87. _______________ refers to the prima facie evidence of the title of the members to such shares

(a) Share Certificate (b)Share Warrant (c) Lien on Shares (d) Calls on Shares

88. Share certificate must be issued with in _______ of the date of allotment

(a) 2 Months (b) 3 Months (c) 4 Months (d) 5 Months

89. Share Warrant is a _______

(a) Document (b) Negotiable Instrument

(c) Certificate (d) Both 'a' and 'b'

90. Which of the following condition relates to the issue of Share Warrant?

(a) It must be authorized by the Articles

(b) The shares must be fully paid up

(c) Only a public company can issue share warrants

(d) All the above

91. Which of the following stamp duty is prescribed by govt. for transfer of shares?

(a) Re.0.50 for every Rs.100 of the value of shares

(b) Re.1 for every Rs.1000 of the value of shares

(c) Re.0.50 for every Rs.1000 of the value of shares

(d) Re.1 for every Rs.100 of the value of shares

92. _______ refers to the passing of the title or property in the shares from one person to another by the operations of law

(a) Blank Transfer (b) Transmission of Shares

(c) Forged Transfer (d) Certified Transfer

93. A document which either creates or acknowledges a debt is _______

(a) Overdraft (b) Cash Credit (c) Debenture (d) Shares

94. Debenture is a _______

(a) Certificate (b) Document

(c) Debenture Stock and Bonds (d) All the above

95. Debentures which are payable to the registered debenture holder are called as _______

(a) Registered Debentures (b) Bearer Debentures

(c) Secured Debentures (d) Redeemable Debentures

96. Debentures which are paid first at the time of winding up are called _______

(a) Preferred Debentures (b) Ordinary Debentures

(c) Secured Debentures (d) Bearer Debentures

97. Debenture which are not repayable during the life time of the company are called as ______

(a) Unsecured Debentures (b)Irredeemable Debentures

(c) Non – Convertible Debentures (d) Redeemable Debenture

98. Stock Exchanges deal in the Securities of

(a) Private Companies (b) Government companies

(c) Select Companies (d) All companies

99. According to Sec.24 of the Companies Act charge is a ______

(a) Security (b) Mortgage (c) Lien (d) All the above

100. Which one of the following way the borrowed money can be secured?

(a) Debenture (b) A floating charge (c) Bond (d) All the above

101. Which one of the following person can not become as a member of company?

(a) Minor (b) Lunatic and Insolvent

(c) Both 'a' and 'b' (d) Sound mind person

102. ______________ is refers to any person occupying the position a director by whatever name called

(a) Promoter (b) Secretary (c) Partner (d) Director

103. The minimum number of members of the Board of Directors for a Public Company is ________

(a) 3 (b) 5 (c) 2 (d) 4

104. Which one of the following persons not eligible to become a Director?

(a) It he is an undischarged insolvent

(b) It he has applied to be adjudged as an insolvent

(c) Both 'a' and 'b'

(d) An individual with sound mind

105. One can act as a Director of _______ at the same time

(a) 30 Companies (b) 20 Companies (c) 10 Companies (d) 25 Companies

106. Which one of the following position is not allowed by the Directors of a Company?

(a) Directors as Agents (b) Directors as Trustees

(c) Directors as Employees (d) All the above

107. Managing Director of a Public Company can hold office for a maximum periods of ______

(a) 3 Years (b) 5 Years (c) 6 Years (d) 4 Years

108. Which of the following is not related to the Manager?

(a) He is the paid executive of the company

(b) He is not a mere head or foreman of a sections

(c) He is subject to the control of the Board of Directors

(d) He is not an agent who is to do a particular thing

109. In the case of Managing Director's remunerations the maximum limit is fixed at _______ of the annual net profits

(a) 15% (b) 5% (c) 10% (d) 20%

110. An Optimistic Speculator is

(a) Stag (b) Bear (c) Bull (d) Lame duck

111. The maximum remunerations payable to a manager of a company can not exceed _______ of the annual net profit

(a) 5% (b) 10% (c) 7% (d) 3%

112. _______ is a Supervisory body established to regulate Indian Stock Market

(a) Reserve Bank of India (b)Securities and Exchange Board of India

(c) State Bank of India (d) Finance Commission

113. Which of the following is not relates to the meeting of the shareholders?

(a) Statutory Meeting (b) Annual General Meeting

(c) Class Meeting (d) None of these

114. Extra – Ordinary General Meeting is the _______

(a) Meeting of the Shareholders (b) Meeting of the Board of Directors

(c) Meeting of the Creditors (d) Meeting of the Debenture Holders

115. _______ is the first General Meeting of the company

(a) Annual General Meeting (b) Class Meeting

(c) Statutory Meetings (d) Extra – Ordinary General Meeting

116. Which of the following legal provision is the Statutory Meeting?

(a) Statutory report sent to all members

(b) Send notice of the meeting at least 21days before date of meeting

(c) Certifications of the report

(d) All the above

117. Annual General Meeting is usually held in _______

(a) Once in a year (b) Twice in a year

(c) Not compulsory (d) Once in two years

118. Time gap between two Annual General Meeting is

(a) Twelve moths (b) Fifteen months

(c) Fourteen months (d) Sixteen months

119. _______ is held by the shareholders of a particular class of shares

(a) Annual General Meeting (b) Statutory Meeting

(c) Class Meeting (d) Meeting of Creditors

120. The quorum for the meeting of the Board of Directors should be _______ of the whole total strengths or _______ Directors whichever is higher

(a) Two Third, Three (b) One Third, Two

(c) Two Fourth, Three (d) Three Fourth, Four

121. The length of the notice required for convening a General Meeting is not less than _____ days

(a) 21 (b) 31 (c) 41 (d) 11

122. ________ is a certain number of members whose presence is necessary for the meeting of company to commence its deliberations

(a) Notice (b) Board (c) Quorum (d) Motions

123. The term Agenda refers to ________

(a) Things to be done

(b) Business to be transacted at a meeting

(c) Business to be drafted at the meeting

(d) All the above

124. ________ is the propositions which is formally made at a meeting and which is liable to attestations before it is adopted by the meeting

(a) Motion (b) Resolution (c) Notice (d) Agenda

125. A motion when passed with or without amendment is called ______

(a) Motion (b) Resolutions (c) Agenda (d) Notice

126. Which of the following resolutions are passed in the General Meeting?

(a) Ordinary Resolutions

(b) Special Resolutions

(c) Resolutions required with special notice

(d) All the above

127. Proxy is an agent or representative of a ______

(a) Share holders

(b) Debenture holders

(c) Creditors

(d) Board of Directors

128. Which of the following right is relates to Proxy?

(a) Right to speak

(b) Right to vote

(c) Right to participate in discussion

(d) All the above

129. _______ is an act of putting off or breaking off for a later resumptions

(a) Adjournment

(b) Postponement

(c) Suspensions

(d) Amendment

130. Which of the following is Adjournment?

(a) If no quorum is present

(b) If the meeting passes a resolutions to this effect

(c) If it is not possible to obtain the required information within the date of the meeting

(d) All the above

131. Pairing Method use in ______

(a) British Parliament

(b) Indian Parliament

(c) French Parliament

(d) German Parliament

132. ________ is the written record of the business done at a meeting

(a) Report (b) Minutes (c) Discussions (d) Resolution

133. In the case of Board Meetings, the minutes can be signed by ________

(a) Chairman (b) Directors (c) Shareholders (d) Secretary

134. ________ is an officer to whom confidential matters can be entrusted

(a) Auditor (b) Secretary (c) Directors (d) Executive Director

135. ________ is the sum paid and received as the quotient, forming the share of the divisible sum payable to the recipient .

(a) Profit (b) Interest (c) Dividend (d) Subscription

136. The cheque issued by the company to the shareholders for the amount of dividend is known as ________

(a) Dividend Mandate (b) Dividend Warrant

(c) Interim Dividend (d) Dividend Request

137. Dividend Mandate is also called as________

(a) Dividend Request (b) Dividend Warrant

(c) Interim Dividend (d) Unpaid Dividend

138. Final Dividend is________

(a) declared by the shareholder in the annual general meeting

(b) relates to the full year

(c) declared only after the accounts are prepared

(d) All the above

139. Which of the following is not relates to Interim Dividend?

(a) is declared by the Board Directors

(b) is declared before the preparation of the final accounts

(c) is declared by the shareholders

(d) its relates to the full year

140. Any unpaid or unclaimed money is transferred to ________

(a) Un paid dividend account (b) Dividend account

(c) Profit and loss account (d) Shareholder A/c

141. Which of the following is the legal provision relate to the Annual Accounts and the Balance Sheets?

(a) True and Fair view (b) Filing with Registrar

(c) B/S and P & L A/c signed by Secretary (d) All the above

142. Which one of the following documents is submitted by the Board of Directors at every Annual General Meeting?

(a) Profit and Loss Account (b) Balance Sheet

(c) Report of the Directors (d) All the above

143. If the persons responsible for the maintenance of accounts are in default, they will be liable for ________

(a) Imprisonment up to six months (b) Fine up to Rs.1000

(c) Both 'a' and 'b' (d) Fine up to Rs.5000

144. Annual Return should be filed with in ________ form the date of the Annual General Meeting

(a) 60 days (b) 180 days (c) 18 months (d) 6 months

145. Which of the following books is Statutory Book ?

(a) Register of Charges (b) Register of Members
(c) Index of Members (d) All the above

146. Which of the following book is not Statutory Book?

(a) Log Book (b) Books of Accounts
(c) Minutes Books (d) Cost Account Records

147. Which of the following book is Optional Book?

(a) Register of Transfers (b) Register of Certifications
(c) Proxies Record (d) All the above

148. Which of the following is Membership Rights?

(a) Right to attend the general meeting (b) Right to Vote
(c) Right to share the profits (d) All the above

149. Which of the following right is granted to the minority members under the Companies Act?

(a) Rights relates to reconstructions
(b) Rights to remedy
(c) Rights to apply central govt. for investigations of the company
(d) All the above

150. _________ is the process whereby the life of a company is ended and its property administered for the benefits of its creditors and members

(a) Winding up (b) Insolvency (c) Both 'a' and 'b' (d) None of these

151. A company can be put to an end only through a legal process known as _______

(a) Winding up (b) Liquidations (c) Both 'a' and 'b' (d) None of these

152. In a Compulsory Winding Up by Court, the liquidator is known as ______

(a) Voluntary Liquidator (b) Company Liquidator
(c) Liquidator (d) Official Liquidator

153. __________ is appointed and he takes the control of the company collects its assets profits and debts and finally distributes any surplus among the members is accordance with their rights.

(a) Administrator (b) Liquidator (c) Officer (d) Both 'a' and 'b'

154. Which of the following is a method is of winding up of company?

(a) Compulsory Winding Up (b) Members Voluntary Winding Up
(c) Creditors Voluntary Winding Up (d) All the above

155. ________ is a person who is liable to contribute to the assets of a company in the events of its being wound up.

(a) Liquidator (b) Contributory (c) Officers (d) Secretary

156. _________ refers to an amicable settlement of differences by mutual concessions by the parties to dispute or differences

(a) Compromise (b) Arrangements (c) Amalgamations (d) Deconstruction

157. ________ takes place when two or more companies are joined to form an entity or one is absorbed into or blended with another

(a) Reconstructions (b) Holding

(c) Amalgamations (d) Absorptions

ANSWERS

1. (a) According to Sec 3 (1) i of Indian Companies Act
2. (b) Natural persons, legal person
3. (c) Grower
4. (d) Company
5. (d) All the above
6. (d) All the above
7. (b) Long drawn process
8. (a) Official Signature of the Company
9. (b) The Veil of Incorporation
10. (d) All the above
11. (b) Companies Act
12. (c) Not compulsory
13. (c) Mere abstraction of law
14. (a) Freely transferable
15. (c) 2
16. (b) 50
17. (c) 7
18. (a) 2,20
19. (b) Schedule I
20. (c) Public
21. (d) Share
22. (a) Registrar
23. (c) Subscription
24. (d) Paid up
25. (c) Court
26. (a) Citizen
27. (c) Joint – Stock Company
28. (d) Both 'a' and 'b'
29. (b) Sole Trader Concern
30. (c) To render service to its members
31. (a) $6_{1/4\%}$
32. (b) 10
33. (d) Public Company
34. (a) Public Issue
35. (d) All the above
36. (a) Chartered Company
37. (d) Both 'b' and 'c'
38. (a) Statutory Companies
39. (c) State Bank of India
40. (b) Registered Companies
41. (c) Unlimited Company
42. (a) 2,50
43. (c) 7
44. (b) Public Companies
45. (a) Private Company
46. (b) 11%
47. (a) 5
48. (c) 5
49. (b) Holding Company
50. (c) 50%
51. (c) Not les than 50% of paid up share capital
52. (c) Both 'a' and 'b'
53. (b) Central Government
54. (c) Controller of Auditor General of India
55. (d) Winding Up of a Company
56. (a) Promoter
57. (c) Both 'a' and 'b'
58. (b) Registrar
59. (a) Certificate of Incorporation
60. (c) Both 'a' and 'b'
61. (c) Secretary
62. (c) Approval of the proposed name

63. (a) Memorandum of Association
64. (c) Document
65. (d) Management Clause
66. (a) Doctrine of Ultra Virus
67. (b) Sec 2 (2) of the Companies Act
68. (b) Secondary Document
69. (d) Both 'a' and 'c'
70. (a) Alteration is difficult
71. (c) Both 'a' and 'b'
72. (a) Authorized Capital
73. (b) Subscribed Capital
74. (c) Calls in arrears
75. (d) By making securities with third parties
76. (d) Securities and Exchange Board of India
77. (b) Guidelines for Disclosure and Investor Protection
78. (b) Share
79. (d) Both 'a' and 'b'
80. (c) Risk Capital
81. (c) Deferred Shares
82. (d) Preference and Equity share holders
83. (b) No par share
84. (d) All the above
85. (d) All the above
86. (b) Lien on Shares
87. (a) Share Certificate
88. (b) 3 Months
89. (d) Both 'a' and 'b'
90. (d) All the above
91. (a) Re.0.50 for every Rs.100 of the value of shares
92. (b) Transmission of shares
93. (c) Debenture
94. (d) All the above
95. (a) Registered Debentures
96. (a) Preferred Debentures
97. (b) Irredeemable Debentures
98. (c) Select Companies
99. (d) All the above
100. (d) All the above
101. (c) Both 'a' and 'b'
102. (d) Director
103. (a) 3
104. (c) Both 'a' and 'b'
105. (b) 20 Companies
106. (d) All the above
107. (b) 5 Years
108. (d) He is not an agent who is to do a particular thing
109. (c) 10%
110. (c) Bull
111. (a) 5%
112. (b) Securities and Exchange Board of India
113. (d) None of these
114. (a) Meeting of the shareholders
115. (c) Statutory Meetings
116. (d) All the above
117. (a) Once in a year
118. (b) Fifteen months
119. (c) Class Meeting
120. (b) One Third, Two
121. (a) 21
122. (c) Quorum
123. (d) All the above
124. (a) Motion
125. (b) Resolution
126. (d) All the above
127. (a) Shareholders
128. (b) Right to vote
129. (a) Adjournment
130. (d) All the above
131. (a) British Parliament
132. (b) Minutes
133. (a) Chairman
134. (b) Secretary
135. (c) Dividend
136. (b) Dividend Warrant
137. (a) Dividend Request
138. (d) All the above

139. (d) Its relates to the full year
140. (a) Un Paid Dividend Account
141. (d) All the above
142. (d) All the above
143. (c) Both 'a' and 'b'
144. (a) 60 days
145. (d) All the above
146. (a) Log Book
147. (d) All the above
148. (d) All the above
149. (d) All the above
150. (a) Winding Up
151. (c) Both 'a' and 'b'
152. (d) Official Liquidator
153. (d) Both 'a' and 'b'
154. (d) All the above
155. (b) Contributory
156. (a) Compromise
157. (c) Amalgamation

*****

XIII

INDUSTRIAL LAW

1. **The first Factory Act in India was passed in the year _______**
(a) 181 (b) 1881 (c) 1882 (d) 1883

2. **_______ is a premises where ten or more persons are engaged if power is used, or twenty or more person are engaged if power is not used, in a manufacturing processes**
(a) Factory (b) Work place (c) Concern (d) Organizations

3. **_______ means a person employed, directly or by or through any agency with or ' without the knowledge of the principal employer**
(a) Individual (b) Worker (c) Employee (d) Business Man

4. **A person who has completed his eighteen year of age is _______**
(a) Adolescent (b) Child (c) Adult (d) Competent person

5. **______ means a person who has completed his fifteen year of age but has not completed his eighteenth year**
(a) Child (b) Adolescent (c) Adult (d) Young person

6. **_______ means the period of twelve months beginning with the first day of January in any year**
(a) Calendar Year (b) Financial Year (c) Assessment Year (d) None of these

7. **________ means a person who is either a child or an adolescent**
(a) Old person (b) Young person (c) Adult (d) Child

8. **______ is any engine, motor or other appliance which generates or otherwise provides power**
(a) Hazardous process (b) Manufacturing processes
(c) Prime Mover (d) None of these

9. ____________ of a factory means the person who has ultimate control over the affairs of the factory

(a) Employer (b) Chief Inspector of Factories

(c) Occupier (d) Labour Commissioner

10. Who are the following persons appointed by state Govt. for the inspecting staff

(a)Chief Inspector (b) Additional Chief Inspectors

(c) Joint Chief Inspectors (d) All the above

11. Which of the following are the powers of the inspectors under Factories Act?

(a) Make examinations of the premises plant etc

(b) Inquire into any accident or dangerous occurance

(c) Seize or take copies of any register, record necessary in respect of offence

(d) All the above

12. Certifying surgeons can be appointed by __________ under factories Act?

(a) State Government (b) Central Government

(c) Quasi Government (d) All the above

13. Separate latrines and urinals provided for men and women in a factory where in more then ______ workers are employed

(a) 350 (b) 300 (c) 250 (d) 200

14. Which of the following sections of the Factories Actdeals with the provisions ensuring the health of the workers?

(a) Sec. 22 to 41 (b) Sec. 11 to 20 (c) Sec. 41A – 41H (d) Sec.42 to 50

15. Which of the following provisions does not relate to health under Factory Act?

(a) Cleanliness (b) Disposal of wastes and effluents

(c) Ventilation and Temperature (d) Fencing of Machinery

16. Drinking water facilities provided by the factory where in more than ________ workers are employed

(a) 250 (b) 200 (c) 300 (d) 350

17. Which of the following sections of the Factories Actdeals with the safety provisions?

(a) Sec. 11 to 20 (b) Sec. 21 to 41

(c) Sec. 41A to 41H (d) Sec. 42 to 50

18. Which of the following provisions of Factories Actdoes not relate to Safety?

(a) Fencing of machinery

(b) Work on or near machinery in motion

(c) Employment of young persons on dangerous machines

(d) Lighting facilities

19. Safety Officers can be appointed by the State Government in a factory where in more than _______ workers are employed

(a) 500 (b) 1000 (c) 1500 (d) 2000

20. Under Sec 41A to 41H of the Factories Actdeals with

(a) Provision relating to hazardous process

(b) Provision relating to health of workers

(c) Provision relating to safety of workers

(d) None of these

21. As per the Factories Act sit Appraisal Committees for the purpose of ______

(a) To consider applications for grant of permission

(b) Interfere in a factory involving a hazardous process

(c) To Grant permission for the expansion of any factory

(d) All the above

22. Sit Appraisal Committee can be appointed by

(a) State Government

(b) Central Government

(c) Local Bodies

(d) Central Board of Prevention and Control of Water Pollutions

23. Under Sec. 42 to 50 of the Factories Act deals with ______

(a) Facilities for the welfare of workers

(b) provisions relating to hazardous process

(c) Provisions relations to safety measures

(d) Provisions ensuring the health of the workers

24. Which of the following are the facilities for the welfare of the workers under Factories Act?

(a) Washing facilities (b) First aid appliances

(c) Facilities for sitting (d) All the above

25. As per the Factory Acts, canteen facilities are provided by the Factory where more than ______ worker employed

(a) 200 (b) 250 (c) 275 (d) 300

26. As per the Factory Act, shelters, rest rooms and lunch rooms facilities are provided by the Factory where more than ______ workers employed

(a) 150 (b) 200 (c) 250 (d) 300

27. As per the Factories Act, a welfare officer can be appointed by State Government in a Factory where more than ______ workers are employed

(a) 400 (b) 300 (c) 500 (d) 600

28. According to Factory Act, no adult worker shall be required or allowed to work in a Factory for more than ______ in any week

(a) Thirty hours (b) Thirty Eight hours

(c) Forty Eight hours (d) Fifty hours

29. According to Factory Act, no woman shall be required or allowed to work in a factory except between the hours of ______ and ______

(a) 6 A.M, and 7 P.M (b) 5 A.M, and 6 P.M (c) 7 A.M, and 6 P.M (d) 8 A.M, and 7 P.M

30. As per Factory Act , the State Government has power for

(a) Payment in advance in certain cases (b) Power to make rules

(c) Mode of recovery of unpaid wages (d) All the above

31. According to Factory Act, no adult worker shall be required or allowed to work in a factory for more than _______ in any day

(a) 10 hours (b) 9 hours (c) 8 hours (d) 11 hours

32. Workmen's Compensation Act passed in _______ was the first step towards social security of workmen

(a) 1924 (b) 1923 (c) 1925 (d) 1926

33. Which is the main object of Workmen's Compensation Act 1923 ?

(a) To provide for the payment of compensations

(b) Payment of compensations by the certain classes of employers

(c) Compensations for injury by accident

(d) All the above

34. _______ means loss of capacity to work or to move

(a) Disablement (b) Injury (c) Accident (d) Sickness

35. According to Workmen's Compensation Act 1923, Disablement may be _______

(a) Partial Disablement (b) Temporary Partial Disablement

(c) Permanent Partial Disablement (d) All the above

36. _______ means any disablement as reduces the earning capacity of a workman as a result of some accident

(a) Partial Disablement (b) Temporary Partial Disablement

(c) Permanent Partial Disablement (d) None of these

37. Any disablement which reduces the earning capacity of a workman in any employment in which he was engaged at the time of accident which resulted is called as _______

(a) Partial Disablement (b) Temporary Partial Disablement

(c) Permanent Partial Disablement (d) None of these

38. _______ is one which reduces the earning capacity of a workman in every employment which he was capable of undertaking at the time of injury

(a) Partial Disablement (b) Temporary Partial Disablement

(c) Permanent Partial Disablement (d) None of these

39. As incapacitates a workman for all work which he was capable of performing at the time of the accident resulting in such a disablement is _______

(a) Partial Disablement (b) Total Disablement

(c) Permanent Partial Disablement (d) Temporary Partial Disablement

40. _______ means some unlooked for mishap or untoward event which is not expected or designed by the injured workman himself even though there may be negligence on his part

(a) Personal injury (b) Accident (c) Hazard (d) None of these

41. A person engaged in any process involving use of lead tetraethyl is liable to contract poisoning by lead tetra – ethyl, and a person employed as a telegraphic operator may contract telegraphist's Cramp. All such diseases are known as ______

(a) Occupational Diseases (b) Occupational Contact

(c) Personal Injury (d) Accident

42. According to Workmen's Compensations Act, the amount of compensations for death can be calculated by ______

(a) $\frac{40 \times \text{Monthly wages} \times \text{Relevant factor for age 20}}{100}$

(b) $\frac{50 \times \text{Monthly wages} \times \text{Relevant factor for age 20}}{100}$

(c) $\frac{60 \times \text{Monthly wages} \times \text{Relevant factor for age 30}}{100}$

(d) $\frac{40 \times \text{Monthly wages} \times \text{Relevant factor for age 20}}{100}$ or Rs.20,000 whichever is more

43. According to the Workmen's Compensation Act, the amount of compensations for permanent total disablement calculated by

(a) $\frac{40 \times \text{Monthly wages} \times \text{relevant factor}}{100}$

(b) $\frac{50 \times \text{Monthly wages} \times \text{relevant factor}}{100}$ or Rs.24,000 whichever is more

(c) $\frac{50 \times \text{Monthly wages}}{100}$ or Rs.24,000 whichever is less

(d) None of these

44. The first employees state insurance act was passed in the year ______

(a) 1947 (b) 1948 (c) 1949 (d) 1950

45. Medical Benefit is provided under

(a) Factories Act (b) Employee's State Insurance Act

(c) Industrial Disputes Act (d) Minimum Wages Act

46. Which of the following benefit is not covered under the Employees State Insurance Act?

(a) Sickness Benefit (b) Maternity Benefit

(c) Medical Benefit (d) Entertainment Benefit

47. The inability of employer to give employment on account of shortage of raw material is known as

(a) Lock Out (b) Lay Off (c) Strike (d) Award

48. Contribution to ESI fund is made by

(a) Employer only (b) Employees only

(c) Both a and b (d) None of the above

49. Weekly hours of adult workers as provided under Factories Act, are

(a) 56 (b) 50 (c) 45 (d) 48

50. A Factory has to provide crèches when the number of women workers exceed

(a) 40 (b) 50 (c) 30 (d) 20

ANSWERS

1. (b) 1881
2. (a) Factory
3. (b) Worker
4. (c) Adult
5. (b) Adolescent
6. (a) Calendar year
7. (b) Young person
8. (c) Prime Mover
9. (c) Occupier
10. (d) All the above
11. (d) All the above
12. (a) State Government
13. (c) 250
14. (b) Sec. 11 to 20
15. (d) Fencing of Machinery
16. (a) 250
17. (b) Sec. 21 to 41
18. (d) Lighting Facilities
19. (b) 1000
20. (a) Provision relating to hazardous process
21. (d) All the above
22. (a) State Government
23. (a) Facilities for the welfare of workers
24. (d) All the above
25. (b) 250
26. (a) 150
27. (c) 500
28. (c) Forty – Eight hours
29. (a) 6 A.M, 7. PM
30. (d) All the above
31. (b) 9 hours
32. (b) 1923
33. (d) All the above
34. (a) Disablement
35. (d) All the above
36. (a) Partial Disablement
37. (b) Temporary Partial Disablement
38. (c) Permanent Partial Disablement
39. (b) Total Disablement
40. (c) Hazard
41. (a) Occupational Diseases
42. (d) $\frac{\text{40 x Monthly wages x relevant factor for age 20}}{\text{100 or Rs.20,000 whichever is more}}$
43. (c) $\frac{\text{50 x Monthly wages}}{\text{100 or Rs.24,000 whichever is less}}$
44. (b) 1948
45. (b) Employee State Insurance Act
46. (d) Entertainment Benefit
47. (b) Lay Off
48. (a) Employer only
49. (d) 48
50. (c) 30 Workers

*****

XIV

OFFICE MANAGEMENT

1. **Printing the value of postage is the function of ______**
   (a) PBX (b) Franking machine
   (c) Hectograph (d) Pigeonholes
2. **Making and using records is one of the primary functions of ________**
   (a) Administration (b) Stores (c) Office (d) Management
3. **A good office layout is suitable for ______**
   (a) Smooth Flow of Operation (b) Effective Administration
   (c) Executions of Management Polices (d) Proper Material Handing
4. **Which of the following refers to Inward Mail?**
   (a) Mail received in the office (b) Mail received by employee for personal
   (c) Mail sent by the employee (d) None of these
5. **Which of the following refers to Outward Mail?**
   (a) Mail received in the office (b) Mail sent out to customers
   (c) Mail sent by the employee (d) Mail sent by the employee for personal
6. **Office work is more concentrated in a ______**
   (a) Line Organization (b) Line and Staff Organization
   (c) Decentralized Organization (d) Centralized Organization
7. **Internal Mail relates to ______**
   (a) Mail sent in the local city
   (b) Mail sent with in India
   (c) Written correspondence made with in an organization
   (d) Written correspondence made outside the organization.

8. **Which of the following method is the best system of filing?**
(a) Horizontal (b) Vertical (c) Flat (d) Box Files

9. **Blue Print is also called as _____**
(a) Diazo (b) Fax (c) Lithography (d) Telephone

10. **The concept of Punched Cards was invented by _______**
(a) Koontz (b) Gulshan (c) Hollerith (d) Diskee

11. **Which of the following is the main objectives of Office Management?**
(a) Improvement of flow of work (b) Codifications of work procedure
(c) Importance existing workout (d) All the above

12. **______ is defined, includes forms, reports, reproductions of written materials, filing, records retention, microfilming and related services**
(a) Records Management (b) Office Management
(c) Management Information System (d) Business Communication

13. **Preparation of Record Manual aims at**
(a) Control records effectively
(b) To elimination of waste in all activities
(c) To make the staff efficiency conscious
(d) All the above

14. **______ is described as a statement prepared to present facts relating to planning co coordinating performance and general state business in an organization**
(a) Technical Reports (b) Business Report
(c) Project Reports (d) Written Reports

15. **______ is a document copying process which involve preparing a master copy from which further copies are run-off.**
(a) Duplicating (b) Word processor (c) Computer (d) None of these

16. **_______ is defined as the process of arranging and storing records so that they can be located when required.**
(a) Recording (b) Filing (c) Programming (d) Indexing

17. **Which of the following major objectives of filing?**
(a) Proper arrangement of records (b) Careful storing of records
(c) Easily availability of the records (d) All the above

18. **Who is the another of the book on Development in Office Management?**
(a) L.A. Allen (b) J. Batting (c) L. Cortside (d) O. Donnel

19. **O & M stands for _______**
(a) Organization and Management (b) Office Management
(c) Output and Management (d) Organization and Motivation

20. **Indexing refers to _______**
(a) Method of filing (b) Collection of records
(c) Aid to filing (d) All the above

21. Loose – Leaf binders is very useful for ________

(a) Filing (b) Indexing (c) Both a and b (d) Recording

22. ______ defined as an exhaustive review and evaluation of Office Management

(a) Cost Audit (b) Office Audit (c) Company Audit (d) Internal Audit

23. Office Manuals is important for _______

(a) Elimination of repetition of instructions (b) To aid employee training

(c) Collection of facts (d) Both a and b

24. _______ can be described as a definite course of actions or a principle of procedure

(a) Policy Manual (b) Organizational Manual

(c) Multi-Purpose Office Manual (d) Administrative Practice Manual

25. _______ is defined as manual that deals with organization and procedure of a individual department

(a) Organization Manual (b) Department Practice Manual

(c) Multi-Purpose Office Manual (d) None of these

26. An individual is legally permitted to take an actions is means _______

(a) Technical Authority (b) Legal Authority

(c) Ultimate Authority (d) Operational Authority

27. An authority that deals with the original source from which one derives the right to take certain actions is called_________

(a) Legal Authority (b) Technical Authority

(c) Ultimate Authority (d) Operational Authority

28. In communication cycle, if any response is communicated back to the sender it is called as ___

(a) Decoding (b) Freed Back (c) Received Response (d) Encoding

29. Filling is an important aspect of

(a) Record Keeping (b) Book Keeping (c) House Keeping (d) Time Keeping

30. Which of the following method does not relate to Upward Communications?

(a) Open-door Policy (b) Social Gatherings

(c) Reports and Counseling (d) None of these

31. Complaints – and – Suggestions Boxes is a methods of _______

(a) Downward Communication (b) Upward Communication

(c) Horizontal Communications (d) Vertical Communication

32. Grapevine is an example of ______

(a) Formal channel of Communications (b) Vertical Channel of Communications

(c) Informal channel of Communications (d) None of the above

33. Which of the following is not Grapevine?

(a) Single strand (b) Gossip

(c) Probability and Cluster (d) None of these

34. Grapevine is important for _______

(a) A safety value (b)Organizational Solidarity and Cohesion

(c) Quick transmission and feed back (d) All the above

35. _____ is defined as the process of focusing attention on some details and omitting others

(a) Abstracting (b) Slanting (c) Bias (d) Inferring

36. Communication log is like a _______

(a) Diary (b) Record of Events (c) Both a and b (d) Catalogue

37. Which of the following is essential for Business Letter?

(a) Appropriateness (b) Accuracy (c) Curtsey and Tact (d) All the above

38. Which of the following does not relate to Body of Letter?

(a) Opening paragraph (b) Object (c) Main paragraph (d) Subject

39. State the important function of an office

(a) Receiving information (b) Recording information

(c) Arranging and analyzing information (d) All the above

40. 'Order Blanks' are used to _______

(a) Enquiries (b) Replies (c) Place Orders (d) Follow up

41. Which of the following situation is not relating to the need of Circular Letters?

(a) Change in address or premises (b) Introducing a new article

(c) Obtaining agent (d) None of these

42. Which of the three p's are used in Sales Correspondence?

(a) Prospect, Product and Proposition (b) Product, Price and Promotion

(c) Place, Product and Proposition (d) Product, Price and Publicity

43. Which of the four C's are necessary for sound Credit Policy?

(a) Character, Capacity, Capital and Creditors

(b) Character, Capacity , Capital and Commitment

(c) Character, Capacity, Capital and Credit worthiness

(d) Character, Clarity, Capital and Commitment

44. A Sales Letter is aimed at _______

(a) Educating and convincing (b) Securing action

(c) Stimulating desire (d) All the above

45. Any office function common to all sectional offices are physically concentrated in one department known as___________

(a) General Office (b) Centralization of Office

(c) Decentralization Office (d) Both a and B

46. Functional Centralization of office refers to

(a) General Office

(b) Centralization of Office

(c) Combination of Centralization and Decentralization Office

(d) Decentralization Office

47. Organization Manuals is also known as ______

(a) Procedure Manuals (b) Office Manuals (c) Policy Manuals (d) both a and b

48. ______ is defined as the arrangement of furniture and equipment within the available floor space.

(a) Office Layout (b) Production Layout

(c) Stores Layout (d) Factory Layout

49. Which of the following is not relating to Interior Decoration?

(a) Colouring of the walls (b) Design of furnishings

(c) Floor coverings (d) None of these

50. ______ means large rooms where the staff and equipment of several departments or sections are accommodated

(a) Large Office (b) Open Offices (c) Private Office (d) Both a and b

51. ______ refers to the gathering, recording and manipulation of natural data for purposes of planning, coordination's and control of activities

(a) Data Processing (b) Records Management

(c) Filing (d) Record System

52. ______ is the process of arranging and storing records.

(a) Index (b) Filing

(c) Data Processing (d) Records Management

53. Pigeon – Holding is Out of the method for ______

(a) Indexing (b) Filing (c) Data Processing (d) None of these

54. Docketing Filing System is suitable for

(a) Big Concern (b) Medium Concern (c) Small Concern (d) All the above

55. ______ is the process of determining the name subject or other caption under which the documents are to be filed.

(a) Recording (b) Indexing (c) Data Processing (d) Filing

56. Book Index is also called as ______

(a) Fixed Index (b) Card Index (c) Bound Index (d) None of these

57. Any index of files on the basis of A,E,I,O,U, refers to

(a) Book Index (b) Vowel Index

(c) Fixed Index (d) Loose-Leaf Book Index

58. Card Index System was invented by ______

(a) Abbe Jean Rozier (b) J.C. Denyer

(c) Caruth and Holmes (d) B.T. Daster

59. Inward Mail Register is also called as

(a) Keeping Track of Mail (b) Letters Received Book

(c) Mail Room List (d) Receiving and Opening Mail

60. Dispatching is also described as ______

(a) Mailing of Outward Correspondence (b) Sending Off the Mail
(c) Both a and b (d) Delivery of the Mail

61. Which of the following is the main function of the Dispatch Sections?

(a) Folding letter and inserting into envelops
(b) Sealing and stamping
(c) Entering in Outward Mail Register
(d).All the above

62. Open – Shelf Filing System is used mainly in ______

(a) Libraries (b) Offices in Large Concern
(c) Stores in Large Concern (d) Officials in Government

63. ______ refers to a file which contains papers to be attended to on a particular day

(a) Loose – Leaf Binders (b) Visible Card Index
(c) Tickler (d) None of these

64. Oral and written communication may be conducted on the basis of ______

(a) Means adopted (b) Methods used
(c) Directions of flow (d) Relationship

65. ______ refers to the transmission or exchange of thought and message between persons and department of the same organization

(a) Internal Communication (b) Inter Communication
(c) Both a and b (d) None of these

66. Conveyors and overhead wire conveyor are devices used for ______

(a) Oral Communication (b) Written Communication
(c) Informal Communication (d) Formal Communications

67. ______ is defined as a printed sheet of paper or card with marked headings for entries to be made in hand or by typing.

(a) Office Forms (b) Form Set (c) Form Design (d) Indexing

68. Orders, Invoices, Statement and Vouchers are examples of ______

(a) Internal Office Forms (b) Outside Contract Forms
(c) Single Copy Forms (d) Multiple Copy Forms

69. Which of the following mechanical device is not used for Oral Communications?

(a) Call bell (b) Buzzer (c) Light (d) Conveyor

70. PABX stands for ______

(a) Private Branch Exchange (b) Private Automatic Exchange
(c) Private Automatic Branch Exchange (d) PAX Switchboard

71. 'Intercom' telephones system was devised by ______

(a) Indian Telephone Industries Ltd-Bangalore
(b) Indian Telephone Industries Ltd-Tiruvanduram
(c) Indian Telephone Industries Ltd-Mumbai
(d) Indian Telephone Industries Ltd-New Delhi

72. Telephone is also called as ____

(a) Tele – Typewriter (b) Tele Printer (c) Telex (d) Both a and c

73. Which f the following machine is used for transmitting sketches is drawing

(a) Tele Autograph (b) Tele Fax (c) Tele Printer (d) Tele Writer

74. Memorandum forms, requisitions accounting forms and rport forms are the examples of ______

(a) Outside Contract Forms (b) Internal Officer Forms

(c) Single Copy Forms (d) Multiple Copy Forms

75. Continuous Form set is also known as ______

(a) Sets in Gangs (b) Continuous Stationery

(c) Set in Books (d) Unit Sets

76. ______ may be defined as a device where by office forms are produced in a continuous strip and separate forms are divided from one another by perforations

(a) Form Sets (b) Form Design

(c) Continuous Stationary (d) Set in Gangs

77. Hectograph is also called as ______

(a) Gelatine Duplicator (b) Stenotype

(c) Ditto Process (d) None of these

78. Which of the following method is used for dictating letters by the executive?

(a) Dictating to a shorthand-writing stenographer

(b) Dictating recorded in a dictating machine

(c) Dictation directly to the typist

(d) All the above

79. Stencil Duplicator was invented in ____

(a) 1881 (b) 1891 (c) 1911 (d) 1921

80. 'Diazo' is also known as ______

(a) Ozalid (b) Blue-Printing (c) Both a and b (d) Photostatic Process

81. _____ means the photographing of papers, documents in miniature on a thin strip of film

(a) Microfilming (b) Xerography (c) Diazo (d) None of these

82. Signature Stamps, Date and Time Stamps are the devices for ______

(a) Addressing Machines (b) Impression Stamps

(c) Signature Machines (d) None of the above

83. Full Band/ Keyboard type and Ten – key type are used in______

(a) Adding/Listing Machines (b) Calculating Machines

(c) Cash Register (d) None of these

84. Which of the following is not relate to Cash Registers?

(a) Press – Down – key Register (b)Lever Register

(c) Press – in – key Register (d) None of the above

85. ______ which is used for recording of information on cards by means of punched holes

(a) Mailing Machines (b) Folding Machines
(c) Punched Card Machines (d) Dictating Machines

86. Franking Machine is used for ______

(a) Affixing postage stamps on envelops
(b) Inserting the folded letters into the envelops
(c) Opening envelopes of different sizes
(d) None of the above

87. Messages can be communicated quickly and inexpensively from one place to another by means of ______ through the Post and Telegraph Office

(a) Telegrams (b) Phonograms
(c) Reply-Paid Telegram (d) All the above

88. Telegrams sent from a Telegraph Office in India to another situated in a foreign country are known as ______

(a) Foreign Telegrams (b) Overseas Telegrams
(c) Both a and b (d) Inland Telegrams

89. Which of the following method is not used for sending and receiving telegrams?

(a) Phonogram (b) Reply-Paid Telegrams
(c) Multiple Telegrams (d) None of the above

90. Foreign Telegrams can be sent through ______

(a) Cablegrams (b) Radiograms (c) Express Telegrams (d) Both a and b

91. When a common message is sent to more than one addressee it is called ______

(a) Phonograms (b) Reply-Paid Telegrams
(c) Inland Telegrams (d) Multiple Telegrams

92. V.P.P is stands for _____

(a) Value Payable Post (b) Value Postal Parcel
(c) Value Postal Packets (d) Value Payable Packets

93. Market Research Report is an example of ______

(a) Informational Reports (b) Analytical Reports
(c) Research Reports (d) Office Reports

94. ______ is a person who is responsible for the conduct of others in the achievement of a particular task

(a) Office Supervisor (b) Administrative Manger
(c) Personnel Manger (d) None of these

95. Which of the following is the main objective of Circular Letter?

(a) To obtain publicity for a cause or merchandise
(b) To make the reader interested in their contents
(c) To gain the confidence of the reader
(d) All the above

96. Which of the following function is not relate to Sales Letter?

(a) Attracting attention (b) Arousing interest (c) Stimulating desire (d) None of these

97. The purpose of an office is to perform essential services to the _____

(a) Government (b) Public
(c) Management (d) Office and Administration

98. Which of the following relates to Filing?

(a) Record – Keeping (b) Book – Keeping
(c) House Keeping (d) Time Keeping

99. Index is an important aspect of _____

(a) Dictates (b) Predicts (c) Connects (d) Indicates

100. Which of the following machine is used for adding multiplying and dividing of arithmetical figures ?

(a) Typewriter (b) Tele printer (c) Telex (d) Calculator

101. The task of planning, Co-ordinating and motivating the efforts of others towards the specified objectives in the office is achieved by__________

(a) Office Management (b) Administrative Management
(c) Indexing (d) Book Keeping

102. The Mechanical device which helps for personal contact and direct exchange of ideas and information is called______

(a) Telex (b) Telephone (c) Calculator (d) E-Mail

103. Xerox machines is useful for________

(a) Exchange information (b) Produce several copies
(c) Additions and subtractions (d) Record keeping

104. Efficient system of filing helps the Management for

(a) Effective record keeping (b) Effective communication
(c) Effective correctness of records (d) Effective decision making

105. ______ facilitates easy location of records and files

(a) Index (b) Telex (c) Filing (d) Chekograph

106. Which of the following machine is used for writing, crossing or signing the cheques to prevent frauds

(a) Fax System (b) Checkograph (c) Computers (d) Index

107. Which of the following machine helps to get exact copies of a document ?

(a) Tele Printer (b) Checkograph (c) Xerox (d) Telex

108. ______ is a machine through which typed messages can be reproduced at a distant place on a similar machine.

(a) Tele printer (b) Telex (c) Both a and b (d) E-Mail

109. Fax is also known as _______

(a) Facsimile Automatic Xerox (b) Communication
(c) Quickly Transmitted Machine (d) All the above

110. Which of the following is an important function of an office?

(a) Recording Information (b) Furnishing Information
(c) Arranging and Analyzing Information (d) All the above

ANSWERS

1. (b) Franking Machine
2. (c) Office
3. (d) Proper Material Handling
4. (a) Mail received in the office
5. (c) Mail sent by the employee
6. (d) Centralized Organization
7. (c) Written correspondence made with in an organization
8. (b) Vertical
9. (a) Diazo
10. (c) Holleirth
11. (d) All the above
12. (a) Records Management
13. (a) Control records effectively
14. (b) Business Report
15. (a) Duplicating
16. (b) Filing
17. (d) All the above
18. (b) J. Batting
19. (b) Office Management
20. (c) Aid to filing
21. (c) both 'a' and 'b'
22. (b) Office Audit
23. (d) Both 'a' and 'b'
24. (a) Policy Manual
25. (b) Departmental Practice Manual
26. (b) Legal Authority
27. (c) Ultimate Authority
28. (b) Feed Back
29. (a) Record Keeping
30. (d) None of these
31. (b) Upward Communication
32. (c) Informal Channel of Communication
33. (d) None of these
34. (d) All the above
35. (a) Abstracting
36. (c) Both 'a' and 'b'
37. (d) All the above
38. (b) Object
39. (d) All the above
40. (c) Place Orders
41. (d) None of the above
42. (a) Prospect, Product and Proposition
43. (a) Character, Capacity, Capital and Conditions
44. (d) All the above
45. (d) Both 'a' and 'b'
46. (c) Combination of Centralization and Decentralization Office
47. (d) Both 'a' and 'b'
48. (a) Office Layout
49. (d) None of these
50. (d) Both 'a' and 'b'
51. (a) Data Processing
52. (b) Filing
53. (b) Filing
54. (c) Small Concern
55. (b) Indexing
56. (c) Bound Index
57. (b) Vowel Index
58. (a) Abb'e Jean Rogier
59. (b) Letters Received Book
60. (c) Both 'a' and 'b'
61. (d) All the above
62. (a) Libraries
63. (c) Tickler
64. (a) Means adopted
65. (c) Both 'a' and 'b'
66. (b) Written Communication
67. (a) Office Forms
68. (b) Outside Contract Forms
69. (d) Conveyor
70. (c) Private Automatic Branch Exchange
71. (a) Indian Telephone Industries Ltd-Bangalore
72. (d) Both a and c
73. (b) Tele Fax
74. (a) Outside Contact Forms
75. (b) Continuous Stationery
76. (c) Continuous Stationery

77. (a) Gelatine Duplicator
78. (d) All the above
79. (a) 1881
80. (c) Both a and b
81. (a) Microfilming
82. (b) Impression Stamps
83. (a) Adding/Listing Machines
84. (d) None of the above
85. (c) Punched Card Machines
86. (a) Affixing Postage Stamps on Envelops
87. (d) All the above
88. (c) Both a and b
89. (d) None of the above
90. (d) Both a and b
91. (d) Multiple Telegrams
92. (a) Value Payable Post
93. (c) Research Report
94. (a) Office Supervisor
95. (d) All the above
96. (d) None of these
97. (c) Management
98. (a) Record-Keeping
99. (d) Indicates
100. (d) Calculator
101. (a) Office Management
102. (b) Telephone
103. (b) Produce Several Copies
104. (d) Effective decision making
105. (a) Index
106. (b) Checkograph
107. (c) Xerox
108. (c) Both a and b
109. (a) Facsimile Automatic Xerox
110. (d) All the above

****